GW00599343

Computer Auditing

Computer Auditing

Second Edition

Andrew D Chambers BA FCA FCCA FBCS
Sub-Dean Administration and
BP Professor of Internal Auditing, City
University Business School

John M Court BA FCA MBCS
Secretary of the Information Technology Group
of the Institute of Chartered Accountants in
England and Wales

Pitman

PITMAN PUBLISHING LIMITED
128 Long Acre, London WC2E 9AN

A Longman Group Company

First published 1981
Second edition 1986

British Library Cataloguing in Publication Data
Chambers, Andrew D.
Computer auditing.—2nd ed.
1. Accounting—Data processing
2. Auditing
I. Title II. Court, J.M.
657'.453 HF5679

ISBN 0-273-02418-3

Printed in Great Britain at The Bath Press, Avon

Contents

Preface to the Second Edition

In writing this book we have attempted to give a clear guide to computer auditing for the practitioner as well as the student. There is no need for the reader to start with an understanding of commercial data processing or with a grasp of data processing jargon. It is, however, our intention that the careful reader should obtain a thorough grasp of the principles involved and acquire the confidence to start work on all aspects of computer auditing. To help such a reader on the way, the book contains guides and checklists which we have tried to present in a systematic way. Our other objective has been to say what must be said in as few words as possible.

This second edition represents a significant revision in several respects. First, we have updated the text from the first edition by a process of adjustment, insertion and sometimes elimination. Significant revisions include a greater focus upon proprietary software and a more contemporary rather than historical analysis of computer fraud. Secondly and very importantly, while retaining the same overall structure of the book, we have reorganized the material in particular to incorporate interactive methods of data processing into the main body of the text rather than treating these methods as special, advanced topics. Thirdly, it has been necessary to develop a number of new chapters to reflect developments in the practices of data processing and computer auditing. To this end there are new chapters on 'Systems Software', 'Networks and Teleprocessing' and 'Automating the Audit'; also a further new chapter on 'Data Protection' based on the European Convention as implemented in the UK.

Finally we decided that the book should appropriately begin with a consideration of 'Overall Management Objectives'—a chapter which includes a new general questionnaire for use in the audit of management information systems.

We have retained certain features of the first edition, such as our discussion of the control and audit problems of databases and our consideration of computer flowcharting methods, as we have taken the view that these still represent important aspects of the skills and knowledge base of the computer auditor.

We believe that audit complexities are likely to become compounded as data processing technologies and methodologies advance. Each auditor is advised to make his or her own evaluation of the priorities that need to be given to the procedures and techniques we describe in the light of the audit problem areas present in his or her data processing environment. We believe this book will be a useful aid to identifying both the problem areas and also the likely appropriate audit responses.

We have found this material to be useful in the classroom and seminar situation, and with this in mind we have included numerous discussion topics as well as some exercises with suggested answers.

It would be difficult for us to express adequately our gratitude to those who have shared with us their computer auditing skills. We are particularly grateful to E. A. Evans, W. List, B. Matthews, P. W. Morriss and G. Ward. We are also grateful for the opportunity to refer in this book to the writings of others: in each case we have endeavoured to attribute the reference to its source and to obtain permission to use it. If we have failed to do so, it is an oversight of ours for which we would ask your forbearance until we can remedy it in the next edition.

Our thanks are also due to Pergamon Infotech Limited, in particular to Ivan Berti, Colin Steed and Frank Chambers, for their encouragement in the development and use of most of the material contained contained in this book.

A.D.C.
J.M.C.

Part 1 **Audit Objectives and Approach**

1 Overall Management Objectives

Summary

Illustrations of data processing for commercial purposes. The importance of the financial accounting function. The equal or even greater importance of management control. The need for management to act in accordance with an overall control objective. Suggestions of the sort of questions which management should ask in order to achieve such an objective.

Commercial computing

Computer applications are widely used to support commercial activities, in both large- and small-scale business environments, and functionality depends largely on software. This is why both internal and external auditors are almost certain to become involved in the design or evaluation of such systems, the use of such systems in the course of their work and the implementation and checking of procedures adopted to ensure that the use of such systems is properly controlled.

For example, sales order entry and accounting systems are among the most promising applications. The idea is that the user keys in the details of an order, maybe at the moment it is received, and then the system generates the delivery note and invoice, updates the sales transaction records for the day and the customer's account in the sales ledger, and maybe updates the relevant stock records in the process.

The invoice can then be delivered along with the goods, instead of having to be sent out afterwards. In this way it gets into the customer's system, and hopefully out again with the customer's payment, as quickly as possible.

The user should usually have to intervene at two subsequent stages, although of course errors may have to be corrected, or other adjustments made, at other times.

First, the user will need to input information when the goods have been delivered, and the receipted delivery note comes back from the customer (or when the customer collects the goods). It may be necessary to modify the transaction record, for example, because the wrong quantity was delivered, or part of the delivery was faulty, and issue or generate a credit note. (Systems differ in respect of how much is done.) If the system is integrated with a stock recording system, it is very important to ensure at this stage that, if resaleable goods are returned by a customer, then they are immediately re-entered in the stock records.

Secondly, intervention will be required in order to record the payment received from the customer after an order has been delivered. Again, at this stage, a credit note may need to be issued, or a discount generated.

The system should generate the relevant daily and periodical accounting reports, and will also produce customers' statements, debtors' analyses, and in some cases management information about the frequency and categories of goods ordered.

All this is what an integrated sales order entry system can achieve. Indeed, this sort of thing is what is implied by calling a system 'integrated'—that it updates all the interrelated records simultaneously, without the need for further manual intervention.

Such a system should also be interactive. The user should be able to call back details of any transaction onto the screen, including full information about its current delivery and payment status, without any technical difficulty.

The user certainly has to be aware of some of the pitfalls of such a system—why it may not work well in practice. For example, some systems do not cope well with non-standard packaging or containers, if these have to be included in the amounts to be invoiced. Sometimes it is difficult to cater for more than the simplest type of discount calculations: differential discounts for different customers, or different periods of credit, may cause all sorts of complication. (This is an example of why it is difficult to evaluate software in isolation from the conditions of its use—it all depends in such a case on how flexible the user wants to be).

Retailers, of course, do not normally need such systems. However, together with manufacturers and credit traders, they may be able to use the stock recording software with which order entry systems are often themselves integrated. One of the major features of good stock recording is the ability to stimulate re-ordering, purchasing or the need for production of stock lines as soon as a critically low stock level is reached, and indeed to discourage unnecessary re-acquisition while stocks remain above this level. Good stock control is, of course, an important component in maintaining liquidity.

The system should produce an appropriate re-order listing. It must be able to differentiate between stocks which have been allocated for delivery, even though they are still held in the storeroom or warehouse or are in transit to customers, and stocks which have actually been delivered. Re-order levels are affected as soon as stocks have been allocated, not when they leave the premises, particularly if an invoice has already been produced by the system in respect of the sale.

The main pitfall is that unless the user is very conscientious in entering every single stock movement, in or out, the benefits of such a system will very quickly turn counter-productive. The quantities recorded by the system, and compared with the re-order levels in order to generate the re-order listing, will be incorrect and the re-order listing will therefore be of no value. The effects of not being very accurate in record-keeping will be out of proportion to the number of individual mistakes. It will then be better not to use the system at all than to try to compensate for the incorrect management information which it, through the users' own fault, will have generated. Or at least it will be better to make the effort to bring the records maintained by the system back into conformity with the real world.

Such systems, together with those which deal with sales, bought and nominal ledger maintenance, are at the heart of computerized financial accounting procedures. Other computer systems, dealing with such matters as payroll computation, fixed asset accounting and share registration, are also often crucial in this connection.

This recognizes the importance of the financial accounting function. However, at least equally, and in some ways often even more important than financial accounting, is the function of management control.

Stated in general terms, the most important aspect of commercial data processing is, or at least should be, the production of accurate and useful management information to assist all levels of management within the business to maximize profit and minimize loss. This may perhaps be stated in the form of a control objective, as follows.

Control objective

That management utilizes information (which is of optimal value in terms of timeliness, completeness, accuracy, consistency, clarity, conciseness, relevance, security and economy) in assisting them to meet their objectives.

This is the primary purpose of all support activity, including computer auditing, and all detailed work should be planned and implemented with this overall objective in mind.

The questionnaire which follows is designed to assist in the fulfilment of this overall control objective. It does not deal directly with any specific aspect of computer processing, but provides a framework within which an auditor may make judgements about the objectives, relevance, applicability, relative priority and comparative resource justification with reference to the particular circumstances and conditions of the business or organization being audited.

Key questions

1 *General*

(a) Has responsibility for management information been formally designated to a member of the management team?

(b) If 'Yes', does this person's brief include an appraisal of the following:

(i) quality of management information?

(ii) satisfactory utilization of management information?

(iii) continued appropriateness of management information in the light of changing political, legal, economic and technical circumstances?

(c) Are there adequate written procedures on the preparation and use of management information?

(d) Is management information originated at the correct sources?

2 *Timeliness*

(a) Are deadlines laid down for the preparation and distribution of management information?

(b) Is management information produced at the most appropriate intervals?

(c) Is management information based upon up-to-date data?

(d) Is management information produced promptly in accordance with laid-down deadlines?

(e) Is management information kept no longer than necessary? (For instance, out-of-date price lists are dangerous)

3 *Completeness*

(a) Does the management information system enable management to ascertain the following:

(i) that all important laid-down procedures have been complied with?

(ii) the extent to which significant errors have occurred?

(iii) the extent to which all control points have operated satisfactorily?

(b) Does the information system cover all aspects of the business?

(c) Is there a budgetary control system?

(d) Does the information system adequately cover the operational needs of managers?

4 *Accuracy*

(a) Is all management information based upon adequately reliable data with no practical ways of improving upon the reliability of the data?

(b) Are the data upon which the management information is produced, and the management information itself, checked as necessary for reliability?

(c) Is an appropriate balance struck between the often conflicting objectives of accuracy and timeliness?

5 *Consistency*

(a) Is there adequate consistency between each edition of periodic management reports?

(b) Are the data used as a basis for management reports mutually consistent—especially when drawn from different sources?

6 *Clarity*

(a) Are all management reports:
(i) unambiguous?
(ii) legible?
(iii) attractive?
(iv) clearly titled, dated and captioned?

(b) Is clarity achieved with respect to the presentation of figures which relate to each other:
(i) in comparison of the results of periods?
(ii) in comparison of 'actual' with 'budget'?
(iii) in comparison of cumulative data with prior cumulatives?

7 *Conciseness*

(a) Are all management reports as concise as possible without being too brief?

(b) Is full proper use made of reporting only by exception?

8 *Relevance*

(a) Is all management information relevant to:
(i) the business?
(ii) the responsibilities of those who receive it?

(b) Is the requirement for the information known to those receiving it, as well as to those preparing it?

9 *Usefulness*

(a) is the information provided all capable of being acted upon?

(b) Does the information, actionable by those to whom it is provided:
(i) relate to the manager's span of control?
(ii) generally come within the manager's sphere of responsibility?

(c) Is management information acted upon by management;
(i) promptly?
(ii) appropriately?

(d) Are exceptions on exception reports all followed up?

(e) Are comparative figures provided where appropriate?

10 *Security*

(a) Are adequate arrangements in force and applied to provide satisfactory security over (A) the preparation, (B) the distribution, (C) the custody, and (D) the disposal of information, in order to preserve the requirements of confidentiality with respect to the following:

(i) the business?
(ii) employees?
(iii) third parties?

(b) Is there an inventory of information at risk?

(c) Are retention periods for information adequately correctly defined, and are they minimized commensurately with all necessary requirements for their retention?

(d) Is information securely disposed of?

(e) Is access to sensitive information restricted to defined personnel?

(f) Are all staff handling sensitive information (A) carefully selected, (B) fidelity bonded, and (C) closely controlled?

(g) Is the release of information (A) to insiders, and (B) to outsiders, properly authorized?

(h) Are there official channels for handling requests for sensitive information, and are these followed?

(i) Are all company secrets kept securely locked up?

(j) Is there adequate security over keys, including spare copies?

(k) Are there appropriate building access controls?

11 *Economy*

(a) Is all produced information necessary and none of it excessive?

(b) Is all information prepared with maximum economy (consistent with other requirements) with respect to:

(i) collection of data?
(ii) recording of data?
(iii) processing of data?
(iv) presentation of management information?
(v) distribution of management information?
(vi) custodianship of management information?
(vii) utilization of management information?
(viii) disposal of management information?

Discussion topics

1 What is the relationship between management objectives and management information, including computer-produced information?

2 How can computer processing be used to assist management in the achievement of its objectives?

3 How is data related to information?

4 How is computer auditing related to management objectives?

2 Internal and External Audit Objectives

Summary

The scope and objectives of audit in relation to computers. The meaning of audit and of internal control. *Protective* auditing concerned with compliance with laid down procedures and the safeguarding of assets. *Constructive* auditing concerned with efficiency, effectiveness and economy. The relevance to the auditor of what happens within computer programs and within the data processing department generally. The relationship between internal and external audit—particularly with regard to computer auditing.

This chapter is deliberately more about auditing than about computers. It sets the scene for the rest of the book by defining the purpose of auditing.

It is a truism that audit objectives remain the same when computers are in use, for computers are only tools which assist management to achieve its objectives. There is a growing number of instances where the potential of the computer has been so remarkable that managements have modified their objectives, even to the extent of moving into new lines of business which have become feasible and profitable due to the speed of the computer and its greater ability to store, retrieve, correlate and process information. In these cases, of course, the internal auditor's work will be modified to meet the evolved objectives and policies of management. But for a given business activity the *objectives* of the auditor are unchanged whether or not the computer is used. His *approach* to his audit work will be markedly different, and we discuss this later.

Establishing audit objectives

The auditor, whether internal or external, must have a clear picture of his general objectives before he can delineate the boundaries of his interest in computers. These audit objectives must be clearly established, accepted by top management and effectively communicated to managers throughout the organization at all levels. Internal auditors are frequently not clear about their objectives; but even if there is no doubt in the auditors' minds, there will be problems if internal audit's objectives are not understood and accepted throughout the organization. For instance, data processing management may say 'Hands off!' to any internal audit enquiries about data processing organization, administration and efficiency. That may be a legitimate response if internal audit has no mandate from top management to do this sort of work or if this mandate has not been communicated effectively to management at all levels.

In the last analysis, internal auditing is what management wants it to be. It is management's perception of internal audit's role which will define the limits of what internal audit can do. Different managements design the terms of reference of internal audit in different ways, particularly with respect to scope and responsibilities.

Internal audit is widely held to be the independent appraisal of internal control. This leaves a number of key questions which must be answered prior to arriving at a clear perspective on internal audit's objectives and scope with respect to computers. First, what is meant by independence? Secondly, what sort of appraisal does the internal auditor make? Thirdly, what is internal control?

Audit independence

There is no such thing as complete independence for the internal auditor. Internal audit, along with external audit and other professional advisers, is somewhere along a continuum which stretches from complete dependence at one extreme to total independence at the other extreme. The place of internal audit on this continuum is a function of the work it is required to do, the position of internal audit within the organization, the personal qualities of the auditors themselves, and of management's perception of internal audit.

Internal audit will be less independent if it has operating responsibilities for routine controls. For instance, if internal audit has been built into the system it is not well placed to audit that system—and certainly not that part of the system for which internal audit has day-to-day responsibility. Internal audit may have responsibility for conducting a pre-audit of payments from a computerized payments system prior to those payments being made by the concern. At some point management decided that this was a key control and vested it in internal audit, on the basis that internal audit, being independent from other parts of the system, was well placed to operate this control objectively. While that reasoning is correct, it deprives that control of subsequent, objective review by internal auditors, who are badly placed to review their own work. It is unfortunate that it is usually the most essential controls which internal audit is asked to operate; these are the controls which warrant an internal audit review most, but which are thereby deprived of it. If management identifies a key internal check operation it should make its own arrangements to staff that operation and should not use internal audit. Other examples of the misuse of internal audit in this way are the routine review of the console log to spot unauthorized computer processing or inefficient utilization of the computer resource, the administration of access control to the computer centre or passwords for terminal use, the conduct of stock taking of data processing materials, and the supervision of good housekeeping practices in the media (magnetic tape and disk) library.

The independence of the internal auditor is also constrained if he is restricted in what he is allowed to review. He should be able to follow an enquiry wherever it takes him. He needs to have access to computer operations and to have the active co-operation of data processing staff. This is not to say that there should not be controls over the internal auditor himself: unbridled independence may mean that the internal auditor is less productive than he would otherwise be, that he devotes too much time to non-essentials or that he is tempted by the opportunity provided for him to engage in fraudulent activities. The internal auditor should be the first to subscribe to the principle that his work should be controlled, as this is the precept he applies to others. Data processing management will always be wary of allowing the internal auditor indiscriminate, unsupervised access to computer operations, systems, media and programs. The auditor should not be in a position to gain unauthorized access to the computer area. He should not be able to remove tapes and disks at his own volition from the computer centre. He should not be able to use the audit terminal for the amendment of data on current computer files. He should not be entrusted with an audit enquiry program which also provides the facility to modify the data to which he has access. A clearly responsible attitude by the auditor himself to working in a controlled manner is a necessary prerequisite to persuading management to take the control problem seriously.

For the data processing of a concern to be effectively audited it is necessary for internal audit to be independent of that activity, while at the same time being acceptable to those who work within data processing. Internal audit frequently is part of the finance and accounting function of a concern. This is fundamentally unsound. Not only does it make it more difficult for internal audit to conduct objective audits within the finance function (it will probably only succeed in auditing effectively at an operational level below that of the chief internal auditor) but it makes internal audit less acceptable in other functional areas of concern. For a similar reason data processing itself is usually set up, independent of any other function, in order that it might provide an effective service to the concern as a whole. If the terms of reference of the internal audit department restrict it to a review of financial and accounting matters at a fairly low level, and if the concern has set up its data processing department within the finance function, then it can work tolerably well for internal audit to be part of finance. If there is a separate data processing department outside the finance function, then it is not so straightforward for an internal audit department based in the finance function to audit the data processing activity. Data processing is likely to see internal audit as a snoop from a rival department, even to the extent of making out a case for the exemption of data processing from internal audit attention. There are cases where computer auditing is done by a separate unit set up within the data processing function and not reporting to the chief internal auditor. A financially based internal audit will also find it difficult to persuade data processing that the operational efficiency of data processing is a matter of audit interest: there will be the feeling that audit attention should be restricted to a review of the accounting and financial applications which are computer based. In fact the effective control of these applications depends not only upon controls built into the computer programs but also upon the general controls of the data processing department—those concerned with the development of systems, their operation and their security. Computer systems cannot be effectively audited from the user end only.

The ideal situation for a modern internal audit department is for it to be set up outside any functional area, reporting directly to the chief executive or to a committee of the board such as the audit committee. Such an internal audit would embrace all the concern's activities, including data processing. A less satisfactory compromise is for internal audit to belong to one of the service activities (such as finance, accounting or management services) for administrative purposes (office space, staffing and such like) while being clearly vested with higher authority reflected in a right to refer matters to a higher level, such as to the chief executive or the audit committee, if necessary.

Independence is a means to an end: it is intended to make the auditor *objective*. If his findings and recommendations are not objective they will be worse than a waste of time. The auditor also wants to be *constructive* in order to provide a service to management; sometimes he will compromise his independence in order to be so. He will want to get involved with computer systems at the design stage, making recommendations for the incorporation of control features. Whether he makes these recommendations before or after implementation of the computer system, there is no doubt that he is getting involved in the design process of the system. To that extent his independence is compromised, as on subsequent occasions he will return to audit systems which already bear his imprimatur. Whether at that stage he can act objectively depends in part upon his personal qualities. If internal audit management has sent a different team on the return visit it will be less difficult to be objective. If the auditor has maturity, integrity and candour he is more likely to be objective. It goes without saying that the better his technical grasp of data processing the less likely it is that he will make ill-judged recommendations in the first place, and the more likely it is that he, and therefore his recommendations, will be acceptable to data processing management.

Protective auditing and constructive auditing

The auditor's appraisal is objective and constructive. It may be conducted before the event (pre-event auditing) as it is too late to make initial suggestions after the system has gone live (historical auditing). The nature of his appraisal will, in the last analysis, be determined by management's viewpoint about internal auditing. In some concerns it is limited by management to being a *protective* service. Such an audit service in the context of computerized systems will be restricted to the development of audit procedures which check compliance with laid down procedures and check that the assets of the concern are safeguarded. Although in principle such an audit approach could be concerned to confirm that data processing procedures, as laid down in the computer standards manual, are being complied with and that data processing physical resources are being safeguarded, in practice this style of auditing focuses its attention almost exclusively on the user end of the computer systems, to check for compliance with laid down user procedures and to confirm that assets within the custody of the user are adequately safeguarded. This is because traditionally this style of auditing has been linked with accountants and with the accounting function, and on the whole has not extended its scope to become interested in compliance and security within the data processing area.

Where internal audit has a wider scope it will not be limited to checking for compliance with laid-down procedures but will review those procedures themselves to determine whether they could be modified in order to become more effective, efficient or economical. It would be nonsense to restrict such a review to user department procedures, as these are interdependent with the procedures which have been built into the computer programs themselves. Where a computer is in use the three 'E's' (effectiveness, efficiency and economy) are dependent to a large extent upon how the computer is used. Such an internal audit will therefore be concerned to review the controls built into the computer programs of computer applications.

Efficiency auditing

If internal audit is restricted to checking for compliance with laid down accounting and financial procedures and assessing whether these financial and accounting procedures could be improved, it is unlikely that such an internal audit will review the computer centre itself by conducting what is known as an operational or installation audit of the computer centre. This is unsound as the control standards of the data processing department are central to the issue of whether the '3 E's' are achieved with respect to user systems. On the other hand, if the scope of internal audit is interpreted as being concerned with compliance and efficiency of *all* a concern's activities, not merely the financial and accounting ones, then audit work will be done outside the accounting area and the computer centre will become one of the operational audits along with other operations such as production, distribution, marketing and personnel.

Internal control

For over thirty years auditors have defined internal control as a number of close variants of 'the methods and measures established by management within a business to safeguard its assets, ensure the reliability of its records, promote operational efficiency and encourage adherence to laid down policies'. Under this umbrella internal auditors have widened their horizons to embrace all aspects of management. Indeed it is difficult to visualize any part of the management process which does not come within their definition of internal control. The progressive stance is that internal audit is the independent review of the management process, which of course includes the data processing operation.

Despite the broad definition of internal control, internal auditors have always retained a special interest in management control *per se*. An attractive alternative definition of internal auditing is that it is 'the process of appraising the information flow to the monitoring function of a system for its quality and completeness. It is carried out by checking that the information is both self-consistent and mutually consistent and by the irregular generation of test information flows'. This definition restricts internal audit to the narrower 'control' or 'monitoring' activity of management and makes it plain that internal audit is responsible not for doing monitoring itself but for the review of the information flow to the monitoring process. Following on from this definition we can say that *external* audit is concerned with monitoring functions in so far as these are relevant to the financial reports on which external audit is called to express an opinion, and in terms of that opinion.

Information

Whichever definition of internal auditing we adopt, two things stand out. First, what happens in the computer department is to be included within internal audit's review. Secondly, information is of special significance: not only is information needed for control but for the other management activities of planning, organizing and directing. The internal auditor has always had a special interest in *safeguarding assets:* it can be argued that a concern's information, which is part of its intellectual property, is its most valuable resource to be safeguarded. When the pyramids were built manpower was the resource that had to be commanded; at the time of the industrial revolution the key resource was capital; now it is information. The security of corporate information is largely a matter of computer security, which is therefore of direct concern to the internal auditor. Computers are ideally suited to storing, processing and transferring the vast quantities of data which are a feature of today's business environment, and they do this at high speed.

The relationship between internal and external audit

One of the areas of co-operation between internal and external auditors is computer auditing. The objectives of the two auditors are different but they overlap. The external auditor provides an opinion on the statutory accounts. The internal auditor is concerned with compliance and efficiency, both financial and operational. The internal auditor does not focus his attention on the year-end results.

Both auditors are interested in the internal control of the financial accounting system. Whereas the internal auditor is concerned with the operational efficiency of non-financial operations such as production and computer operations, the external auditor does not share this concern beyond satisfying himself that operations, efficient or otherwise, are properly accounted for. In accounting matters the external auditor is interested in completeness and accuracy of updating, satisfactory maintenance of data and accuracy of processing. The internal auditor is also concerned with efficiency and economy.

With respect to assets the external auditor is concerned about existence, ownership, valuation and inclusion in the financial accounts. The internal auditor is concerned about security, appropriateness and utilization as well.

The internal auditor can assist the external auditor in computer auditing work by his special knowledge of the concern's computer systems and the people and politics involved, by his special ability to monitor continuously, and of course by virtue of work he has already done to meet his own objectives, or which he is prepared to do on behalf of the external auditor. The extent to which external audit will rely on internal audit work is related to the degree of internal audit independence, the extent to which the external auditor is able to supervise the internal auditor, the materiality levels to which the internal auditor works—they should not be greater than those of the external auditor if the external auditor is to rely upon the internal auditor's work—the internal auditor's inclination to take on work for the external auditor and the quality of his work, the level of professionalism of the internal auditors—from the external auditor's point of view they should have similar qualifications to himself—and external audit staffing and fee constraints.

On the other hand external audit can help internal audit departments in a variety of ways. They are familiar with statutory requirements and with other methods of running similar systems. They often have more influence with management and may be used discreetly by internal audit as a vehicle of persuasion. In the area of computer auditing the external auditor may be particularly helpful for the services he can provide—training, research, audit aids (such as internal control questionnaires for computer auditing, computer enquiry programs), recruitment, consultancy advice. Finally, there have been many instances of external audit undertaking special assignments for internal audit departments when internal audit resources were overstretched or the internal audit department lacked the competence to tackle certain work.

The internal auditor should ensure that by undertaking work for the external auditor he does not fail to meet his own objectives. In particular, heavy involvement in checking computer listings on behalf of the external auditor may, for instance, mean that the internal audit department spends too much time on compliance auditing and not enough on operational auditing for efficiency and effectiveness, with a consequent lowering of internal audit job satisfaction. An increasing proportion of internal auditors are in close touch with external audit. The partnership should be between equals and founded upon mutual respect.

Discussion topics

1 With respect to computer auditing, why does the internal auditor want to be independent? What do we mean by internal audit independence? How does the internal auditor achieve the independence he needs for computer auditing?

2 How do the laid down objectives and scope of the internal audit department affect its computer auditing work?

3 Discuss the relationship of internal and external audit with respect to computer auditing.

4 Suggest, in general terms, the objectives of an adequate management information system.

5 'There is a tendency for computer auditing to be thought of as a separate discipline from other types of auditing. Upon consideration, this will seem to be an incoherent concept. An audit is a single unified exercise, as a result of which the auditor provides an opinion on the accounts or a report on various aspects of the organization. It is very unusual for audit opinions to contain any direct reference to the organization's data processing activities . . .' Do you agree with this sentiment?

3 The Audit Approach to Computers

Summary

An explanation of the systems approach to auditing and its relevance to computer auditing. Risk analysis. The place of the vouching and verification approaches. The distinction between application controls, computer centre controls and controls over the development of systems. The importance of segregation and supervision techniques in achieving satisfactory control over computer affairs.

The vouching approach and audit trail

Having established in chapter 1 the purpose of auditing, we are now in a position to relate auditing to computers by examining the audit method with respect to computers.

Most auditing activity falls into one of three possible categories, the vouching approach, the verification approach and the systems approach, of which a useful variant is the analysis of risks and appropriate countermeasures. The vouching approach is typified by the ticking and checking of quantities of transaction documents to ensure that they have been processed accurately and correctly. With computerized systems some testing of this type will still be required as part of the auditor's task, but it would be exceptional if the external auditor could obtain the reassurance he needed that results were true and fair by orienting his work to the vouching approach. Similarly the internal auditor, even if his audit objectives are restricted to protective auditing (confirming compliance with established procedures and obtaining reassurance that the concern's assets are safeguarded), will not be able to provide an effective service if he concentrates upon the vouching approach. Computer systems may process huge quantities of data which are beyond the resources of the internal audit department to vouch even on the basis of dependable statistical sampling. With computer systems much of the paper-work will be missing or available in an unwieldy form.

The auditor must have audit trail in order to pursue the vouching approach—and with computer systems this may be inadequate. The vouching approach when applied to computer auditing is often called 'the black box approach'. With this approach the auditor avoids any scrutiny of the computer system itself and depends upon the audit trail to audit round the computer system. He will also supplement this with direct verification of assets and other accounting items. Of course this approach can only be applied to accounting audits and would be quite inappropriate for efficiency audits. It is also only feasible for straightforward computer systems where it is possible to vouch in detail the transactions which have been processed. It is a time-consuming approach to computer auditing: the best that can be said for it is that it is better than overlooking computer systems altogether. A recent survey in the UK showed that internal auditors have been avoiding computerized systems, devoting most of their effort to those parts of their concern's affairs which have not been computerized. The 'black box' approach to computer auditing is a reflection of many internal auditors' lack of confidence about getting involved with what happens within the computer programs themselves and within the computer department itself. What is really needed is the courage to take the plunge and start to do genuine computer auditing based upon the systems approach.

Audit trail implies the preparation and retention within an organization (a) for an adequate period, (b) in a reasonably accessible form, and (c) in enough detail to satisfy the auditors, of records which allow each detailed element of any transaction to be tracked from its source through each intermediate stage to its final disposition (or dispositions); and vice versa—that is, the facility to use records to trace back in detail from the final outcome (or outcomes) through the intermediate stages back to the initial source (or sources) of the transaction.

The systems-oriented auditor will want to find adequate audit trail for the limited amount of testing that he finds essential. He will not use the audit trail as the principal means of obtaining his audit reassurance as he no longer places his emphasis upon the vouching approach. If audit trail is deficient the auditor would consider making recommendations to remedy the position. This is one reason why audit involvement before computer systems are implemented is sound—it is too late to think about audit trail for the first time after the system has gone live. It should be realized that the information that auditors call the audit trail is also the information that management needs for detailed control. If it is deficient it is likely that there is a control weakness. The auditor usually avoids recommending amendments to systems purely to assist his audit work; in this case he can usually present his recommendation as being in the interests of effective management control.

Control costs money. Management has a cost-benefit outlook on control. With computer systems the provision of complete audit trail may be considered by management to be too expensive for the benefits it may provide.

In these cases it is not constructive for the auditor to insist on audit trail purely for audit purposes, though he should consider in depth whether management's judgement is sound.

With manual systems audit trail was usually present almost by chance as the system depended upon the audit trail in order to function. Early computer systems tended to be automated copies of old manual systems, so once again audit trail tended to be present. Modern computer systems do things differently. For instance, it is unusual for carbon copies of invoices to be produced on the line printer. That is not to say that there is no audit trail: it is quite acceptable for audit trail to be held on magnetic tape or disk or on microfiche, so long as it is available in a reasonably accessible form. A good control principle is that a record should always be produced of the conversation between a terminal operator and the computer—but once again it is acceptable for this to be held on media other than paper—and this may be inevitable if visual display unit (VDU) terminals are in use. Audit trail would only be absent if this record were not available in any reasonably accessible form; in those situations management control would invariably be weakened.

Where the auditor encounters an audit situation with inadequate audit trail he must compensate by modifying his methods. He may use an audit enquiry program to conduct his own interrogations of client computer files. His use of enquiry programs would not be limited to occasions where audit trails were deficient. He may consider developing methods of auditing in 'real-time'—that is, conducting his audit tests before the data is lost. This may involve building modules of audit programming into application programs or, in the case of on-line real-time systems, incorporating an on-line audit monitor program into the system.

The auditor needs to be aware that control costs money and should not be built in regardless of cost. He should be sympathetic to management's anxieties about the cost of control, and as willing to recommend economies of control in appropriate circumstances as enhancement of control. Control should be tailored to need: for instance, in computer systems tighter control is needed over account numbers than over most narrative descriptions of data. Avoid duplication of control: controlling the same thing twice is no better than controlling it once. Watch out for examples where the purpose of the control has been superseded but the control is still operated. Search for cheaper ways of achieving the same control effect. Above all, be vigilant for control features which have been built into computer systems but are worthless because they are not being applied, such as the computer control report which is never looked at.

The verification approach

The modern auditor does not depend exclusively upon audit trail in order to conduct his audits, as his emphasis has moved away from the vouching approach to the systems approach. Even for the auditor whose objective is to conduct protective audits for compliance and security only, the systems approach provides much greater audit reassurance. For the auditor whose objectives include an evaluation of the efficiency and economy of systems, the systems approach is inevitable.

Before discussing the systems approach it is necessary to describe the verification approach. With this audit approach the auditor devises independent means of verifying the existence, ownership and valuation of assets. Verification techniques can also be used for other balance sheet and income and expenditure account items. As examples, the auditor might use his enquiry program to obtain a sample printout of the computerized accounts file and then circularize the account holders to obtain their own confirmation of the balances on their accounts. The verification approach is particularly important for the external auditor as he is providing an opinion on the balance sheet and on the income and expenditure statement. This approach is also applied by the internal auditor.

The systems approach

The systems approach to auditing entails an appraisal of the control features which govern a system in order to determine the extent to which the objectives of the system will be met. By an examination of the system itself, the auditor gains his reassurance that, for instance, transactions will be processed completely, accurately and once only. Alternatively, he will identify the weaknesses in the system which threaten the effective processing of data. Even where there are huge volumes of data being processed through the system, there will be only one system: so with the systems approach the time needed to conduct the audit is independent of the volume of data that the system processes. If audit reassurance on compliance and security is gained by means of the vouching and verification approaches, at best this reassurance is restricted to an audit finding that *up to the time of the audit* procedures have been complied with and assets have been safeguarded. The vouching and verification approaches allow no assessment as to whether procedures will be complied with in the future or whether assets will be safeguarded in the future. As the auditor has not conducted a systems review he will only have detected those system weaknesses which have actually been violated; he will be unaware of the latent weakness which is lying waiting to be exploited at a future date either deliberately or accidentally. The systems approach avoids this problem, which may sometimes be less significant for the external auditor, who has a less direct interest in future events.

Under the systems approach the auditor asks three questions:

1 What is the official system?

2 Is it operating according to plan?
3 Is it adequate?

To answer the third question he also needs to keep three things in mind:

1 What *should* happen (to achieve the objectives of the system)?
2 What can go wrong (in view of the way the system has been designed)?
3 What has been done to stop it?

The systems auditor will use vouching and verification techniques as subordinate tools to his systems approach. For instance, he will conduct limited tests to confirm his understanding of the system by checking the processing of a limited number of transactions through the system. These are sometimes called walk-through tests or 'cradle-to-grave' tests as they usually trace the processing of data right through the system. This testing may not be feasible if audit trail is defective.

The philosophy of the systems approach is that there is only one system and if the auditor can assure himself that the controls are effective then he does not need to look at the data itself, as it is bound to be processed correctly. This is too simplistic. No system of controls is ever watertight. The auditor who devotes all his attention to the systems approach in this way is likely to overlook even material cases of control violation. Managements expect internal auditors to reassure them not only that their systems are sound but that they have been complied with.

Testing

The auditor should therefore conduct compliance tests of apparently strong controls upon which he hopes to place reliance. These will be performed after the evaluation of the system and are designed to discover whether these controls have in fact operated throughout the period under review.

Where the auditor has identified a weakness in control either during his review of the system or due to an unsatisfactory result of a compliance test, then he will conduct weakness or substantive tests: these are designed to identify and assess the effects of control weaknesses or control violations.

Risk analysis

One very productive variant of the systems approach is known as risk analysis.

In summary, the issues to be addressed in risk analysis are *integrity*, *security* and *privacy*. *Integrity* means completeness and accuracy, *security* means guaranteeing continued integrity, and *privacy* means protection from unauthorized access. Of course these issues overlap—in particular because of overlap of the means by which they are achieved.

All systems have good and bad, deliberate and unintended, characteristics or design features. Unsatisfactory characteristics (i.e. weaknesses) may result in unacceptable consequences which are often called *contingencies*. Whether or not these contingencies occur, and the extent to which they matter if they do occur, is a measure of the *risk* to which the enterprise is exposed as a result of its system weaknesses. Sensible enterprises will develop a *contingency plan* to reduce or eliminate the weaknesses and risks and to facilitate recovery if a contingency nevertheless does occur. *Recovery* simply means restoring integrity, security and privacy.

Finally, it is not enough to set up systems and contingency plans and then to go away. To avoid degradation of either, there must be a pattern of *monitoring* in order to review these arrangements independently and objectively, and this monitoring must itself be formally provided for.

It should be noted that different types of business have different degrees of exposure to the same risks. For example, a bank is more likely to be exposed to the violation of its computer systems than, say, a retail shopkeeper. This is partly because, in the former case, the data themselves are often invested with value (e.g. a customer's bank account may not exist in any form *except* the data on the bank's computer file, whereas the data on the shopkeeper's computer files are likely only to *represent* assets in the form of stock in a storeroom or cash in a till. The shopkeeper may therefore be much more at risk of a physical attack than an attempt to gain improper access to computer records).

Moreover, different businesses rely on their computer systems to different extents: this affects the scale, if not the type, of risks to which they may be exposed.

Auditors should encourage management to carry out a full analysis of risks and appropriate countermeasures. In any event, auditors may find it useful to perform their own risk analysis, not only as a check on that of management, but also to help them optimize the mix of audit tests and procedures to be performed.

Both management and auditors should bear in mind that risk analysis may be particularly effective when directed towards achieving greater security and confidentiality of *data*. It may be of less use, though it will always be of some value, in connection with the detection and prevention of programming errors and with the effects of operational errors and faults.

Controls in computer systems

As the methods of processing used in computer systems are different from those which apply to manual systems, so the means by which control is achieved are different. The auditor must be familiar with the vast variety of control techniques available within a computerized environment. The objective of these control methods is to ensure the accuracy, completeness, security, timeliness, effectiveness and economy of records and reports generated by the data processing function, and the efficiency of the data processing function itself.

To assist comprehension of these methods some form of classification is required. First, there are application controls. These are controls which are built into individual systems or applications and include the following:

1 Controls over input data.
2 Controls over computer processing.
3 Controls over computer files.
4 Controls over computer output.

These controls may be either manual controls or programmed into the systems themselves. They may be operated within the user department or within the computer department, and they may be designed to control the work which takes place in either of these departments. The auditor must examine these controls whenever he undertakes an audit of a computerized system: these controls are not independent of applications—they may be built in satisfactorily in one application but be missing from another.

Apart from application controls there are general controls. These are sometimes called data processing procedural or administrative controls. They relate to the acquisition, development, use and maintenance of the data processing resources—hardware, personnel, software and data. They can be subdivided between:

1 Computer centre controls.
2 Application development controls governing the development and maintenance of computer applications (or systems).

These controls are also of vital interest to the internal auditor. At the minimum they are procedures which should be complied with and which relate to the processing of accounting, financial and other data. They also relate to the safeguarding of assets in several ways:

1 The security of the assets of the concern is dependent upon effective data processing and information storage and retrieval.
2 The data processing department itself is a major user of resources.
3 The information resource of the concern is probably its most valuable resource.

It is apparent that even an internal auditor with horizons limited to protective auditing will be concerned with general controls over data processing. If he has a wider perspective, being concerned with the efficiency, effectiveness and economy of all operations of the concern, then he will have a deeper interest in these general controls. As these controls are independent of individual computer applications they will not be audited whenever the auditor encounters systems which have been computerized. These controls will not change with different applications. The audit of these general controls should be set up as a special audit.

Auditability

A new term has recently been coined: 'auditability'. From the viewpoint of the auditor, auditability implies the facility for a competent and qualified auditor to independently convince himself of the proper design and functioning of a system and its internal controls, in order to form an opinion on the propriety of generated information for the user and the efficiency of the process by which it is produced, within reasonable time limits and without undue difficulty. From the viewpoint of the systems designer, auditability requires that the designer be able to convince an auditor that the system under review is sound and under control.

Control by supervision and segregation

We have stated that audit objectives do not change with computers but the audit approach does. The control techniques have altered, yet the fundamental principles that govern the control techniques are very similar. Control is achieved either by segregation or by supervision, or both. A summary of the different types of segregation follows and shows how these may apply in a computerized environment. If satisfactory control cannot be achieved by one means of segregation, then another means should be considered.

Some forms of segregation are more satisfactory than others as several have negative side effects such as reduction of job interest and job satisfaction. Of course the principle of avoiding over-control applies here: once one has achieved control one stops looking for additional control devices over the same item. If satisfactory control cannot be achieved by segregation then supervision must be applied. Many forms of programmed control amount to automated forms of supervision.

Examples of control by segregation in a computer environment

Control techniques	Examples
1 Segregation of knowledge: on a need-to-know basis.	Computer operators should not learn to code. Computer operators should not have access to program files. Computer operators should not run programs without proper operating instructions.

2 Segregation of operations: certain tasks should be organizationally separate.	Input generation to be separate from: (a) input control (not easily achieved if input is entered on-line); (b) computer operating; (c) output control; (d) media-library control (data and programs); (e) application programming; (f) system programming.
3 Segregation of duties: no one person to be exclusively responsible for a complete operation.	A computer operator should not work single-handed. A computer operator should not be allowed to restart a computer program which has failed, without supervisor intervention to ensure that all is in order. Never allow a console typewriter log to be removed and insist that all paper breaks are initialled by two people. Ensure that the program code is desk-checked by another programmer. Modular programming gives more scope for sharing the programming of an application. Have cover for key positions, such as that of database administrator.
4 Segregation of staff: staff should be segregated between operations and other duties. It is too easy for staff to step informally across boundaries between operations, or to take on a complete task single-handed.	Do not allow a programmer to assist with computer operating. Avoid the willing, lone operator on the night shift.
5 Segregation of records: in order to protect them and to avoid unauthorized access.	Provision of security copies of data and programs away from the computer centre in a safe place. Password control to the database, and to parts of the database.
6 Segregation of record-keeping and control from physical operations and from physical custodianship: reduces the risk of poor or fraudulent work or custodianship being concealed.	The media library of data and programs should be separate from the computer room. Program and data files should only be present in the computer room when they are needed for computer operations. The physical operation should be segregated from the accounting responsibility for the operation at the user end with respect to purchasing, store-keeping, receipt or disbursement of cash etc. This principle is easily violated when computer systems are designed. The user department should be in a position to control their application with respect to input, processing, computer files and output, and it should be their responsibility to do so. Data processing provides a separate processing service.

7 Bookkeeping steps: some bookkeeping operations are incompatible with each other for control purposes if done by the same person.	Separate DR from CR on personal accounts (opportunity to violate this control may exist in the user department usually at the input generation stage, in the input control section, or in the data preparation section). Separate original entries from adjusting entries (computer rejections should be carefully controlled, independently from their original generation). Separate journal from ledger.
8 Separation of review from operating responsibilities	Audit should not be responsible for operating controls, however important they may be. Audit should not be part of the data processing department, but should be independent of it. Supervision should be effectively independent of the work which is being supervised. Programmed controls should be protected against manipulation by those whose work they are designed to control.

Discussion topics

1 Compare and contrast the vouching, verification and systems approaches to auditing.

2 Is it practical to apply the 'black-box' approach of auditing around the computer?

3 When would you consider to be the right time to audit the controls in a computer system:
(a) before the system goes live?
(b) after it goes live?

4 If the auditor makes recommendations for the incorporation of improved control features within a computer system, what are the implications of this from an audit viewpoint? Is he becoming one of the system's designers?

4 Obtaining and Developing Computer Auditing Competence

Summary

Should every auditor be a computer auditor? Is there also a need for specialist computer auditors? How should auditors be developed as computer auditors? What are the practical ways of obtaining computer specialists for audit work and incorporating them into internal audit departments and external audit firms?

Computer auditing by computer auditors

All internal auditors should be computer auditors. As most systems become computerized there is little room for the internal auditor who is unable to cope with the audit of computerized systems.

The recognition of the relevance of computer specialists for internal auditing is part of a general process of recognition of the value of non-accounting specialists.

This is associated with a widening scope of internal audit—to embrace efficiency auditing as well as compliance auditing and to embrace the audit of non-accounting activities as well as the accounting activities.

The computer specialist as an auditor

Even for the internal audit of accounting activities there is an irrefutable case for the employment of computer specialists as auditors. Whereas before the advent of computers it was the accountant who understood both the business of processing accounting data and also the conventions of presentation of that data, now he no longer has a complete understanding of these matters. He shares responsibility for the processing of accounting data with the data processing professional. Before computerization it was logical that the auditor would be an accountant, if only on the basis that you set a thief to catch a thief. Now it is more sensible for the audit activity to be shared on a team basis between accountants and computer specialists. This applies to external audit as well as to internal audit. For internal audit, and given an adequate size of the internal audit department, there will also be a need for other specialists such as production specialists, as internal audit moves into other operational audit areas.

While all internal auditors should be computer auditors, in the sense that they should be capable of auditing systems which are computerized, not all internal auditors will be computer specialists. The general internal auditor must be trained to cope with computerized systems. In addition there is a place for the computer specialist in internal audit. He will provide technical advice to the other auditors. He may be responsible for the selection of the appropriate computer audit enquiry package or packages for use by the internal audit department. While he will subsequently be available to advise on the use of these packages, all internal auditors should be competent to use them. He would also be responsible for the development of other technical audit tools such as integrated audit monitors, integrated test facilities, or parallel simulation and normative internal audit models.

With the complexity of data processing it is no longer realistic to expect one man to have all the competence required to conduct all audits. Audit competence must be put together on a team basis. The audit department may use computer specialists as members of audit teams even if these specialists are inexperienced auditors. In this case the audit competence is provided by the other auditors.

The need for auditors who are both technically competent in a specialist field and also experienced as internal auditors comes when the audit department tackles operational audits. Survey data shows that 70 per cent of internal audit departments use specialists for operational audit work. Sometimes they are co-opted from other departments of the company, or even from outside for one-off audit assignments. It is better that the audit department should have its own specialists.

More internal audit departments are now conducting operational audits of data processing—reviewing the computer centre, the system for the development of new applications and also the general controls over teleprocessing where this exists. These audits are set up as special operational audits, whereas the review of controls built into computerized applications would be part of the audit of user department systems. The latter is what every internal auditor should be competent to undertake—perhaps with some assistance from computer specialists over technical problems. The former requires computer specialists.

Operational auditing

Survey data confirms that operational auditing generally, and the audit of the computer centre in particular, is increasing. In 1968, 64 per cent of internal audit departments worldwide reported audit work in this area: this had risen to 79 per cent by 1975. While these figures are high, it should be realized that although the study surveyed almost four hundred internal audit departments worldwide, most were within the United States where internal audit has tended to be practised more progressively. It is also likely that the 79 per cent figure includes positive responses from internal audit departments which do not audit the computer centre as a special audit but merely as a consideration which they bear in mind in all their audit work. The important point is that the trend is upwards.

Training and development

Two questions remain to be dealt with—from where do we obtain computer specialists for computer audit work, and how do we develop all our internal auditors to be competent to audit systems which have been computerized?

Specialist computer auditors are increasingly being drawn from the data processing profession. A glance at the job adverts in the professional computer press confirms this. Chief internal auditors should consider approaching their concern's data processing manager with a view to arranging the transfer of one or two of the data processing staff into internal audit. Care must be taken to ensure that internal audit does not thereby end up with the 'dead wood' of the data-processing department—those who can most readily be spared are not likely to be the right people. The proposal should not be without its attractions to the data processing manager. The deal would involve a temporary transfer to internal audit for between three and five years. During that time the computer specialist could be given the opportunity and encouragement to qualify as an accountant. Upon his ultimate return to data processing the computer manager would have the advantage of a qualified accountant on his staff, and one who understands the principles of internal control and the priorities of the internal audit department. It is ideal from the perspective of career development, both for the individual involved and also for the data processing department. The individual has a guarantee of eventual transfer back into data processing—which is his principal professional interest. The transfer will occur before he has been away so long that it is almost impossible for him to update himself. It should be noted that he will not be out of touch with developments in computer technology during his stay in internal audit and will therefore not become too dated in his computer knowledge. All the same, this plan does avoid internal audit ending up with an out-of-date specialist, which might result if he stayed in internal audit permanently.

A recent survey showed that the average stay of all internal auditors in internal audit is between three and four years, with 64 per cent staying less than three years. The suggested stay of the computer specialists would if anything be above average. There is no reason why he should not subsequently return to internal audit for a further spell a few years later. This is generally a good way of ensuring that internal audit is staffed by auditors who are both experienced in auditing and up-to-date both in management principles and in the principles and approach of their specialist areas. Should the computer specialist turn out to be unsuitable for internal audit he may be returned to the computer department more quickly than originally intended, without too much loss of face.

The other way to obtain computer audit specialists is to train existing internal auditors in the skills of computing. If this method is followed, the auditor is placed in a data processing environment for an extended period—preferably for two years but certainly for at least six months. During this time he must be given valuable work experience. It is exceptional for computer audit specialists to be developed exclusively within the audit department, where they can only learn *about* data processing rather than be exposed to doing most of the job.

Leaving aside the computer audit specialist, the methods of developing all other internal auditors so that they are competent to handle computerized systems is different. This can be done from within the internal audit department. The formula should include satisfactory on-the-job exposure to computerized systems. There is no better way to learn than by doing. Membership of an audit assignment team which includes a computer audit specialist is also valuable. General training courses on computer auditing, either mounted internally or available outside, should also be used. More specifically, each internal auditor should attend a course of instruction in the use of the computer audit enquiry package which is in use within the internal audit department. It is regrettable that so little emphasis is often given to in-house training, even in times of relative economic affluence.

Discussion topics

1 How would you as an audit manager ensure that the computer audit competence within your department was up-to-date?

2 What is the best way to produce a computer auditor:
(a) train an auditor in computer techniques?
(b) train a computer man in audit techniques?
(c) other?

Part 2 **Control and Audit of the Computing Process**

5 Auditing Systems Development and Maintenance

Summary

The meaning of pre-event auditing and its application to auditing a system at the development stage. Providing audit reassurance that the stages of systems development have been complied with in accordance with laid down policy and are adequate to ensure well-controlled systems. A discussion of the auditor's interest in the stages of development including the feasibility study, program specifications, programming, testing, training, file conversion, audit 'sign-off', implementation, post-installation audits and subsequent maintenance.

Our classification of computer controls is as follows:

1 Application controls
2 General controls
 —computer centre controls
 —application development controls

Here we are concerned with application development controls, i.e. controls over the development cycle of a new computer system (application) and its subsequent maintenance. We shall concentrate on those matters which are of special relevance to the auditor. The principles involved are identical for systems developed for use on all types and sizes of computer. However, the emphasis may well be different, and special factors relating to the audit of systems for microcomputers are considered in chapter 8.

In this discussion we will make a few assumptions for convenience. We will assume that a new computer system is replacing an old manual system. Increasingly, new computer systems are replacing old computer systems, but the audit issues are the same. Many computer systems have to be superseded because of poor control over their original development and subsequent maintenance. In costing out the computer system as part of the feasibility study it is unwise to assume a system life of much more than five years.

We will use the term 'master files' to refer to the 'permanent or semi-permanent data' of the system held usually on magnetic media.

Finally we have taken the perspective of the internal auditor. The external auditor should also be involved at the development stage, and enterprises should consider whether they should also ask their external auditor to sign-off a new system.

Pre-event auditing

In auditing at the development stage of a system the auditor is engaged in pre-event rather than historical auditing. First, he is auditing the development process itself while it is under way rather than after the event. His objective is to satisfy himself that the *process* of development is both satisfactory and has been complied with: this is what we are considering here. Secondly, he reviews the controls which are being built into the new system in order to satisfy himself that the system will be reliable and secure as well as auditable: we look at the audit of these application controls elsewhere.

In a recent US survey it was found that 73 per cent of internal auditors audit computer systems while they are under development. It is too late to make the initial audit recommendations for improvements in the controls which are built into the application if this is left until after the system has gone live. By then the damage may have been done: once a system has been implemented with defective controls, or is deficient in controls, an out-of-control situation will probably quickly occur which may be very difficult to remedy. Typical examples are (a) an unknown debt position of customers, (b) inaccurate payslips and no computerized means of correcting the position, (c) excess or out-of-stock situations.

In practice, unless the auditor audits at the pre-event stage he will frequently fail to audit the system until one or two years later. Audit recommendations involving redesign of computer systems are unlikely to be popular, and data processing resources will probably not be available at that time to devote to the task. So pre-event auditing is something that computer professionals should commend to internal auditors, if the auditors themselves are not setting the pace. It is, however, something that auditors should be doing in other areas as well. The following are a few examples;

1 The audit of contract terms before contracts are signed, ensuring that laid down procedures have been complied with.
2 The audit of capital investment proposals before commitment.
3 The audit of corporate plans for the future.

The first two are of course relevant with respect to computer contracts and investment in computers.

Auditors are sometimes reluctant to get involved with pre-event auditing: this reluctance may be a mask for avoiding any commitment! It has been suggested that if the auditor expresses a firm view before the implementation of a system that the application has adequate controls incorporated and that the development of the system has taken place in a controlled way, then he has 'put his head on the block'. If subsequently the system is found to be deficient, management will be able to blame the auditor, amongst others. However the auditor should not seek to avoid being accountable. As with any other professional man, he is responsible for the quality of the advice that he gives and he should not seek to avoid giving that advice when it is most needed.

Does audit involvement before the event make the auditor less independent of the system, since he has been involved with it during development? There is no doubt that his independence is compromised to some extent, but we should not guard the auditor's independence at all costs. In this instance it is more constructive for the internal auditor to take on this work than to reject it. Further, the auditor's independence was compromised when he first started to make recommendations for improving control in systems. He first made these recommendations as a result of historical auditing after the event. Switching the timing of his work to before the event does not compromise his independence any further, so this is no argument against pre-event auditing.

In the same US survey, 58 per cent of internal audit departments reported that they were involved in the testing of new systems prior to implementation. Thirty-five per cent had formal responsibility to sign-off a new system before their concern would implement it. Only 19 per cent had a similar responsibility to sign-off subsequent modifications to systems—an indication that modifications during the maintenance stage of a system are not so well controlled as the initial design of the system.

Network for the introduction of a new computer application

Figure 1 follows the style of a network used in critical path analysis or in PERT (program evaluation and review technique) scheduling. The circles are points in the time (i.e. 'activities'). The schedule shows the activities and events in the sequence in which they should occur. Dotted lines are a charting convenience known as dummy activities: there may be 'zero-time' dummies or 'real-time' dummies. Zero-time dummies are denoted by a '(0)' and simply connect two events together where these two events may occur at the same time—i.e. no time is consumed by a zero-time dummy. Where no '(0)' is shown, the dummy is real-time—i.e. some time must elapse between the two events at either end of a real-time dummy activity. Dummy activities are, of course, used to aid the charting of activities which may occur in parallel with each other. Each event is numbered to facilitate identification, but the numbers should not be used to determine the sequence of activities:

the ordering of the flowlines themselves denotes the sequence of the activities. Times can be assigned to all activities and in this way the critical path may be determined—i.e. the path which has no spare time.

The user department

The stages in the development of a new computer system are shown in Fig. 1. The auditor who is reviewing the development process will want to satisfy himself that each of these stages is being completed in a controlled manner. The network does not show adequately the importance of heavy user department involvement in the development of the system. It is an important control principle to assert that *computer systems are user department systems*, not computer department systems. It is true that the network shows a user department test of the system, the training of user staff and a later sign-off by the user department. But the user department's involvement should be much more pervasive. Computer systems foisted upon reluctant users are unlikely to be successful. Imposed change has a high risk of failure. Technically elegant systems which do not meet user requirements will fail. The auditor will want to satisfy himself that the user has been fully involved from the outset. The project team developing the new system should have representation from the user department and care should be taken to ensure that key user personnel are assigned to this task rather than 'the person who can be spared'. In addition to the project team comprising user representatives, systems analysts and programmers (unless they belong to a separate pool), there may be a case for setting up a liaison committee to meet periodically to review progress and resolve problems. If this all sounds too expensive, beware of cutting corners as it will work out more expensive in the long run!

The auditor will want to satisfy himself that the user department is fully aware of the implications of the computerization. This is not easy to achieve. A typical user department is shy of computers and probably reluctant to admit it. In addition it still has its normal work to do running the old system, and has probably been assigned no additional resources to cope with the development of the new system. Frequently user departments only wake up to the new system when it is about to be implemented—or later, with plaintive cries that it does not do what they want, or could do it much better. Small wonder that computer people have designed computer-oriented systems rather than user-oriented ones! Communication is a two-way process and computer people as well as users must be bullied into talking and listening to each other. The auditor is well placed to assist in this direction.

The feasibility study

Every concern should have a set procedure for the development of new systems. There should be no presumption that a computer solution is necessarily

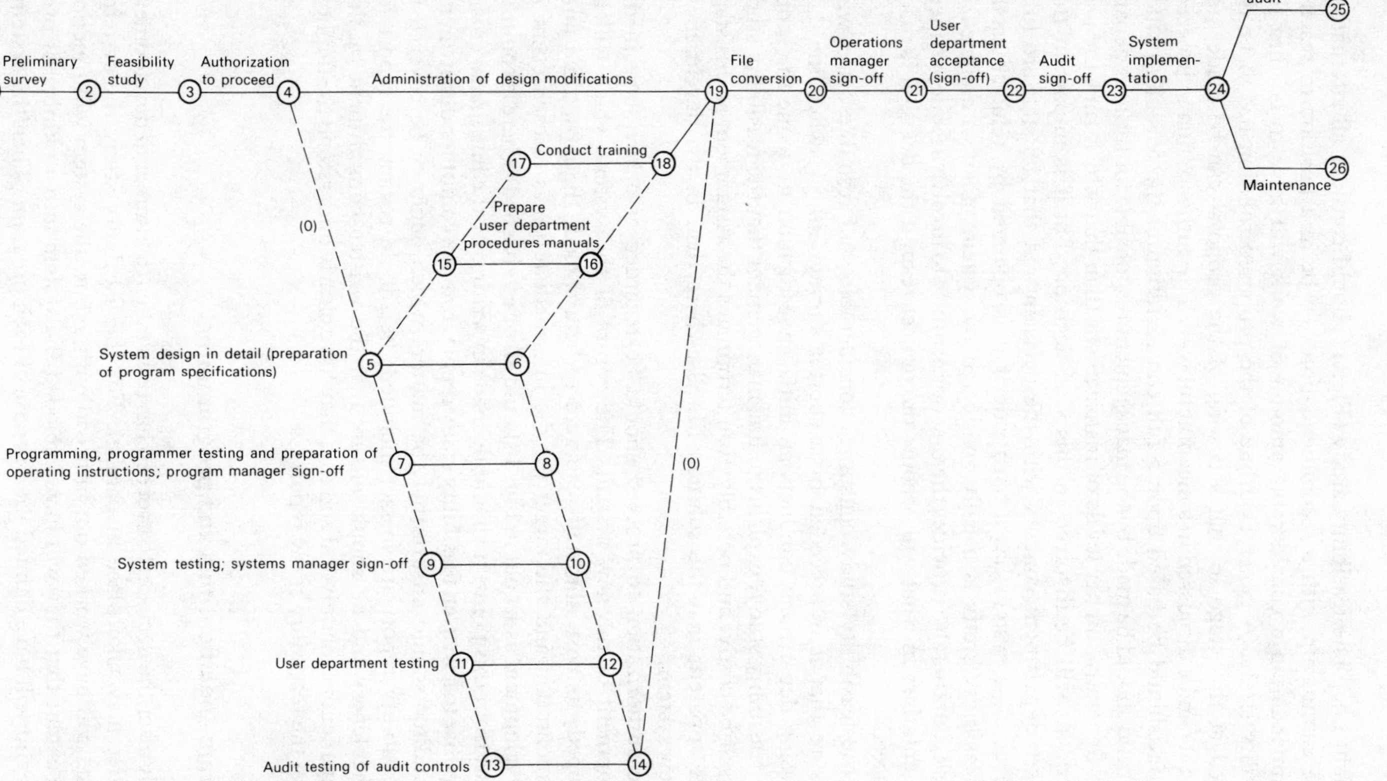
Preliminary survey
Feasibility study
Authorization to proceed
Administration of design modifications
File conversion
Operations manager sign-off
User department acceptance (sign-off)
Audit sign-off
System implementation
Post-installation audit
Maintenance
Conduct training
Prepare user department procedures manuals
(0)
System design in detail (preparation of program specifications)
Programming, programmer testing and preparation of operating instructions; program manager sign-off
System testing; systems manager sign-off
User department testing
Audit testing of audit controls
(0)
1
2
3
4
5
6
7
8
9
10
11
12
13
14
15
16
17
18
19
20
21
22
23
24
25
26

Fig. 1. Network for the introduction of a new computer application.

the right one. The feasibility study (Fig. 1) should consider all alternatives before coming up with a recommendation. To be in a position to reach a recommendation a considerable amount of work will have to go into the feasibility study. A general outline of the proposed solution has to be developed at this stage so that a costing of the proposal can be made, and so that it can be discussed in a meaningful way. The authorization to proceed, if made, should be based upon a full consideration of the feasibility study report and should be made by the management responsible for the user department. Generally, higher levels of management than that which runs the user department will be involved in this vital decision, but it is important that the user department concurs with the decision and that its staff are fully aware of it—a system has a hard ride if it is operated by reluctant staff. The feasibility study is usually conducted by systems analysts assigned to the task, but this also provides the first opportunity to involve user department representatives in what will become the project team if the decision is made to proceed.

As the feasibility study consumes considerable staff resources, it is wise to ensure that it is preceded by a shorter survey (Fig. 1) when the data processing department conducts an initial investigation to define the scope of the feasibility study, explains to line management that the feasibility study will itself be costly, and possibly even terminates the assignment at this stage if it is apparent that the solution lies elsewhere than in the development of a new system.

The authorization to proceed should be regarded as a key stage in the development of the new system. The nature of the system which will be developed, its cost, the staff resources to be assigned, the lapse time until implementation and the target for the intermediate times of each event in the development as set out in Fig. 1 should all be established. There is commitment as from this point: it should be made in writing by the line management in response to a written feasibility study report from the computer department. The auditor should ensure that the matters which ought to be covered in the feasibility report are in fact included; he should review the report for reasonableness and he should ensure that the written commitment by line management is unequivocal and that they have clearly understood the implications of the feasibility study report.

Program specifications and programming

Shortly after the decision to proceed has been taken, a number of development activities may take place in parallel. For the feasibility study the systems analysts will have worked out in broad outline how the system will function to the extent that they will have exploded the system into a number of programs and will have defined the purpose of each program. Then the systems analysts and user representatives, working together as a project team, will develop a detailed program specification for each program; from this the programmer will write his program. There is some control advantage in having the programmers working not as members of the project team but as a separate pool reporting to a programming manager. In this way the systems analysts are compelled to prepare thorough program specifications, as the programming section will not accept them if they are inadequate. It will be the programmers' responsibility to write workable programs, so the programming pool will be inclined to be firm before accepting program specifications.

Once again there should be a formal acceptance by programmers of program specifications, in order to ensure that lazy ways do not creep in. The auditor should check that formal acceptance occurs and that the standards laid down for program specifications have been complied with. These standards should be included in the data processing standards manual. In brief, a program specification should describe the input data the program will process (e.g. by means of record layout charts), the processing required and the format of the output data to be produced. It should also provide a brief summary of the system, particularly of the programs which link into the program described in the specification. While a program specification describes *what* is to be done by the program, it is not usual for it to describe *how* it is to be done: this is left to the programmer. A program specification would not therefore usually include a flowchart of program logic.

Any commercial computer system will comprise a number of programs. Program specifications can be handed over to the programmers as they are written, so that programming can commence. In practice a control problem here is that analysts find they need to modify program specifications in the light of factors which only become clear as they are designing later program specifications. Modifications to issued program specifications should be avoided wherever possible as they lead to bad programs and bad programming—apart from bad human relationships, which are also damaging to the system. It is wise to compromise and to release a group of programs to the programmers when the systems designers are reasonably sure that no significant amendments will have to be made to them. Despite this caution, later amendments will doubtless still have to be made; these should be controlled in the same way as the initial program specifications—formally documented by the analysts and formally accepted by the programmer and appended to the program specification. Some modifications are triggered by technical requirements of systems analysts: others are suggested by user requirements.

The auditor should review the issuing of amendments to program specifications and satisfy himself that they are being processed in a formal way. If the level of amendments appears high or if it is causing undue aggravation, it may be a warning signal of more fundamental problems—such as material changes from the agreed system as documented in the feasibility study report, or weak program specification by the systems analysts.

The auditor will depend at this stage on the program specifications to indicate to him whether adequate programmed controls are being built into the system. From his point of view the main purpose for these controls will be to ensure the completeness and accuracy of data processing as well as its security. It is as well to underline here that if the auditor is conducting his audit of these application controls at the pre-event stage, it is at this stage that he will do much of his investigation of these controls. He will continue this investigation when the system is being tested.

The auditor will review the programming work to satisfy himself that standards laid down have been complied with. It is unlikely that he will review the program code itself for this purpose, but he will confirm that all programming work has been desk checked by other programmers. In the US survey referred to earlier, 64 per cent of internal audit departments review program code, although only 10 per cent do this regularly. They review it as part of their work on application controls rather than to confirm that programming standards have been complied with. This is rather grandly referred to as 'program auditing'.

Testing

The programmer is responsible for testing his program against test data which he creates in order to test all logical combinations of data and programming. He should also link test his program with the programs on either side of his in the program suite. It is also his responsibility to write the operating instructions for his program. Perhaps most important of all he is required to put together a program file which will contain the following:

1 The program specification.
2 All authorized amendments to the specification.
3 A computer listing of his program coding.
4 His flowchart or logic diagram.
5 His test data and the test results.
6 The operating instructions.

The programming manager should sign-off each program when he is satisfied that it works and documentation is complete.

The program file is vital for subsequent maintenance purposes as it describes how the program works. It is one of the most important things that the auditor should review.

The systems analysts' understanding of the system requirements will be different from the programmers', so the former must conduct their own system test. Data should be passed through all the programs from the first to the last; at least three cycles of the system should be tested as the programs may use different logic for the first time through from the next cycle, and the third cycle is the first occasion that the system will process data which has already been updated. The system test tests all combinations which may occur in practice, whereas the programmer's test is more technical and is designed to ensure that the program will not fail, irrespective of what it is asked to do. Because the programmer is further away from the user environment he may overlook situations which could occur: his perspective is parochial to his own program, so a separate system test is essential.

The user department must also conduct its own test of the system. It is preferable that this should not be merged with the system test. The user also has a different perspective from the systems analyst and it is best that they should both be able to satisfy themselves independently. The auditor will work closely with the user in the development of the user department's test of the system. He will want to satisfy himself that the test is thorough and that it shows convincingly that the system can handle whatever it may encounter in practice. He will also want to confirm that the user has tested the functioning of the programmed controls which have been built into the system. Consideration should be given as to whether the system has been tested to confirm that it can handle the *volumes* (of data and of monetary and quantity amounts) that it may have to handle: testing with small volumes only is easier but grossly inadequate. One approach to the user department test is to run genuine data through the new system and check to see that the computer produces the same results that have been produced manually; on its own this will be inadequate as no cycle of the system contains all the possible logical combinations of transactions.

If the auditor has specified his own programmed audit controls, he must test that they are functioning satisfactorily. He may do this to monitor records and print out exceptional transactions which may be symptomatic of fraud or other out-of-control situations.

It has been suggested that the use of a *separate* system-testing group will provide a quality assurance over systems being developed.

Controls over development

The initial development stage of an on-line system is the time when the auditor should be involved in order to satisfy himself that a number of rules are clearly established. It is for instance necessary to determine what information in the system is to be regarded as highly confidential and how this is to be achieved. Specific rules relating to who will be permitted to *add* to data, *change* data or *delete* data must also be developed, and the nature of the reports which the system will produce to show the effect of these changes must also be specified.

Many developments of on-line systems are additional developments to already existing, integrated systems. An integrated system must be able to cope with regular hardware changes and software modifications, as well as developments of new applications. Data structures and terminal arrangements will also be subject to modification from time to time. The testing and commissioning of these changes may cause problems. Simulation software is available to assist in this task. A teleprocessing software simulator enables the use of test files to check out a new system. A network activity simulator allows an on-line system to be tested in batch mode without using terminals; it also allows the testing of the interaction between systems.

Manuals and training

Systems design, programming and testing can take place in parallel with the less technical but very important tasks of preparing user department manuals and training user department staff. The user department representatives on the project team should be involved in the preparation of these manuals and the training of user staff. Audit can be invaluable in ensuring that no system goes live with inadequately trained staff and without a full procedures manual. These two aspects tend to be the ones that are neglected as all resources are committed to the technical aspects of systems development. The only effective form of training is for user staff to be trained *using* the new system. This means that the programs must be working, input forms available, and any remote job entry terminals functional before training can be completed. The trainer's style should not be to tell them *about* the system: he should get them to work the system, as this is the only effective way to learn. The system must not go live with poorly trained staff. The extent to which the training can overlap with the development of the system (as shown in Fig. 1) will vary with the circumstances.

File conversion

The network in Fig. 1 perhaps misleadingly shows the crucial file conversion task as commencing quite late. In fact it can commence as early as possible with the collection of data for later encoding and transfer to master files. But the layout of the input forms will have to be known before much progress can be made and at least some of the programs will need to be working before the files can be created. The earlier the task is commenced, the greater the problem in updating the data which has been loaded onto the computer. The later the task is commenced the more hurried it will be, but there is some data which cannot be converted until the last minute—carry forward figures from the last cycle of the old manual system being an example. The GIGO principle is relevant here—garbage in, garbage out. It is not easy to over-emphasize the importance of investing resources in good file conversion.

The auditor must satisfy himself that the size and nature of the task has been allowed for. It may even have been overlooked! Systems have been designed which have depended upon data which, in the event, was not available. On a payroll and personnel statistics system requiring the creation of a one-thousand-character record for each employee, a concern with 25 000 staff has the task of loading onto the computer 25 million characters of data.

The file conversion steps are as follows:

1 Obtain the data.
2 Transfer the data to computer input forms.
3 Check for accuracy.
4 Encode the data.
5 Verify the encoding.
6 Use a computer program to read and validate the data and transfer to a master file.
7 Print out rejected data.
8 Correct rejected data and resubmit.
9 Print out the data which has been accepted.
10 Check all accepted data for correctness by comparison with the source of the data.
11 Maintain accepted data up-to-date by raising modifications and processing in a similar way.

The user department's test of the system should ideally be done on the live master file as it is a good test of whether the file is complete and accurate. This has not been allowed for in Fig. 1. At an early stage in the development of the system the auditor should start asking questions about the planning of file conversion. Where he is required to formally sign-off the system he would only do so if he were satisfied as follows:

1 That the system meets user requirements; and the programs, which function satisfactorily and have been tested thoroughly, have been developed with adequate controls incorporated and are auditable.
2 The master files are complete and accurate.
3 A satisfactory implementation program has been devised.

Implementation

Implementation is often done in phases, possibly linked to a phased construction of the master files. Initially a pilot implementation may be followed section by section until implementation is complete. Parallel running of the old and new systems should occur, at least for the first sections to be implemented until confidence is built-up. The decision must be made as to whether to use the computer results or the manual results, if parallel running is taking place. Parallel running doubles the task of the user department at a time when they are ill-placed to cope and may have lost staff due to a premature run-down in anticipation of staff savings through computerization. The auditor should be vigilant for impending problems in the staffing of the user department.

Maintenance

After implementation a post-installation audit should take place. It is not the responsibility of the internal auditor to conduct this audit but he should conduct a review to ensure that it is done by the project team. The user department should be involved in this and approve the findings. The objective of this audit is to check that design objectives have been met. The audit is made much easier if data was collected about the performance of the old system before it was superseded.

The on-going maintenance task of a computer system is facilitated if the initial development of the system was well controlled. Good documentation, proper authorization of all program modifications and the continued analysis of performance data of the system are the hallmarks of sound maintenance which the auditor will look for. In some cases the auditor will feature in the program change control process even though in theory this is unsound. This will be discussed when we consider computer auditing techniques.

Discussion topics

1 Do you accept that the internal auditor should review the development process of a new system, and if so how would he administer such an audit? Would he be a member of the project team? Would he attend liaison meetings? Would he issue a report? Does he need to be a computer specialist?

2 What are the most important matters to be controlled in the development and implementation of a new system?

3 Much of the work of any computer-user department is now done within the computer department. What are the implications of this from a control viewpoint, e.g.:
- (a) whose system is it?
- (b) who is responsible for system controls?
- (c) who is responsible for organizational controls such as segregation of duties in the data processing department?

6 Auditing the Computer Installation

Summary

This chapter examines the procedures which should be followed by the data processing department in order to achieve effective security over processing and data. This is the approach the internal auditor in particular will take in his operational audit of the data processing function.

Our classification of controls in computer systems is as follows:

1 Application controls
2 General controls
 —computer centre controls
 —application development controls

Although these sub-categories overlap a little, the problem of overlap is not serious. Here we consider computer installation controls.

It should be stressed that these considerations are equally applicable in principle to all computers. A computer may be small in size but still be large in capacity and power, and the data processed on it may be of great importance. It is inevitable that there will be differences of emphasis between controlling a large computer installation and controlling a small one, and consideration is given to this matter in chapter 8. However, *the principles involved are identical*, and this issue should not be fudged or blurred by wishful thinking.

Installation controls

The internal auditor will want to conduct an audit of the computer centre (sometimes called an 'installation audit', 'operational audit' or 'audit of general controls') for the many applications which he audits all depend on good control standards within the computer centre itself. We have earlier said that he will set up this audit as a special audit and will not of course cover these points whenever he audits any computerized application, or whenever he audits the development process of a new application.

An 'Internal Audit Control Evaluation Checklist' for auditing computer centres is given at the end of this chapter. No general checklist can ever be regarded as complete for any particular user, who must devise a specific checklist to suit his own particular circumstances and conditions. However, a general checklist can help to provide guidance on the nature of the points the auditor should look for. For consistency, ease of completion and ease of review the checklist has been designed so that a 'Yes' answer is a good answer in each case.

Internal audit use of checklists is well established. There is really no difference between a checklist of this sort and the traditional internal control questionnaire—all the questions on both lists are intended to provide insights into strengths and weaknesses in internal control. It is essential that an auditor should understand the relevance of each question; it is preferable that he tailor his questionnaire for a particular audit rather than use a standard one without modification.

The basic premise is that *data processing needs good security*. While this may seem obvious, in practice it is not fully accepted. Data processing may account for only between one and two per cent of turnover, and managements are reluctant to invest effort and possibly resources into improved security when it is difficult to demonstrate a direct payback from this investment. Security arrangements over inventory, cash, plant or investments are more self-evidently necessary. Nevertheless data processing security is vitally important. In part it is the information resource which is at risk—it has already been suggested that this is the most valuable resource of many concerns, even though it is not carried as an asset in the balance sheet; and in part it is that businesses are becoming increasingly computer-dependent—it is not merely the computer facility which is being safeguarded but all the commercial operations which depend upon the computer, as well as the assets which are recorded and controlled by computer systems.

Most security measures implemented within the computer department will not be significant net users of resources. It is often no more costly to do something in a controlled way than it is to do it badly—frequently the opposite is the case.

Accounting

In this summary it is intended only to add to the points which appear in the checklist. With respect to accounting it must be emphasized that effective control is likely to be missing if data processing is regarded as a cost centre that does not need to recover its costs by charging out to customers. The charge out system in practice often causes some aggravation as users are reluctant to accept on trust whatever costs data processing is inclined to pass on. It is quite consistent with the principles of internal auditing that internal audit may be asked to audit the charges made. Accounting for re-runs is particularly important as excessive re-runs probably indicate that something is fundamentally out of control in either the programs or the files of data.

Disaster recovery

One senior executive is on record as saying that if anyone were out to get his company the way to do it would be through his company's $25m computer set-up. Another has said that if one of his oil refineries were rendered inoperative he could continue to function but not if one of his key data centres became inoperative.

Top management support is a necessary prerequisite for effective contingency planning. Once this has been obtained, a team should be set up to identify the risks or threats that should be guarded against in contingency plans. The user departments must be involved, as it is their systems which are at risk. The user department is in a position to quantify, at least in approximate terms, the impact of the loss of the computer processing facility. Data processing management and audit personnel should also participate in this process. Then the team should develop contingency plans to cope with the risk, and these should be costed. Once top management approval has been obtained, implementation of the contingency plans can commence. When implemented, responsibility should be assigned to maintain the plan and to test it regularly.

Environmental controls and physical security

Under this heading we consider physical protection measures against hazards, whether natural or otherwise. These are mainly preventative measures and this marks them out from disaster recovery plans.

Fire extinguishers

Water-based fire extinguishing systems, such as automatic sprinklers set into the ceiling, are back in favour even for computer installations. The alternatives of carbon dioxide and other gases have more serious drawbacks. A water-damaged set of hardware is often easier to clean than one which is smothered with foam. There is an asphyxiation risk with CO_2 or other gas, whereas the risk of electrocution with water can be avoided by the automatic shut down of power when the extinguishers are activated.

Back-up power

The most important consideration of back-up power provision is that the switchover should be automatic without loss of processing. One way in which this can be achieved is for a flywheel to be continuously in motion, serviced by grid current. When there is a cut in the grid supply the flywheel continues to supply the electricity to the computer, while a diesel dynamo is started up to service the flywheel. Equipment provision to avoid fluctuations in grid supply may include the provision of an electricity substation devoted entirely to the computer.

Access control

Access control is a thorny issue. It has been suggested that managements pay lip service to this only in order to be seen to be taking the security problem seriously. Managements themselves are often the worst offenders in violating access control procedures. In such cases they only demonstrate their apathy regarding security.

The available methods of access control are:

1 Man recognition.
2 Badge of key system.
3 Personal identification number (PIN).
4 A radio token.
5 Combinations of these.

Some consider an access system worked by security staff to be the best—but it is open to abuse and staff are not consistently reliable. A badge is quite effective but in many systems it must be surrendered when an employee ceases to have right of access. If the system is computer controlled it will be possible to instruct the computer that the badge is invalid from that instant. With a badge its surrender does at least effectively debar entry, but it should be recognized that all these systems of automated access control are controlling equipment and not people: it is the badge that is authorized, and the hope is that it is being carried by the right person. A combined system of badge and personal identification number is more secure but more costly. A personal identification number on its own is not satisfactory as it is difficult to keep numbers secret.

All these methods involve active participation by the person who is seeking access: this may be irksome and the radio token avoids this problem as it activates the access control from its location in a person's pocket. It has the added advantage of being discreetly hidden and perhaps not alerting prospective gate crashers to the fact that a security system is operating. In this context it is perhaps worth pointing out that controlled access systems can be set up with man traps which detain unauthorized entrants. Radio tokens are open to the abuse of irresponsible siting adjacent to the access point in order to keep the doors permanently open. Care must be taken to ensure that, despite sophisticated security, there are no ways round the system—perhaps by forcing the lock or entering by another route. Care must also be taken to ensure that the system for the issuance of badges, keys, tokens or PINs is secure.

Security people are placing more emphasis on coupling these access control methods to a security minicomputer, which allows the system to be more sophisticated and more reliable. There are also hopes for the commercial development of systems which will be more difficult to fool as they will interpret personal characteristics of people, such as voice or signature.

Access control can be considered to be only one of several protective barriers. Outside perimeter protection may also be appropriate. Once in the computer area the intruder should not have it all his own way. Data should be protected in safes. Crucial data may also be encrypted.

An effective test of the security arrangements relating to access is for the internal auditor to try to achieve unauthorized access.

With remote job entry the equivalent of access control is the password system which authorizes terminal use. Passwords are difficult to keep confidential and are vulnerable to 'discovery', perhaps by a computer which has been given the task to break the security of the system on a trial-and-error basis. If the password itself is encrypted it will prevent unauthorized use of the password by line-tapping.

Insurance

Insurance for material damage of computers and equipment may be taken out against a standard list of perils or against all risks. While the standard list usually covers malicious damage by employees, usually only the all-risks cover includes accidental damage by employees. While this cover includes magnetic media it does not include the data held on the media. Consequential loss insurance is necessary to compensate indirectly for the loss of data as it covers loss of fees, increased costs of working and loss of gross profit.

Breakdown insurance is on an all-risks basis due to the difficulty of defining the risks involved. The remaining relevant category of insurance is legal liability to third parties; this covers liability due to contract, negligence or fraud and would be relevant if the computer were in use as a bureau.

The cover needed will vary depending upon the risk. Excessive cover is wasteful as insurance companies will not pay up beyond the actual loss. If a machine is hired it may not be the responsibility of the user to effect material damage insurance, except perhaps on a negligence basis only. There is an excellent chapter on computer insurance by Allen in the book *Keeping Computers Under Control* edited by Chambers and Hanson (Gee, 1975).

Media library controls

Media are more likely to be damaged by improper handling when they are out of the library. In view of this, and for general security reasons, only the minimum of media should be out of the media library at any one time. When not in actual use, any data in the computer room should be kept in a local safe able to withstand attack and fire.

The records of media kept by the librarians should contain the following information:

1 The media-use record (identified by serial number).
    The number of passes of this tape or disk etc.
    The number of read/write errors.
    A maintenance history record.
2 The file record (identified by file identification).
    Creation data.
    Release date.
    Generation number of the replacing file.
    The transaction file(s) used to update this generation.
    Serial numbers of the media used.
  (Each record will show multiple occurrences of the same data, as all generations of the file are recorded together).

Terminals

The same computer room physical controls should also apply to terminals, as should the same back-up arrangements. There may be as good a case for the terminals to have standby terminals, standby power and standby personnel to operate them as there is for the central computer itself. Reserve terminal operators should be thoroughly trained. Terminals may be grouped to provide automatic terminal standby. Alternative lines from the terminals to the central computer should also be considered.

Frequently the central computer itself will be duplicated, with one computer servicing the on-line system while the other does routine batch work on other applications. The peripherals and the teleprocessing control units will be switchable between the computers. Similarly there may be two teleprocessing control units switchable between both lines and processors. Ideally, duplicated mainframe equipment and software should be located separately to reduce the risk of both sets being 'down' at the same time.

Some on-line systems update continuously two copies of permanent data. The two copies may both be used to speed up some on-line processing steps, such as the production of reports, although clearly there is a sizeable overhead involved in maintaining both copies. One acts as a back-up for the other.

With many real-time systems a calculated commercial decision is taken that it is not feasible to have a manual fall-back system should the real-time system be rendered inoperative. However if it is feasible it should exist, and preferably it should also be tested.

Controls over performance

A log file will be maintained which is used to produce statistics of all activities in the system; this provides a powerful opportunity for management control. One target is that the system should be available for 100 per cent of the time that it should be working. In practice, efficiency factors of over 98 per cent can be achieved.

Organizational control

There is no single correct way of organizing a data processing department, but the chart shown as Fig. 2 follows the control principles suggested in this section of the audit checklist.

Auditing the Computer Centre: an internal audit control evaluation checklist

(1) Accounting.
(2) Disaster recovery.
(3) Environmental controls and physical security.
(4) Hardware utilization control and maintenance.
(5) Input and output control.
(6) Insurance.
(7) Media library controls.
(8) Operations.
(9) Organizational control.
(10) Personnel.
(11) Programming.
(12) Resources planning.
(13) Security controller and risk manager.
(14) Standards manual.

Accounting

Objective: To provide the means for controlling and monitoring the performance of the EDP function.

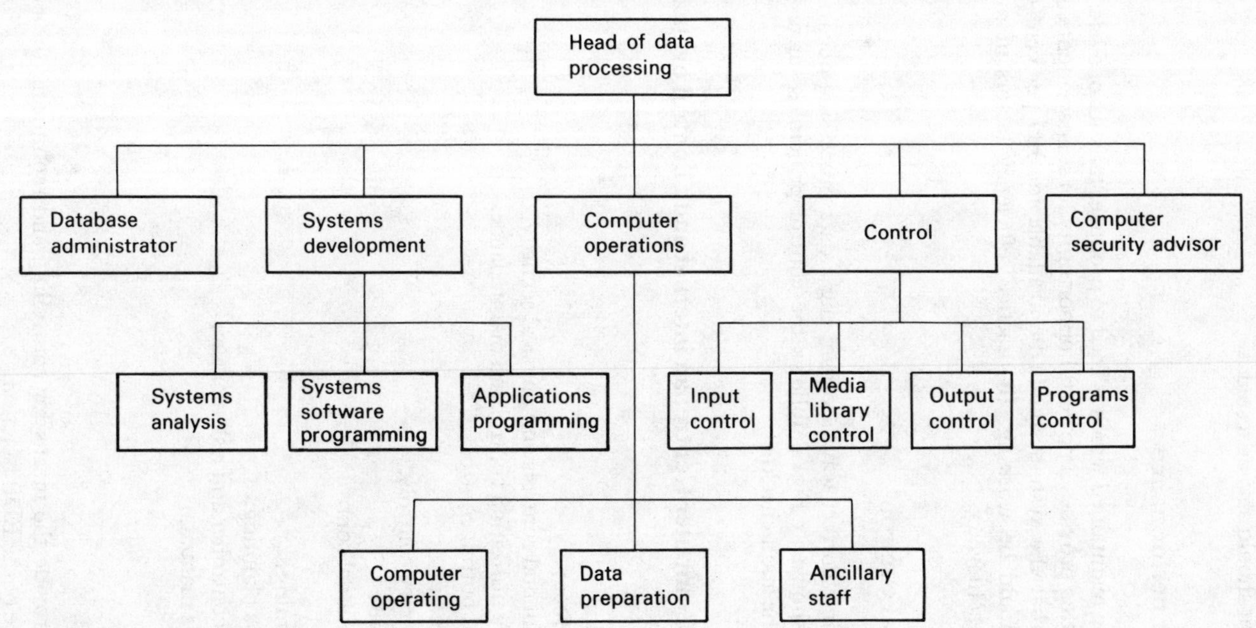

Fig. 2. Organization of data processing.

1 Are all computer costs charged back to the user departments?
2 Are program testing costs subject to budgetary control?
3 Are system development costs charged to user departments?
4 Is it the practice for formal agreements or contracts to exist between EDP and the user?
5 Is a programmed system of job accounting and machine usage analysis in operation as a basis for evaluating EDP performance and determining charges to users?
6 Is tight control maintained of the following computer uses:
(a) 'down-time' and 'up-time'?
(b) re-runs and other processing?
(c) computer time lost through operator error?
(d) application development and production work?
(e) development wrongly treated as production?
(f) unauthorized work?
7 Is EDP billing of user departments subject to evaluation and verification by:
(a) internal audit?
(b) others?

Disaster recovery

Objective: To ensure continuity of essential processing if the resources of hardware, software, facilities, personnel, power or application programs are rendered inoperative.

1 Is there a system in operation whereby a security copy of each of the following is maintained in a strongroom at a separate, secure location:
(a) computer files?
(b) computer programs?
(c) computer run documents?
2 Is the back up afforded by 1 (above) adequate to ensure that all necessary information is available to retrieve the situation in the event of loss of any information at the main computer centre?
3 Has a contingency plan been developed, tested and maintained which will allow processing to continue, assuming different levels of disruption ranging from partial disruption for one to four days up to total disruption for over a month?
4 Does the contingency plan allow for the re-establishment of the EDP function using duplicated facilities?
5 Does the contingency plan allow for manual fallback procedures for computer applications?
6 Is there a contingency plan for each application?

7 Have the user departments been involved in the development of contingency plans and in their testing?

Environmental controls and physical security

Objective: To minimize the risk of loss of data processing capability.

Fire

1 Are the precautions against fire in the computer area adequate, namely:
   (a) use of fireproof doors and fireproof partitioning?
   (b) a regularly tested, satisfactory alarm system?
   (c) a regularly practised, satisfactory fire drill?
   (d) displayed notices?
   (e) heat and smoke detectors?
   (f) fire fighting equipment:
      (i) hand extinguishers?
      (ii) fire blankets?
      (iii) permanently installed, automatic fire extinguishing system?
2 Is there a satisfactory, working system for testing fire detection and fire fighting equipment?
3 Is electrical power automatically isolated before the fire extinguishing system operates?

Flood

4 Has the flood risk from burst pipes and tanks as well as from external sources been allowed for in the development of the computer centre? If not, what are the risks and how are they being tackled? (see also 23 (c)).

Storm

5 Has the risk, if any, from storm been evaluated and catered for?

Power interruption

6 Is there back-up power supply adequate to operate the computer, air conditioning, heating and lighting—by means of:
   (a) standby generator?
   (b) switching arrangement to another section of the electricity grid?
7 Is switch-over to back-up electrical supply automatic without loss of power?
8 Have back-up electrical arrangements been tested regularly?

9 Has electrical equipment been augmented as necessary to improve the quality of the regular supply in order, for instance, to avoid voltage fluctuations?

Air conditioning

10 Is there tested back-up for the air conditioning system?

Access control

11 Is there outer perimeter control against unauthorized access, and has this been tested?
12 Is there access control at *all* entry points to the computer area, and is this effective?
13 Is the computer centre secure against penetration by intruder, bomb, gun, missile or arsonist attack from outside?
14 If unauthorized access is achieved, are program and data media in safe storage?
15 Is access to the computer area restricted to the minimum number of people who should have access?
16 Is there a satisfactory system in operation for controlling the access of authorized visitors to the computer area? Are visitors always accompanied?
17 Where on-line terminals are in use is there a satisfactory system of password control to prevent unauthorized use of terminals?

Back-up

18 Is there back-up for the computer installation by, e.g.:
(a) a duplicate computer centre separately housed and powered?
(b) an agreement with other nearby users?
19 Have back-up arrangements with third parties been formally documented?
20 Have back-up arrangements been tested and is there a satisfactory mechanism for ensuring that compatibility between the computer configurations is maintained?
21 Is there an action plan for coping with a strike by computer operators or other key personnel?
22 Is there adequate redundant hardware to ensure in-house continuity of processing if devices fail?

Siting

23 Is consideration given to the security implications of the location of new

computer sites in order to avoid:
(a) proximity to inflammable, explosive or toxic material?
(b) location within an evacuation-prone area?
(c) a location below flood level?
(d) a location vulnerable to terrorist attack (e.g. above a car park, on display from the street)?
(e) location on a flight path?

Hardware utilization control and maintenance

Objective: To provide a means of controlling hardware by measuring the adequacy of preventive maintenance, the level of vendor maintenance service provided and the rate of failure of the equipment—in order to avoid failures which may result in errors or omissions in computer processing.

1 Is a machine maintenance program in operation?
2 Are statistics available on the breakdown of each item of hardware?
3 Does management evaluate the performance of hardware and take any necessary action?
4 Does management evaluate the quality of the vendor maintenance service?
5 Has consideration been given to transferring the maintenance contract to a third party?

Input and output control

Objective: To ensure the accuracy, timeliness, completeness and security of data received and data distributed, and to deal with complaints.

1 Is there an input and output control group segregated from any other responsibilities?
2 Are all off-line jobs prepared outside the computer room?
3 Are re-runs also prepared outside the computer room?
4 Does the control section receive all work which has been processed and control it prior to despatch?
5 Are there laid down job handling procedures?
6 Is the control section responsible for scheduling computer processing?
7 Is adequate attention paid to cut-off date problems with respect to the scheduling of computer processing?
8 Is there physical security over work submitted to and emanating from the computer centre?
9 Is there security over data entering the computer centre by remote job entry (e.g. encryption) and over the return of data to a remote location?

Insurance

Objective: To secure, by means of economic insurance, the risks which cannot reasonably be dealt with in other ways.

1 Does the concern regard insurance (correctly) as a last resort when all other reasonable means have been excluded?
2 Is computer insurance obtained by shopping around rather than by taking a comprehensive insurance package which may give unnecessary or inadequate cover?
3 Are the same policies followed for computer insurance as with insurance in general, e.g.:
   (a) not to insure small risks?
   (b) to carry a large excess?
   (c) to insure at replacement cost rather than second-hand value?
4 Is the computer cover adequate but not excessive?
5 Has consideration been given to all insurable risks:
   (a) material damage to machine and equipment?
   (b) breakdown due to internal causes?
   (c) consequential loss due to down-time?
   (d) legal liability to third parties?
   (e) fidelity bonding of staff in key positions of trust?

Media library controls

Objective: To safeguard the quality of the media and to ensure that no unauthorized alterations are made to, or use is made of, the media.

1 Is there a media library?
2 Is it separated by walls from the rest of the computer centre?
3 Is access to the media library strictly controlled?
4 Is there satisfactory environmental control of the media library, e.g.:
   (a) is smoking prohibited?
   (b) is there adequate air conditioning?
   (c) are fire detection and extinguishing systems comparable with those in the computer room, and adequate? (refer to the section on Environmental Controls and Physical Security for additional points).
5 Are confidential files kept on locked racks (tapes) and in locked cabinets (disks)?
6 Are procedures in force to ensure that no one person is left alone in the library?
7 Are operators excluded from the library?
8 Is tight control kept over the quantity of disks and programs out of the library at any one time?

Operations

Objective: To control the work of operators in order to optimize productive computer time, lessen the risk of error and fraud, eliminate unauthorized work and secure the confidentiality of information.

1 Are programmers prevented from operating the computer?
2 Are operators prevented from working single-handed?
3 Are operators not given the opportunity to learn to write programs?
4 Do operators only operate the computer:
 (a) with the proper program instruction manual in front of them?
 (b) with signed and authorized run instruction sheets?
5 Is it standard practice that operators do not restart programs that have failed without supervisor intervention to ensure that all is in order?
6 Is it laid down and operating that the console log shall not be removed except by the operations manager, and that all paper breaks shall be initialled by two people?
7 In a database environment is the database administrator separate from operations staff?
8 Is there an inventory control of tapes and disks?
9 Is the issuance of media from the library under the sole control of an authorized librarian?
10 Is the release of tapes and disks for overwriting with other data the responsibility of the librarian alone?
11 For each application, are there written instructions specifying when generations of files may be released—such as after expiry date and when a new generation is available?
12 Are records maintained on issue and return of media in order to control:
 (a) media use?
 (b) files?
13 Are there procedures which determine which files should be held in duplicate at remote store?
14 Are all sensitive programs run during normal business hours and under close supervision?
15 Is computer waste paper and carbon paper destroyed by shredding or burning—in a secure manner?
16 Are all write-protect rings removed from new tapes immediately upon delivery and from all other tapes after processing?
17 Is there control over over-writing data on disk files inadvertently?

Organizational control

Objective: To take advantage of the available opportunities to organize the data processing department so as to improve control.

1 Are the following activities organizationally distinct within the data processing department:
(a) systems development?
(b) computer operations?
(c) the control section?
2 Where they exist, are the following positions organizationally distinct from any of the above and from each other:
(a) the database administrator?
(b) the computer security controller or risk manager?
3 Within systems development, is there opportunity to segregate:
(a) application testing from systems design and programming?
(b) systems software programming from application programming?
If so, has due consideration been given to doing so?
4 Within the control section, is there opportunity to segregate:
(a) input control from output control?
(b) media library control from other control activities?
(c) programs control from other control activities?
5 With respect to 1 to 4 (above), where organizational control exists is it functioning satisfactorily?

Personnel

Objective: To achieve a climate and methods of working which maximize the trustworthiness of staff—particularly those in key positions—while minimizing the extent to which control depends upon trust.

1 Are the working conditions and terms of employment of computer staff adequate to maintain high morale and staff loyalty?
2 Are positive efforts made to integrate the computer staff into the concern rather than encouraging them to be an exclusive computer élite?
3 Do personnel recruitment policies ensure so far as they may that the staffing of the data processing department is stable?
4 For applicants for jobs in the computer department, are references taken and followed up by a phone call or visit rather than by letter?
5 Are all applicants interviewed by skilled, trained interviewers?
6 Is it the practice to account independently for all the years and months of an applicant's career in case the missing months give a clue to enforced dismissal, imprisonment or mental instability?
7 Are staff recruited on probation and during this time restricted from:
(a) operating the computer alone (this should apply to all operators)?
(b) operating a system with live data?
(c) operating an on-line system?
(d) maintaining major systems?
(e) testing programs unsupervised?

8 Is there a system of employee review, evaluation and development?
9 Where the above system (see 8 above) exists, can it be said that satisfactory efforts are made to develop staff out of their known weaknesses?
10 Are there adequate staffing levels?
11 Are dismissed personnel immediately released with no opportunity to work out their notice?
12 Is consideration given as to whether a member of staff who resigns should not also be required to leave immediately?
13 Are there standby staff for key positions, and would the use of these staff be free of any dangers caused by violation of segregation principles (e.g. a programmer who acts as a standby operator)?
14 Is there a system in force to ensure that access badges and other materials are returned from staff who are dismissed or leave for other reasons?
15 Is a conscious effort made to maintain good staff and union relations?

Programming

Objective: To ensure that efficient programs, which are readily operated and maintained, are written in a controlled environment which reduces the risk of error or loss whether accidental or fraudulent.

1 Are programmers adequately supervised?
2 Does the data processing department have programming standards which are adequate and enforced?
3 Are programs desk checked by independent programmers after they have been coded?
4 Is program documentation complete and of high quality?
5 Are there standby copies of programs and of program documentation?

Resources planning

Objective: To ensure that adequate computing resources (facilities, equipment and software) are available to provide for continuity of processing and for the development of new systems.

1 Is there an agreed, costed development plan covering all computer resources and related to a time scale?
2 Are data processing commitments being related to this agreed plan?
3 Is the scheduling of hardware acquisitions and application development adequate to avoid serious under- or over-utilization of computer resources?
4 Is due allowance made for acceptance trialling?

Security controller and risk manager

Objective: To vest in one person or section the responsibility for computer security.

1 Is responsibility for computer security included within the job description of anyone in the data processing department?
2 Has any of the following been designated responsible for ensuring that the concern's computer systems have not been the subject of fraud:
(a) the Computer Manager?
(b) the Chief Accountant?
(c) the Security Controller?
3 Is he concerned with all types of risk and not merely with unauthorized access?

Standards manual

Objective: To communicate the best practice to be followed by data processing staff. To encourage uniform and compatible styles of working and to facilitate supervision and re-assignment of work to other staff. To provide a medium for recording and developing the experience of the data processing department and for developing individual staff.

1 Does the data processing department have a Standards Manual covering all aspects of their work?
2 Is this manual kept up to date effectively?
3 Is this manual, or relevant sections of it, issued to all appropriate staff and steps taken to ensure that their copies are kept up to date?
4 Are new staff inducted into the practices and rules contained in the Standards Manual?
5 Is the Standards Manual complied with?

Discussion topics

1 Is it the internal auditor's responsibility to conduct an operational audit of the computer centre covering installation and personnel security as well as methods of work?

2 Should staff be trusted? If so what does this mean in practical terms?

3 Is computer security a resource problem or just a matter of management attitude?

4 Do general controls over the computer centre affect the standard of internal control of user applications?

7 Auditing Computer Applications

Summary

The objectives of controls within computer applications and interface of the auditor with these controls. Controls over input, processing, computer files and output. Overall manual controls, programmed controls, batch control, check digit control, verification, run-to-run controls and other controls.
The meaning of 'on-line' and 'real-time' with examples. The control objectives of authorization, accuracy, completeness, continuity and timeliness. Controls over development, back-up and standby controls, controls over performance, access controls, other input controls, controls over data transmission, controls over programs, controls over permanent data, controls over output, and controls over cut-off. Audit considerations and appropriate audit techniques.

The control areas in computer systems and computer operations may be classified as:

1 Application controls
2 General controls
—computer centre controls
—application development controls

Each of these areas should be the subject of audit review, but here we are concerned only with application controls. These controls can be further subdivided as shown in Table 1.

Table 1. Application controls

Control over	Manual	Programmed
Input	√	√
Processing	√	√
Computer files	√	√
Output	√	√

Control and audit objectives

The objectives of application controls are to ensure that computer systems function efficiently and effectively, and in particular that data is processed completely, once only, accurately and securely. General controls over the computer centre and over the development of applications must also be effective if these objectives are to be met, and these can be reviewed separately by the auditor.

The auditor's objective in the area of application controls is to satisfy himself that the control objectives of the system are being met and, if necessary, to make recommendations. It is clearly essential for the auditor to understand how these control objectives may be met in a computerized environment—and that is what we shall be discussing here.

The auditor's work on application controls will run right through the stages of an audit (Table 2) of a computerized system. It is preferable that he initially

Table 2. The stages in an audit

Stage	Process
1	Determine the scope
2	Learn about the system
3	Record the system
4	Confirm the system
5	Evaluate the control
6	Conduct compliance tests
7	Conduct substantive tests
8	Overall review
9	Report with recommendations
10	Subsequent follow-up

conduct this audit while the system is being designed; he may be required to 'sign off' that, *inter alia*, adequate application controls have been built into the system. He will augment this pre-event audit with subsequent audit visits to confirm that the controls are operating as intended and are achieving the desired results, and to make whatever subsequent recommendations may be necessary.

The fundamental principle is that application controls should be user-oriented. A good system will be transparent in that the *user* will be in total command of it. It is he who should control input data and reconcile output to it. He should also monitor the integrity of computer files and the validity of computer processing. Systems are user department systems: data processing provides a processing service only. This is a basic segregation of responsibilities which greatly strengthens control if it is achieved. Of course the data processing department will control their own work, principally by means of their control section, but this internal 'quality control' by the service department is no substitute for complete control by the user department itself.

Overall manual controls

Controls over input, processing, files and output may in each case be manual controls or programmed controls, and frequently a control mechanism has elements of both manual and programmed control. A very valuable form of manual control is the manual generation of control totals *outside* the computer system for later reconciliation to what the computer has processed as given in computer control totals. This method of control is often referred to as overall manual accounting control—but it may be just as effective for the control of non-accounting data. This control method is best illustrated by an example:

Consider cash coming into a concern. One principle of control is that control should be established as early as possible; afterwards it is less likely that loss or error will occur. Unless there are good reasons why it should not be so, cash may be controlled in the mail room. All mail would be opened by two staff working together. Non-cash mail would be put to one side. Cash would be entered into a mail room cash day book showing the payer and the amount remitted. The day book would be adlisted by an independent operator in order to arrive at our first control total. Other control totals would be produced as the cash is processed through the organization, and finally, assuming the system were computerized, the computer should produce a total of cash posted to the accounts. These totals should be reconciled by someone independent of the generation of any of the control totals. A typical reconciliation might look something like the example in Table 3.

What has been achieved by this overall manual accounting control is that, amongst other things, the completeness and accuracy *in overall terms* of computer postings has been confirmed. It does not prevent an error in the value of a computer posting but it does emphasize that it has happened after the event. It does not pinpoint the actual error and a certain amount of detective work will have to be done to isolate the offending item or items. Of course it does not provide a check that the correct accounts have been posted—the control would be satisfied even if all the cash had been posted to the wrong customer accounts.

For all its limitations this control has the advantage that it is outside the computer system. It acts as a control over the computer system. The computer can be harnessed to control itself in other ways by means of programmed controls but it is reassuring to have manual controls over the computer as well. At system design stage an identification should be made of all the important monetary and quantity amounts which need to be controlled; it will

Table 3. Overall manual accounting control of cash, including computer cash

		$
Cash per mail room day book:		9999.99
Deduct	cash held in suspense	
Add	cash transferred from earlier suspense	(9999.99)
	cash received not through mail room	9999.99
Cash per cash book:		9999.99
Deduct	cash not banked	(9999.99)
Add	cash banked from previous day	9999.99
Cash per deposit slip:		(9999.99)
Deduct	non-computer cash	(9999.99)
	computer cash rejected	(9999.99)
Add	earlier rejections resubmitted	9999.99
Cash per computer control:		$9999.99

usually be found possible to devise some form of manual accounting control over each.

Further examples might be:

1 Overall control of the number of staff on the payroll by maintaining a simple analysis of joiners, leavers and current staff for reconciliation to a computer analysis of the number of payslips produced.
2 Overall control of the number of customer accounts by reconciliation to computer-produced totals. The total value of the computer-based sales ledger can be controlled in a similar way.

Note that manual accounting controls use the computer to some extent, as they depend upon a control (in one of our examples, of cash posted) produced by the computer. Computer-produced control totals should not be taken at face value. If an output control total is accumulated at the time the data is *read* by the computer rather than at the time the data is *posted* to the computer accounts, the total may not be an accurate reflection of actual postings, and cannot be relied upon. Of course the program logic *should* accumulate this control total in the next sequential programmed instruction after the updating takes place in the program. In other circumstances, which we shall consider later, the computer may produce a series of control totals and conduct its own reconciliation of these, reporting discrepancies: it is vitally important that the program logic which produces these control totals is sound and not biased to producing control totals that are bound to agree, whatever the circumstances. In a program which reads the records on a file and writes them all to a new file, the programmer may have inappropriately incremented counts of records read and written *both at the same time immediately after each record is read*. If he has done this, it is inevitable that the computer will report that control totals agree!

The best way for the auditor to check out this potential problem is to conduct some 'program auditing'—that is, to review the program code to determine that control totals have been coded appropriately.

Overall manual accounting controls provide a measure of control over input, processing, computer files and output.

Programmed controls

There is one general programmed control which also has the general potential to control input, processing, computer files and output. This is the incorporation into the programs of coding which is specially designed to monitor what is happening and report unusual developments. One derivation of this technique is the cusum (cumulative sum) technique. With this method the computer maintains a moving average of a particular item which must be controlled and reports any deviation beyond a certain tolerance from the average. Trends in the average may also be reported. Examples are shown in Table 4. This technique may be used as a control over input, processing, computer files and output.

Whereas manual accounting controls and programmed controls such as those using the cusum technique may be applied to the control of input, processing, files and output, other controls are specific to each of these areas of control. Before considering each of these areas in more detail, however, it is necessary to comment on the need for auditors to appreciate differences between computer applications which may superficially appear very similar. These differences have a considerable bearing on the emphasis which may need to be placed on particular types of control in different circumstances.

The meaning of 'on-line' and 'real-time'

Although all on-line systems and real-time systems have many features in common they show considerable variety. While all real-time systems are on-line, not all on-line systems are real-time. At its most basic 'on-line' means the transfer of data from one location to another via a telecommunications link such as a telephone line. On the other hand, 'real-time' is a term best restricted to those systems with simultaneous updating and where a response is also sent down the line *in time to affect the outcome of the transaction itself*, and is intended to do so. Invariably the response must be very quick in order to be in time to affect the transaction: response times of less than one or two seconds are not unusual, even with real-time systems where many hundreds of remote terminals are linked via a satellite telecommunications link to a central computer located in a different continent.

An example of a real-time system is an airline reservation system. In this

Table 4. Cusum technique examples

To be reported	Control over	Programmed control	Interpretation of results
1 Input types	Input, processing and computer files	The program accumulates a count of inputs of specified types and notifies any significant deviations from normal experience. The program maintains a history of input experience, and reports any significant trends.	May indicate new, untrained user or data entry staff. May disclose an unfavourable trend in data entry. May reveal that the integrity of the permanent data files (master files) has deteriorated. May point to a program defect. May indicate changing commercial circumstances or a breakdown in control (e.g. if a disproportionate number of adjusting entries are being input).
2 File conditions	(as above)	The program monitors, for example, the proportion of DR accounts which have CR balances.	May indicate violation of laid down manual procedures. May indicate defective input data. May indicate fraud or other abuse. May point to a program defect.
3 Output volumes	Processing, computer files and output	For example, the average volume of statements per daily run (and perhaps the number of lines per statement) is maintained by the computer, which prints out significant discrepancies and significant trends.	May indicate a program error, a file error or a (possibly otherwise undetected) business trend.

system a member of the public goes to a travel agent to book a ticket. The travel agent keys in an enquiry on the agent's terminal which is linked to a central computer perhaps on a different continent. An apparently immediate response comes back from that computer and is displayed on the agent's terminal. The response may notify the customer that his precise travel request cannot be met and offer an alternative plan. As a result of this information the customer modifies his request and the terminal operator keys in his final requirements.

In this example, a response was made; it was almost immediate, and was intended to provide the opportunity for the transaction to be modified. It is worth pointing out that the system functioned without audit trail being produced as an inevitable by-product—which is often the case and has implications for control and audit which we shall examine later.

Another typical example of a real-time system involves 250 terminals connected to a public utility's central computer which holds one million customer accounts. The system handles 100 000 transactions each day with a peak of 120 000. It is capable of handling 16 000 each hour. Seventy per cent are enquiries, twenty-five per cent on-line updates and five per cent data entries such as amendments of permanent data. Twenty-five transactions can be processed simultaneously and the mean response time is $1\frac{1}{2}$ seconds. In all, the system has eighty on-line files and recognizes seventy transaction types. It operates six days a week for fourteen hours each day.

In general, real-time systems are complex, costly and more difficult to control: a fundamental question the auditor should ensure is asked when he is involved at the pre-event stage is 'Do we really need a real-time system?' Of course, the answer will often be 'Yes'—it is difficult to conceive of an alternative for a modern airline reservation system.

Some on-line systems provide a response which may affect the outcome of the transaction but do not have simultaneous updating, and therefore fail our definition of a fully fledged real-time system. An example would be the cash withdrawal from terminals of some UK banks: the customer can obtain a display of his balance prior to deciding how much to withdraw. If after withdrawal he asks for another display of his balance it will not have changed: what is being displayed is the final balance of the previous night's off-line updating. Other banks provide a genuine real-time service.

Many on-line systems fall short of providing a response which is in time, and is intended, to affect the outcome of the transaction. These are interactive in a more limited way. An on-line system may be designed to conduct instantaneous updating from remote terminals of permanent data held at a central computer: in such a system interaction will occur in order to validate the input data submitted from the terminal. Validation takes place *at the time of data entry* and may be handled by the central computer. This validation is done in a conversational way between the central computer and the terminal operator. Once the data, whether a customer's order or a cash deposit, has been validated it is accepted and the terminal operator moves on to the next item of input. There is a potential control problem here; troublesome input may be put to one side by the terminal operator and may never enter the system. With conventional batch-oriented methods of data entry, offending items would be reported by the computer and held in suspense until they were corrected.

So this form of on-line interactive data entry requires rigorous controls to ensure that all data which should be entered are in fact entered. Although this on-line system provides a response from the destination of the data, the response may only be intended to modify the transaction if the transaction is in error or incomplete, rather than contribute to the construction of the transaction in other respects. Even so, most would designate this a real-time system.

A more modest on-line system would be one which is used for enquiry only. Frequently this is 'Stage 1' of what will later become a fully fledged real-time system with on-line updating and on-line transaction construction. Although an enquiry system is interactive it is not usually called real-time.

Even where batches of data are simply passed down the line from one piece of hardware to another there may be a modest response in the form of control information. Such a system might not involve immediate updating of permanent files: instead the data may be held on magnetic tape or disk for later batch processing when the validation checks will be done, if they have not already been done at the remote location. Processing can be in batches; batch control procedures can certainly be applied. Validation can have been done at the remote terminal location if remote batch terminals with their own independent processing capabilities are in use. Such a system acknowledges that the task of editing input is a user department responsibility, without going to the extent of requiring the development of a real-time system. It presupposes that there must be some constraint which requires centralized processing while allowing local validation. An on-line communication link where a customer's computer sends details of credit transfers (for salary payments, or payments to suppliers) to its bank's computer is an example. Not only is there no real-time updating, there is also no real-time response intended to affect the outcome of the transactions, so the system is merely on-line, not real-time, despite the modest amount of interaction in the form of control information. Another example is the linking of a terminal in a supermarket to a major supplier's computer: daily at an appointed time the supermarket manager keys in stock levels and the supplier's computer computes reorder amounts and triggers a delivery.

The distance of the communications link is not of course very significant. Real-time systems exist within shops with no linkage to the outside world. For instance, a light pen or wand passed by a sales assistant over special markings in a catalogue may trigger a response to the sales point in the form of a tone or a light to indicate whether or not the item is in stock:

the customer goes ahead with his order or modifies it, and stock records are instantly adjusted. Point-of-sales terminals in place of conventional cash registers may be used for cash control, stock control and customer account updating. Process control systems to control production processes were early examples of other in-house real-time systems.

Before we can proceed with an examination of the control and audit implications of on-line and real-time systems it is necessary to provide more background. Usually these systems have terminals at one end of the telecommunications link. These may be intelligent terminals or simply devices for the entry and receipt of data. They may be designed to handle batches of data on paper tape, magnetic tape or punched cards or may simply have a typewriter keyboard. The returned data to the terminal may be displayed on teletype, line printer or VDU (often called a cathode ray tube or CRT). There should be a password control over the use of the terminals; the terminals themselves may be identified to the remote computer by means of hardware responders built into the terminals. Where there are a number of terminals it is usual for one terminal to be designated the master terminal (or master control terminal) for use by the master terminal operator, who has an important internal control role.

The on-line system depends upon a device at the central location known as the teleprocessing control unit, and also upon special software known as teleprocessing system software or the teleprocessing monitor. A real-time system will also invariably depend upon data being held centrally on a database, and therefore the system will also depend upon the database management system (DBMS) software.

The telecommunications link may be by direct private line or it may utilize the public switched lines, in which case dialling may be manual or automatic.

Distributed processing is another term for on-line processing where terminals are situated at remote locations. It may take several forms. It may simply be a matter of remote users having access to joint data held centrally. Alternatively, it may entail the processing of large volumes of data remotely, and the passing of summaries to a central computer, perhaps for consolidation purposes. The opposite may be the case—namely the processing of large volumes centrally and the transfer of summaries only to remote locations for local management control purposes.

Time-sharing services may be on-line or real-time. They are the on-line equivalent of the computer bureau. The special feature of these systems, from a control perspective, is that the central computer has many users from different organizations. Each user must consider the security implications of sharing a computer with other users who may be competitors.

Control in computer systems

The control objectives of computer systems are sometimes expressed in terms of 'security' and 'integrity' but these terms are not precise enough, and instead the following control objectives are adopted:

Authorization—of input, of processing and of output.
Accuracy—of input, of permanent data in the system, of processing and of output.
Completeness—of input, of processing, of permanent data and of output, including the availability of data within the system, especially where a database is in use.
Continuity—the assurance of continued processing.
Timeliness—the processing of input on schedule, the handling of cut-offs, and the production and delivery of output.

To achieve these control objectives there must be satisfactory controls over all the elements of the system.

Input controls

The auditor should be concerned with the appropriateness of the input method. As data gets transferred from one medium to another—such as from coding sheets to magnetic tape—there is always a risk of errors being made. The more transcription stages the greater the risk. Input controls may be designed to pick up this type of error. Prevention is better than cure so attention should be given to reducing the number of stages in the data entry task. If this is successful, both the size of the task and the risk of errors will have been reduced, and it follows that, being more efficient, it is likely that the data preparation task will also be cheaper.

Figure 3 shows the maximum number of stages in the data preparation task. Many of these stages, however, may in practice be merged together. Turnaround documents, originally produced by the computer and then turned around to become input coding documents, are one example. For instance, computer-produced remittance advices can be despatched to customers to be returned with their payments. As these advices already show the customers' account numbers, only the amounts remitted need to be added before they become complete input documents. It is very unlikely that there will be errors in account numbers as these were printed on the advices by the computer. The amounts will be controlled by batch control (which will be discussed later). This can be taken a step further by making the turnaround documents directly readable by a computer peripheral device such as a magnetic ink character reader (MICR), an optical mark reader (OMR) or an optical character reader (OCR). The latter two devices can read an assortment of printing, some of it done by the computer and some of it added manually. With these devices the encoding stage has been eliminated.

Data collection equipment is even more relevant as a means of reducing the data entry bottleneck and contributing to greater accuracy. If employees

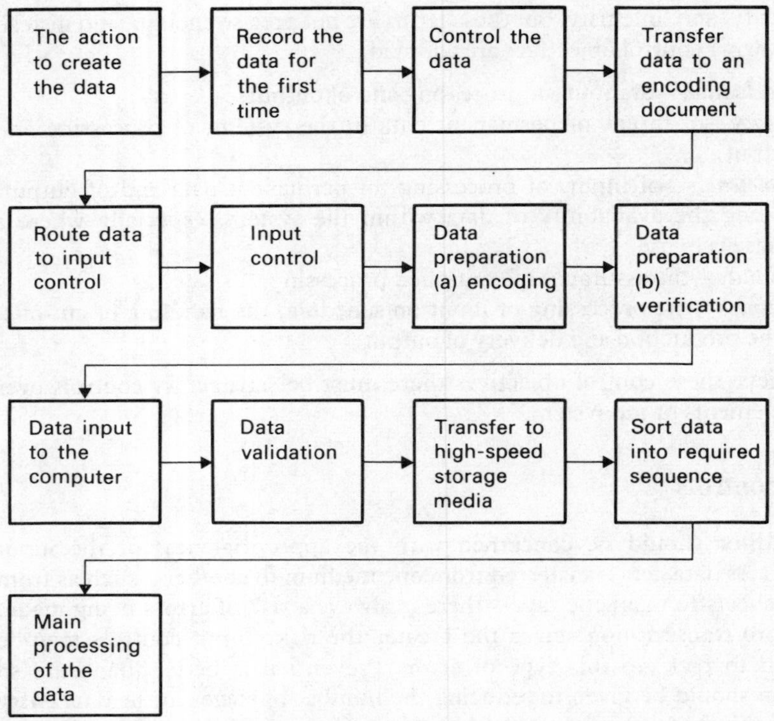

Fig. 3. The stages in the computer input process.

use a badge to clock in at a badge-reading station (a type of computer terminal) the computer receives in 'real-time' the data it will need to produce payslips at the end of the week and most of the steps in the data input process have been eliminated, along with the bottleneck.

As the output of one computer may be the input to another computer it is often possible to avoid producing paper output which has to be converted back to computer media. Instead one user can exchange magnetic tapes with another user, transfer data via an OCR, or have an on-line communications link. The auditor will be particularly concerned to satisfy himself that adequate audit trail is present in such systems.

Key-to-disk installations, where encoders put data onto disks under the control of a minicomputer and a supervisor terminal, provide an opportunity for off-line editing to be done so that the data has passed many validity tests before it reaches the mainframe computer.

The auditor will want to be satisfied that whatever method of data entry is chosen it is known to be reliable and provides the information and records that management needs for control purposes and that the auditor needs for auditing purposes.

Specific controls relating to input are:

1 On-line access controls.
2 Terminal controls.
3 Data transmission controls.
4 Validity and posting checks.
5 Pre-input controls.
6 Batch controls.
7 Check digit and mathematical analogous controls.
8 Verification controls.

Some of these controls are mandatory if the system is to be safeguarded satisfactorily. Some of these controls are mandatory if data input is on-line (though they *may* be used optionally if it is *not* on-line). Others are only mandatory if data input is not on-line (but may be used optionally if it is). Others are only optional, whatever the circumstances.

This may be set out graphically as in Fig. 4.

	ON-LINE INPUT	OTHER INPUT
MANDATORY	On-line access controls Terminal controls Data transmission controls	Pre-input controls Batch controls
	Validity and posting checks	
OPTIONAL	Check digit control	
	Batch control	Verification controls

Fig. 4. Applicability of input control procedure.

Auditors should ensure that each particular application has an appropriate mix of input controls.

1 *On-line access controls*

Access controls limit the action which can be taken by system users and act as a control over sensitive data. Physical access control is the responsibility of the user department. This may include locating the terminals in a lockable room which is kept locked when not in use: it should be vandal- and force-proof. Access may be by badge, key or other controlled access means. Terminals themselves may be lockable, in which case there must be a satisfactory system for the controlled issue and return of keys.

Although the preceding actions are important, the most effective access control routines are those which are programmed into the on-line system. A three-tier system may apply:

1 Control of personnel access and terminal use.
2 Control of terminal access to programs.
3 Control of program access to data.

The access of personnel to terminals may be controlled within the system by means of personal identification to the system of the terminal operator. This is usually done by password control. It is not a foolproof control. Passwords may be communicated to unauthorized personnel in error—perhaps by writing them down as a substitute for memory. The system is often abused by the passwords being posted near the terminals. Occasionally, on-line systems have been designed which print the passwords on demand. Frequently passwords are communicated when unauthorized delegation occurs. Passwords should be under the control of the master terminal operator, who in turn should be subject to control. Passwords should be changed frequently and securely; the program which changes passwords should also be tightly controlled to avoid unauthorized use.

Usually password control is limited to controlling the operation of terminals by authorized personnel and not to determining what they are allowed to do. Control over permissible activity is generally a control over the terminal itself. Each terminal can have a 'responder', i.e. a built-in hardware code which identifies the terminal to the system. The programs a particular terminal is allowed to use are then determined by the system by reference to tables held within the system. There may be a distinction between logical and physical terminals. A *logical* terminal is what the *system* sees as an entry point into the system. Actual physical terminals may be reassigned between logical terminals. Control over logical terminals in a databased system will be under the database administrator: this is because the identification of the logical terminal determines which programs the terminal may use, and the programs which are used in turn determine the processing of the database which takes place. As the integrity of the database is, of course, the responsibility of the database administrator, it is correct that he should also be responsible for the control of logical terminals. It is, however, a user department responsibility, via the master-terminal operator, to control the assignment of particular physical terminals to logical terminals. One physical terminal may legitimately be assigned to more than one logical terminal.

The final access control is over what the programs themselves can do. They may be restricted to what data they can access and limited in what they are permitted to do with that data. The main possibilities are 'read only', 'read and add to', 'read and alter' or 'read and delete'. This control is either by means of restrictions built into the programs themselves, or alternatively by means of tables associated with the database.

All terminal usage should be controlled. A simple means of control is to reconcile the terminal log record of access time with a summary produced by the central computer. The master terminal operator is able to control the work of terminal users by eavesdropping on their interaction with the computer. Any attempts to access programs and data which are prevented by the access control system should be displayed on the master control terminal.

2 *Terminal controls*

Some features of on-line systems are favourable from a control viewpoint. Clerical staff are fully identified with their work. The user department also generally has more effective control over the data input into the system, as data entry occurs in the user department. Input forms and encoding have been eliminated and input is direct to the computer. Validity checks (see below) are made at the data entry stage.

There must still be careful control over data input. Terminal operators must be well trained and they must have detailed written instructions to aid them. There should be a comprehensive terminal log which will include a record of all input. With visual display terminals this log may not be at the place where data is entered but may be held on magnetic tape at the central computer. The log file can be analysed to produce statistics of volumes, exceptions and the occurrence of particular conditions.

Batch control (see below) will often not be practical. Where possible it may entail the establishing of batch balances at the point of data entry in retrospect, *after* the data has been entered and validated. Where batches are found to be out of balance the system may have to 'reverse out' the batch of data, as updating may already have occurred. Alternatively, the error batch may just be reported for prompt corrective action. In on-line systems it is more usual for input control to be by means of exception reporting than by batch control. It is impossible to discuss all the types of exception which might be reported as they will depend upon the nature of the system. Missing or duplicate sequence numbers is one example. In some systems all data is entered twice; an exception would be reported where there was a discrepancy between the two entries. In order to link data with terminal operators, data may be tagged to identify the person who entered it, and tagged again to identify the person who checked it.

Physical housekeeping over the input operation must be to a high standard. Generally a real-time system depends upon input being entered promptly and controls must exist to ensure that this is achieved.

3 *Data transmission controls*

There are routine hardware and software controls to ensure that the data which leaves the terminal is the same as the data that arrives at the central computer, and these need not concern us. It should be noted that public switched lines result in more inaccuracies and are also less secure than private lines. Where public lines are used, a telephone dial lock may inhibit unauthorized use of a terminal but there may be nothing to prevent unauthorized access from another terminal at a different location. If data is transmitted across a public network it is in the last analysis public. However, where data is sensitive it may be encrypted before transmission. Passwords may also be encrypted. Transmissions may also be authenticated by the application of an algorithm mutually agreed between the originator and recipient of an authorized transmission.

4 *Validity and posting checks*

Most validity checks over input are reasonableness tests. The validate program should vouch input data for reasonableness in order to prevent invalid data going further into the system.

Typical tests might include the following:

1 Are all amount fields numeric?
2 Is all data present which should be present?
3 Is data within the correct range of values?

The auditor should examine the specification of the validate program to satisfy himself that it has been thoroughly specified. He may use audit test data to verify that the validate procedures are operating correctly.

Posting checks are failures to find a match for transaction data on master files—for instance, a customer may not exist on the file or there may be a 'stop' on his account. The auditor should satisfy himself that all errors of this variety are satisfactorily dealt with by the computer programs and actioned by the user department. Sometimes these errors only show up late in the system when the master file is accessed for the first time; in this case the system may need to be programmed to reverse the effects of processing which has already been done on the transaction which is in error.

With computer-controlled data preparation using visual display terminals linked to a direct-access master file, posting checks can take place at the data preparation stage even prior to the submission of the data to the mainframe computer.

5 *Pre-input controls*

Pre-input controls, although non-technical, are very important. They are the techniques and procedures which may be applied before the data reaches the entry stage. They include good computer forms design, no more types of input form than are necessary, the use of pre-numbered forms whenever appropriate, avoidance of unnecessary transcription, avoidance of unnecessary codes, the use of turnaround documents, good housekeeping and orderly working methods in the departments which generate computer input and fill in computer coding sheets, trained staff, good clerical procedures manuals and measures to maintain the security of data and forms. Some computer input forms may be particularly sensitive and should be kept securely. Examples would be forms which are used to change rates of pay, to change a price list or to write off a debt.

6 *Batch controls*

Batch control is not necessarily inconsistent with the use of on-line data entry or file updating. Batch control ensures that all data that should reach the computer does in fact do so, and that no unauthorized data gets included. It also acts as a verification of the transcription of selected important items of data on the source documents. It should be established as early as possible so that thereafter there is control. A salesman taking orders would batch them at the end of the day before mailing them to his head office.

While the optimum size for a batch is between fifty and one hundred documents, it would nevertheless be appropriate to establish batch control even on an average of six to eight documents if this is a unit of work. If the salesman takes half a dozen orders a day, batch control should be established by him at the end of the day; from that time the orders he has taken will be safeguarded. The smaller a batch the more work is involved, as more batch control slips must be made out and processed. On the other hand fewer documents will be rejected when the computer encounters a batch that does not balance, and it will be easier to find the offending document.

To establish batch control the salesman would fill in a batch control slip for customer order processing such as the example shown in Fig. 5. In Fig. 5, not all the fields may be essential. The asterisked fields alone may achieve satisfactory control when other controls (such as check-digited account numbers) are taken into account. Similar fields will be used for batch control of other systems. The batch control slips might be in a consecutively numbered

*		*					*	
Batch number (often pre-printed)	Previous batch number	Com-pleted by (staff code)	Date D D M M Y Y	No. of docu-ments	Hash total of (e.g.) account numbers	Hash total of (e.g.) stock item codes	Quantity total	Total price (if applicable) $ $ $ $ $ $

Fig. 5. A batch control slip.

pad. He fills in the number of orders in the batch. As the number of items that customers have ordered must be kept correct, each order form may have a box to enter the number of items ordered and on the batch control slip he inserts the total number ordered on all the orders in the batch. If there were other important quantity or monetary items he would control these in the same way. It is possible to control other data such as account numbers by making hash totals on the batch control slip. However, there are more effective ways of controlling account numbers (such as check digit control, which is discussed later) and a hash total is rarely needed to check that all data has reached the computer, as the number of documents in the batch is usually included on the batch control slip.

The batch control slip, once completed, accompanies the documents it describes as they are routed through the system. It is important that batches are logged in and out of each stage using proper log books so that a lost batch can be traced. Ultimately the computer receives the batch together with the batch control slip and it conducts a check to see if the batch control slip correctly describes the documents in the batch. If there is a discrepancy it will be due to a document being lost or encoded twice, a mis-encoding of data or an inaccurate batch control slip. The computer will also account for the receipt of all batches by keeping note of the serial numbers of batches or by some other means, such as expecting a batch a day from each salesman (in which case the salesman's number should also appear on the batch control slip). Another method is for a grand total batch control slip—which controls all the batches—to be made out and submitted to the computer.

The first program of the system is often called the validation or edit program. It is responsible for batch control, check digit control and the general scrutiny of data for reasonableness. *Exceptions* are reported but allowed to continue processing although they can be stopped by user intervention. *Errors* are rejected. The auditor must satisfy himself that validity checks result in the appropriate response of these two depending upon the circumstances. A batch of data which does not balance should generally be rejected, although there may be occasional instances where minor discrepancies can be treated as exceptions. Rejected data should be printed out. Since it will not be known which transaction is in error the entire batch and the batch control slip must be printed out for correction. Correction is a user department responsibility. The offending batch can be put onto a suspense file (on disk or tape) so that when it is corrected it is only necessary to resubmit the erroneous transaction rather than the entire batch. Whenever possible, programs should be designed to carry on with all the validity tests, even when one error has already been detected in a document or in a batch. This reduces the risk of some errors remaining undetected until the are resubmitted.

It is vitally important that there should be satisfactory control over the clearance of exceptions and errors.

7 *Check digit control*

Check digit control is a control over the continued integrity of a permanent number. It may also pick up bogus numbers indicative of fraud. It is usually not practical to use check digits for variable amounts such as monetary items. Check digit control does not confirm that the number is the right number. For instance a valid check-digited account number may be copied from a list of account numbers but it may be the wrong customer's number: check digit control will not detect this.

The check digit is originally computed according to a special formula. The computation may be done by the computer or by a calculating machine, or even automatically during the form printing process. Once computed the digit is added to the account number and thereafter permanently associated with it. It is conventional for the check digit to be the most junior digit of the number. Due to the nature of the formula most errors which occur in practice relating to the number will be detected by check digit control. One formula known as 'Modulus 11 straight weighted' detects over 99 per cent of typical errors. This is because most errors are transposition errors. 'Modulus 11 straight weighted' picks up all transposition errors and all single transcription errors and other random errors as well. An example of this formula is shown in Table 5 and Table 6 shows a different formula which is used for the UK Value Added Tax (VAT) numbers: in effect this is 'Modulus 97 straight weighted'.

Check digit control is appropriate for important permanent codes where the consequences of error could be serious. it is most commonly used for account numbers and may also be used for stock item codes.

When the computer reads a check-digited number it does a quick proof to test its validity. A proof is shown in Table 5, and the same method would be used for Modulus 97 in Table 6.

It should be recognized that check digits may impose some constraints upon the system. Modulus 11 can result in a 'double check digit'. This can

Table 5. check digit control by 'Modulus 11, straight weighted'

Problem: To compute the check digit for the number '9214' and then to do the computer 'proof'.

Computation:

1 Multiply each digit by descending weights, commencing with five (number of digits + 1)	9	2	1	4	
	×	×	×	×	
	5	4	3	2	
2 Add products	45 +	8 +	3 +	8 = 64	
3 Divide by 11 (the modulus)					64 ÷ 11 = 5, remainder 9
4 Subtract the remainder from the modulus to arrive at the check digit					11 − 9 = 2
5 Check-digited number	9	2	1	4	2
Proof:	×	×	×	×	×
6 Multiply by descending weights	5	4	3	2	1
7 Add products	45 +	8 +	3 +	8 +	2 = 66
8 The result of Step 7 should always be directly divisible by the modulus leaving no remainder					66 ÷ 11 = 6, remainder 0

Table 6. Check digit control on the UK Value Added Tax Number ('Modulus 97, straight weighted')

Problem: To compute the check digits for the VAT number 282 5842 ??

Computation:

1 Multiply digits of the first two fields by descending weights, commencing with '8'	2	8	2	5	8	4	2
	×	×	×	×	×	×	×
	8	7	6	5	4	3	2
2 Add the products	16 +	56 +	12	+ 25 +	32 +	12 +	4 = 157

3 Deduct 97 from the result until a negative number is reached. The result is the check digits. 157 − 97 = 60 − 97 = −37

4 The complete VAT number would be 282 5842 37

be avoided by not issuing any account numbers which would give such a result. Alternatively, an alpha character can be used in place of a '10'.

8 *Verification controls*

Verification is the action of checking the encoding of one encoding operator by another operator. The file of encoded data is mounted on an encoding machine set up in verification mode and the second operator goes through the motions of encoding while the machine checks that he is encoding the same data as has already been put on the tape. If a disk-based system of data preparation is in use, the data already on disk may be assigned to a second operator for verification.

Verification is an effective way of picking up most encoding mistakes—though not when the mistake was caused by illegible input. This control suffers from being dependent on staff of variable reliability. A bonus scheme for encoding staff which is based upon volume of work done will discourage staff from being thorough in verification work.

As control costs money there is no point in over-controlling. Complete verification halves the speed of data preparation. Selective verification may be in order. Unimportant fields may not merit verification, and if an account number has check digit control there may be no merit in including it in batch control and verification control procedures.

Processing controls

Control over processing is achieved by overall manual controls and programmed routines such as the cusum method. There is of course no end to the variety of programmed controls that can be built in to aid control of processing. They should be tailored to the circumstances.

Basic run-to-run controls

A few specific techiques deserve special mention. Run-to-run controls act as a control over completeness and accuracy of processing as well as being a control over the integrity of computer files. These controls take the form of the accumulation within the program of processing totals to which the files which have been read, amended or created are reconciled.

Figure 6 describes a simple computer program which amends a customer master file with amendments which are presented on a magnetic file previously sorted into the same sequence as the customer master file—which would be ascending sequence by account number. The modified file may be re-

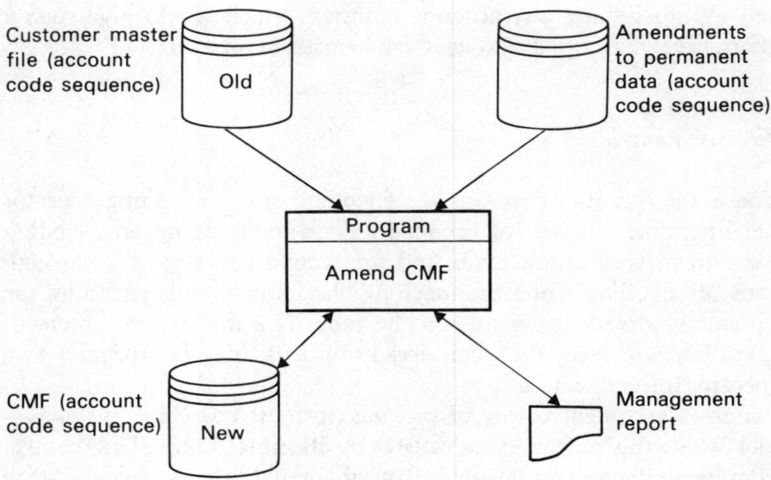

Fig. 6. Amendments to a customer master file.

written to a new file, as updating of the same magnetic file is not a practical computing proposition. Each file has a trailer record which at a minimum has a count of the number of records on the file. As the computer reads the old customer master file and the amendments file it accumulates its own count of the number of records read in each case and, when end of file is reached, compares its totals with the total carried in the trailer records of each file. If they do not agree it is possible that, due to a program fault or hardware failure, a record or records have not been read from one of the files. If undetected this would be serious, as all record might be lost of a customer and his debt. In addition the computer would accumulate a total for the number of records written to the new customer master file and reconcile this with its count of additions and deletions to the old customer master file. An example of this reconciliation is shown on Fig. 4 and Table 7.

It is better that the computer should be programmed to conduct run-to-run controls automatically rather than simply printing out totals for manual review. Machines administer routine controls more faithfully than staff. The computer must of course report whether control totals agree and the auditor will want to satisfy himself that the appropriate consequences occur whenever run-to-run controls are out of balance. Although Table 7 shows this control in action in one program only, the control is fully developed when it is applied to a suite of programs, checking that the files used by one program agree with those processed by later programs. Hence the term 'run-to-run' control.

The data held in the trailer records of files is flexible and can be designed specifically for a particular application. If additional data is required for run-to-run controls then this can be added. Control will usually not only be exercised over the number of records but also over quantity or monetary values

Table 7. Control report

	Per program count CMF	Amendments file	Per trailer records
Total of records on old CMF	10 051		10 051
Records modified		351	
Records added	130	130	
Records deleted	(69)	69	
Total records on new CMF	10 112		10 112*
Total records on amendments tape		550	
Control totals agree			

* Inserted by the computer on this run.

held in particular fields as well. An obvious example would be control over the total value of a customers' ledger.

Control totalling of indexed files and databases

Run-to-run control totals are readily produced when a computer file is read sequentially from beginning to end. Where only selected records are read (either directly or via indexes), it is not so easy to produce control totals of the files. Frequently these control totals are not produced during routine processing but when the disk file is either dumped onto tape for security purposes or is reorganized. Databases pose similar and additional problems. It will frequently be found that not all the data segments of a particular type are read, so no meaningful control totals can be produced of 'total number of segments' or 'total value'. Nevertheless control totals *must* be produced as this is an important way of confirming the continued integrity of the database. These control totals will usually have to be produced as a special run of the database. As with a conventional disk-based system this could be done when the database is dumped daily for security reasons: this in itself is another control overhead of databases which is not found with tape-based systems, where security copies of files are automatically available as a by-product of normal processing. Alternatively it could be done by a special control program. The totalling and the frequency with which it will be carried out must be agreed between the systems designers and all users at the design stage.

It is important to realize that with a database each file, and indeed each record, is constructed specifically for the user application which is being processed: this is done by bringing together individual data entities. Consequently the user cannot so readily satisfy himself that processing has been done completely and accurately. This is an illustration that user controls outside the computer system are not so readily achieved with databases, thus emphasizing the importance of higher levels of inbuilt integrity.

Checkpoints

On very long computer runs where there will not be the time to start processing again or it is likely to be too costly to restart, checkpointing should be considered. This entails the periodic copying onto a magnetic tape of the contents of the computer and of all files in use. Should the run fail after that point—due perhaps to power failure or operator error—the contents of the checkpoint tape can be read back into the computer and onto the files and processing can be recommenced as from the last checkpoint. The interval between checkpointing will vary but may be as little as fifteen minutes in vital systems such as the overnight processing of cheques through the banks' clearing systems. There is an economic issue here: checkpoints cost money as they take computer time. They also delay the completion of the job. It is necessary to balance the risk of processing failure, the cost of checkpointing and the consequences of not checkpointing in order to arrive at a realistic checkpointing interval.

File controls

Header records

In addition to trailer records, files have header records or electronic 'labels' which identify the files and contain generation numbers, expiry dates and other data.

Applications can be programmed to check that the generation number of a file is the right one—in order to avoid, for instance, Thursday's transactions being processed again on Friday. Expiry dates are used to prevent the over-writing of current data. Opportunities exist for inserting other data into the header record for control purposes.

Basic file security

The auditor should examine the arrangements made for the file security of an application. Many of the security arrangements over files, such as media library controls, will be common to all applications and will be covered in the audit of the computer centre. Some security arrangements may vary from application to application. A standard method of file security is the three-generation cycle for file security.

Referring to Fig. 6, if the following day a further file of amendments was processed against the customer master file, the input customer master file on that second occasion would be the file that had been created on the previous day. At that instant three generations of file would exist. At a minimum the earliest generation (grandfather) could now be released for other uses, but father must be retained until son produces his own progeny. The transactions or amendments which were processed against father in order to produce son must also be retained. The objective is to be in a position to recreate the latest generation of the file if the latter were destroyed or damaged. These security copies should be stored at a separate, secure location.

Integrity of data

It is a basic control principle that all amendments to master files should be printed out, checked by the user department and authorized. Each application should allow for the periodic confirmation of all reference data—that is, of the permanent data on master files, and any permanent data held as tables within the computer programs.

Control over indexed files and databases

The control totalling of indexed files and databases is carried out in a different way, because files are not created whenever records are amended, and the complete file may never be read at any one time. File security may be achieved by specific copying to magnetic files which are then stored remotely in the usual way. This is necessary as earlier generations of the files do not automatically become available. Control totalling should be done when this copying process takes place.

Recovery

It is not, of course, enough to take a daily security copy of a database for recovery purposes unless all transactions are also logged. Logging of transactions allows recovery by processing the back-up copy of the database against all logged transactions which have been processed since that copy of the database was made.

Apart from reporting all changes to the database, the contents of a database should be logged before and after changes to it; transaction data which instigated a change should also be logged. This history log should be readily accessible: the auditor may want to access it.

Technical reliability of the database

Most of the other problems relating to continued correctness of the database relate to the technical nature of the database itself. For instance, the database may lose its integrity due to deficiencies in the database management system (DBMS): pointers may go missing, or indexes become defective. Periodically a database has to be reorganized; this is a time when the logical integrity of the database is especially at risk. The database may also lose its integrity due to logical inconsistencies in the way it is handled by users.

Looked at objectively it is a tall order to expect all data on a database to remain intact, accessible and accurate over a long period of time. For instance, a one-premium insurance policy recorded on a database may remain unaccessed for many years until, when it matures, the database is expected to report it. By that time the insurance company will be using a computer several generations removed from the computer which first accepted the details of the policy, and the database itself will be unrecognizable. This highlights the need to exercise great care when new hardware is acquired or when information is transferred from one database to another.

Database control program

The answer to unreliability is partly control totalling, and partly the regular use of a special control program to examine the database for errors. This control program will be useful for the auditor as well. It is sometimes known as a query/report generator and will be a high-level language used to interrogate the database.

Data dictionaries and data maps

Databases are used in conjunction with data dictionaries and data maps. The dictionary defines each data element held within the database and the maps, sometimes called schemas or sub-schemas, describe logical relationships of data items with other data items as well as the physical relationships with other data within the database. When a computer application requires data it is found by reference to *indices* (which point to the place on the disk where the data is located) and/or *pointers*, which allow chaining from one data item to another without the need to work through indices. Auditors should from time to time seek to test the continuing integrity of the database in these respects.

Data definitions

The quality of the database depends upon rigid enforcement of consistent data definitions. At its most basic this means that everyone must refer to a data item by the same name, otherwise duplication of data within the database will probably result: this may lead to serious inaccuracies in processing apart from loss of efficiency and a generally weakened opportunity to integrate applications. In practice this is more of a problem than might appear: what is, to one department, known as an employee number may be known to another department as a staff number, payroll number, clock number and so on; a stock number may be a product number, part number or stock code. Very careful control must be exercised to ensure that like items are held on the database once only, and that no items are deemed to be the same unless they really are. This means that during the design of a database the database administration team, analysts and programmers *and all interested users* must agree a unique definition for each data element. The auditor should confirm that data is used by different departments in accordance with this common definition, otherwise misleading or erroneous management information may be produced.

Validation of input

A database may not allow as much validity testing of input data at the time of input as a batch processing system. The ideal time to validate input is when it goes into the system, or even beforehand with off-line data editing. With a database it is often the case that different elements of data, which together feature in the validation process, may be input at different times. A related problem is that it may be more difficult to achieve proper authorization of input data prior to submission to the system than it is with a batch processing system. In summary, there is a risk that the validation process may not be so thorough as with a batch system, and unauthorized data may be more likely to enter the system.

It is therefore particularly essential that, as a formal design procedure, provision should be made for establishing which validation tests should be conducted upon data, and what authorizations of data are required, and that these should then be built in. All interested users as well as the system designers must be involved in this specification.

'After-the-event' authorization of input

Since it may be impractical to authorize input prior to submission to the computer, an alternative would be to authorize afterwards. Under this method, the authorizing authority receives a listing or a display of all data which was identified at the design stage as requiring his authorization. When he receives this display the data will have entered the computer and will be held on the database, but it will not be processed further (e.g. be amended or used to produce output) until it has been authorized. Authorizing 'after the event' in this way has the advantage of ensuring that *all* data which should be authorized is brought to the attention of the authorizing authority: there is a much reduced risk that input could, deliberately or accidentally, avoid the authorization process.

Controls over permanent data

Real-time systems often have greater concentrations of data and higher levels of activity, so the risks of errors occurring are correspondingly greater. Now that batch control is rarely used there is a problem of authorizing amendments. The authorization process cannot readily occur before the event, and in any case it is better to authorize amendments to permanent data *after* they have been made. This has the advantage of drawing unauthorized, illicit amendments to the attention of the authorizer as well as the proper amendments. Until the after-event authorization has been made there can be a 'stop' on the processing of any transactions which use the modified data.

As a means of unravelling data integrity problems a 'data image back-up journal' may be written whenever permanent data is updated. This is a history file which shows the permanent data as it was immediately before and after each update. In addition, the permanent data would usually be dumped overnight, when it would also be reorganized. The dumped data would be retained for several cycles together with the associated transaction and history files in order to allow for recovery.

An essential control is to ensure that the current version of files is being updated. The master terminal operator is responsible for checking that the files are the correct versions at the commencement of processing before any other user is allowed on the system; but the files themselves are the responsibility of the data control section. One of the problems of database systems is that data is shared by many users: it is no longer possible to assert that the permanent data files are the property of a user department.

The data processing department should not have the on-line facilities which would allow its staff to modify the contents of user files.

Output controls

Output controls are required to ensure that produced output is correct and complete, and that it is then properly and securely distributed to the correct users within a defined time schedule. Once again, overall manual controls and programmed controls such as the cusum technique are used.

Output controls are not technically complicated. The auditor should look for the following:

1 Reconciliation of output to input.
2 Accountability within the user department for all accountable stationery such as cheque stationery.
3 Proper treatment of exception and suspense reports.
4 Controlled resubmission of rejections.
5 Controlled use of microfiche where appropriate.

Controls over output

Even though input may not have been in batch mode, output reports (with the exception of individual enquiries) can be controlled by means of control totals which should reconcile to file totals, and it is important that this should be the case as a means of control over the integrity of the database, the availability of the data, and the completeness of the reports. Output may be confidential: this should be allowed for when the system is designed. It is often a good principle to allow output only at the terminal which provided the associated input.

Controls over cut-off

Accounting cut-off is always a problem with computer systems, the more so with a real-time system for which it may be impossible to suspend the processing of transactions. The problem is to handle the processing of the new period's transactions even though the old period may not have been closed off. It may be impossible to close off the old period as certain items of data relating to that period may not have reached the system. This problem is usually overcome by dating transactions and data elements with their accounting as well as their processing dates. Where this is done, care must be taken to ensure that control reports produced by the system make proper allowance for the dates of items.

Audit considerations

The auditor will clearly want to make use of terminals for audit work on on-line systems. He may use dedicated audit VDU terminals to develop and maintain audit software and to conduct audit tests on the system. There will be access protection so that the audit output is available only at the auditor's terminal and at his command. On-line systems invariably have a general enquiry facility and the auditor will be able to use this. He may also use generalized audit enquiry packages. He may develop his own integrated audit monitor to police the on-line system in his absence and hold data for later display for the auditor on the auditor's terminal.

Access control over the auditor's use of the system via his terminal will, of course, restrict him to reading files only. Even this may have to be negotiated, as an unfettered facility to read the data on a database is contrary to the control principles which auditors themselves impress upon data processing departments and users. It is important that use of the audit terminal should be effectively controlled: not even auditors are beyond temptation.

The auditor's terminal can also be set up for use in eavesdropping on other terminals in a similar manner to the master control terminal.

The test data approach has its place in on-line auditing: for instance, the auditor can attempt to breach the access controls in order to test their effectiveness. If he succeeds he does not need to go as far as placing dummy data on the database. However, the integrated test facility can be developed as an audit tool on an on-line system for testing programmed systems controls.

Parallel simulation and normative auditing have also been used by auditors on on-line systems, although the complexity of these systems make it extremely expensive to emulate the operational coding in a duplicate auditor's system. Computer auditing techniques are discussed in chapters 9–14.

Discussion topics

1 How would you decide what to include in each of these three audits:
(a) The audit of the computer centre?
(b) The audit of the development process?
(c) The audit of a computer application?
Are there any problems in determining which audit work should be done in which audit?

2 Can the computer be left to control itself by means of controls programmed into the system? What are the advantages of such controls and what are their limitations? What other types of controls would you consider necessary to overcome these limitations?

3 Is it possible to over-control and if so what are the drawbacks of over-control? Suggest instances of over-control and ways of avoiding such over-control.

4 What are 'on-line' and 'real-time' systems and what are the most common variants of these systems?

5 Explain the purposes of access control and the means by which it may be achieved in on-line systems.

6 How might batch control be established in an on-line system and what are the drawbacks to its use in such a system? What are the alternatives?

8 The Control and Audit of Microcomputers

Summary

Problems of widespread use of micros, characteristics of microcomputer systems, typical weaknesses and strengths of microcomputer systems, including administrative and technical weaknesses and strengths, planning and other managerial issues, impacts upon files, software and output, countermeasures and controls, contingency planning and monitoring—a recommended approach.

The approach in this chapter is that microcomputer systems have particular characteristics, some of which are at the discretion of the system designer and user (who increasingly are the same people). As with all computer systems, some of these characteristics are *technical*, being associated with technical aspects of hardware and software, and others are administrative, being associated with the way the system is managed and used. The characteristics of the microcomputer system will impact upon files, software and computer output, in turn affecting overall integrity, security and privacy, and so placing the enterprise at varying degrees and types of risk. It is incumbent upon management to plan to avoid or reduce the likelihood of unwanted contingencies and to be well placed to recover if they do occur.

Microcomputers in large organizations

Large organizations may be as much interested as small ones in the control of microcomputers. The use of such equipment may permit individuals in any of the offices, departments, branches or operating companies to have:

1 immediate access to information from the files of a large central computer;
2 the ability to create, update and amend their own data files;
3 their own data processing capability (distributed intelligence, whether with the ability to use data from the central files or not).

Such individuals are, therefore, affected by at least some, and in some instances by all, of the various matters discussed throughout the book.

The facilities used by such individuals may unfortunately not even always be authorized, particularly the use of private data files. Even when such facilities are authorized, individuals may well use their own private programs to produce results which, despite the fact that the programs have never been independently tested, are widely relied upon for management purposes.

Characteristics of microcomputer systems

Since their inception, computers have become cheaper and cheaper—per unit of processing capability. One can recall that even as recently as the late 1960s a mainframe computer costing (then) some £100 000 might have had a RAM (random-access memory) of only 4K. In 1965 a calculating machine capable of calculating a square root cost £1000. 1975 saw the first microcomputer following the introduction of the first microprocessor in 1971. Small microcomputers now have 64K RAM of 8-bit data paths (a kilobyte = 2^{10}, i.e.: 1024 bytes) but the minimum requirement for business applications is likely to be 256K RAM of 16-bit or 32-bit data paths with the capability of expansion to at least 512K, and almost inevitably even this will be superseded by requirements for even greater capacity.

Micros can now be used as terminals to mainframe computers or minicomputers, as component parts of local area networks (LANs), as multitasking processors linked to 'dumb' terminals, as stand-alone processors, or as a combination of these. In the future we are likely to see a growing trend towards decentralized (distributed) data processing on micros, each micro being capable of use as a terminal to communicate with a central mainframe computer or minicomputer for consolidation purposes and to enable it to use central files of data. Of course this is entirely feasible at the moment.

Another feasible option at present is to connect micros on a ring (or in some other way) and allow them to share common databases held perhaps on hard disks of the so-called Winchester variety. These are already capable of holding in excess of 200 MB (a megabyte is 1 million bytes).

Compatibility of operating systems and data formats is becoming more and more important in view of the increasing use of micros in data communications. Industry 'standards' will include those based upon the CP/M, MS/DOS and UNIX operating systems: most packaged software is designed to work on any microcomputer using one or more of these operating systems with the advantage that a wide range of software has become available which works on most microcomputers; a microcomputer user may be able to convert his applications from one computer to another, though this is not as easy as it may sound.

Microcomputers are user-friendly to varying degrees but most to the extent that they are quite capable of becoming standard items of office equipment, automating the desk tops of office workers. Almost all micros are very capable word processors. They can be the basic components for either in-house or external electronic mail systems using modems or hardwiring, the latter allowing for much higher transmission speeds. They are, however, also capable of executing full data processing tasks, such as payroll, sales accounting, general ledger, corporate modelling and so on.

Since the first spreadsheet package in 1977, the availability and improving quality of 'integrated' applications packages has been a prime motor of the microcomputer revolution. These are very flexible, multi-purpose packages which can be coupled to each other perhaps associated with 'window software' which allows simultaneous display of output from multiple programs: the four leading types of package are spreadsheets, word processing packages, graphics and databases.

Packages vary as to the extent to which they are user-friendly; some come complete with a cassette tape-based programmed instruction kit and an excellent reference manual, but others are very poorly documented. In practice this is a very important consideration.

Where user programming is required it is not difficult, and most of the established high level languages (including COBOL) are now available on micros. The BASIC language is perhaps the the easiest to learn and is well suited to the needs of many micro users. However, every microcomputer has its own version of BASIC so that the wished-for standardization has not been completely achieved.

The standard data storage medium for micros is the floppy disk or 'diskette' (either 5 inch or 8 inch) capable of holding from 200K to 1.5MB of data, depending on size, density, and whether one or two sides are used. There is now a 24MB hard disk which fits into the space taken by a standard floppy disk drive. Most microcomputers come equipped (or capable of being expanded) to have between two and four floppy disks on-line at any one time—and many can in addition be on-line to a number of hard disk files.

Another related consideration is to buy a microcomputer which allows for a high degree of interchangeability of peripheral devices such as daisywheel printers and communications devices.

Apart from the microcomputer itself, the user will require a VDU (visual display unit, i.e. screen), a keyboard, a printer and floppy disk drive(s). All of these, except the printer, may be incorporated in the same cabinet or they may be separate.

The screen should be capable of displaying at least 80 columns (in width) of letters if it is to be used for word processing. The larger the screen the better, but a 12-inch diagonal measurement is the minimum that is satisfactory. Check that it is flicker-free and has brightness control, that there is edge-to-edge sharpness, that characters can be displayed with true descenders, that special characters can be displayed as they will be printed, and, if required, that the graphics capability is satisfactory. Some microcomputers and screens can handle multi-colour display which is an advantage for some applications. Tinted screens are more satisfactory to work with over long periods.

Touch-sensitive screens (such as with the HP150 micro), mouses and icons are all designed to make micros more user-friendly by reducing the importance of keyboard skills. A 'mouse' is a small device connected via a cable or 'tail' to the micro which allows the user to move the cursor and make other manoeuvres on the screen without the need to use the keyboard so frequently. 'Icons' are visual representations of operations (such as the picture of a waste-paper basket) which when referenced perhaps by a mouse will instruct the software to perform an operation (in this example, to delete data).

Voice recognition may come to supersede today's important requirement for clerks and managers to be reasonably competent to operate a keyboard. Meanwhile, what to look for with respect to the keyboard includes the following:

1 Is the keyboard detachable from the computer/screen for comfortable work?
2 Has it a numeric pad?
3 If it is to be used for word processing, are there special function keys?
4 Is the use of multiple key depressions minimal?
5 Is there a repeat key which functions on most keys?

The choice of printer will be influenced by quality and speed requirements. Many of the following remarks will be relatively unimportant if the equipment is not to be used for word processing. Daisywheel printers operate at speeds in excess of 60 ch.p.s. If they incorporate reverse printing and intelligent detection of line-ends, but their effective speed may be restricted to the speed at which the computer can send characters to the printer. These printers vary in their flexibility. Some can handle 10, 12 and 15 point printing plus variable spacing, but once again these features may be useless unless the software can service them. Metallized daisywheels are more expensive but last longer and provide a typing quality as good as the best golf ball typewriters. Plastic daisywheels are almost as good and quite adequate for most purposes. There are only a few daisywheel printers on which metallized daisywheels can be used. Single-strike ribbons provide better type quality than multi-strike ribbons which in turn are better than cloth ribbons: not all daisywheel printers are designed to use single-strike ribbons. Other features which may be available include 'bolding' (typing bold characters by typing each letter several times), sub- and super-scripting (thus: 2_3; 4^2), and the facility to use the printer as a stand-alone typewriter in emergencies: for the last feature it does of course require its own keyboard.

Apart from the thimble printer of the NEC Spinwriter (which prints to the quality of a daisywheel and has a larger [148 character] type set, not all of which may be readily usable by a typical microcomputer) the other common printer is the dot matrix printer: this printer is cheaper and may be faster. Characters are composed by a series of dots and the quality of the printing (which is never as good as with a daisywheel printer) is related to the number of dots which form one character position of standard size. A 9 × 5 dot matrix is common. In fact dot matrix printers have almost infinite flexibility as characters and shapes can be composed of non-standard sizes by using a larger number of dots.

In selecting a printer the prospective user should have regard to quality of engineering (for instance, to check whether it is built on a proper chassis) and the track record of the model being considered.

Typical weaknesses and strengths of micro systems

Administrative weaknesses

Perhaps the commonest weakness is the 'one-person syndrome'. There is a danger that one person may choose the micro, learn to program it, actually program it, operate it, maintain the media on floppy disks, etc, keep custody of the media, and distribute the output. Accounts departments who used to be so good at internal checking before the advent of computers, seem to have forgotten all about it now that they have their own micros.

In addition there is a danger that nobody within the organization may understand how complex networks of micros function: be careful to avoid this sort of corporate ignorance. There is a need for a technical background and extensive training.

It is very common that the microcomputer set-up is acquired and used by staff with no prior experience of computing and this may be inadequate depending upon the uses to which the set-up is put. It is likely to lead to an amateurish approach to managing and using the computer resource, together with a casual operating environment with poor control over program changes, system documentation, back-up and recovery, authorization of data, validation checks upon data and system testing. Of these, poor file back-up practices are likely to be among the most serious operational problems.

A further administrative snag may be copyright restrictions which hamper duplication of software for use on different microcomputers: be careful to become familiar with the 'small print' prior to committing the corporation to acquiring software.

Technical weaknesses

The technology of many microcomputers has sometimes tended to be amateurish: not all manufacturers, particularly the small, newer ones, have always produced dependable, thoroughly tested, hardware. Maintenance may be hard to come by, particularly locally, and may cease to be available at all if the manufacturer goes out of business. The industry will undoubtedly become rationalized, as is traditional with new industries, with many fewer manufacturers in the market-place by 1990.

It is likely the enterprise is ignorant of its inventory of microcomputers or what they are being used for and, in the absence of a coherent corporate policy for the acquisition of microcomputing equipment and software, that inappropriate choices of hardware and software have been made, leading to medium- and long-term problems which will be costly to remedy.

Despite the appearance on the market of an increasing amount of plug-compatible hardware which allows other manufacturers' hardware to be connected in particular to IBM micros, it is generally true that an enterprise will have compatibility problems unless it carefully controls the machines it acquires. Incompatible operating systems or incompatible versions of the same operating system, incompatible disk formats, incompatible microprocessors, incompatible keyboard design and incompatibility between different versions of the same software will all cause acute operational difficulties.

Some micros are particularly prone to dust, vibration, temperature, condensation and humidity. Others are vulnerable to corrupting the disks which are on-line at the time when someone accidentally knocks a vulnerable switch at knee height. Voltage fluctuations may also upset a micro.

Administrative strengths

Micros mean greater productivity, better information flow, speeded communication and often a need for reduced office space both because the micro workstation may be more compact than the traditional office and because many personnel are now able to work from home. By linkage to minis and mainframes it is often possible to avoid inputting large amounts of data. Incompatibilities of data between different users can be better avoided.

Most important, data processing capability has returned to user departments who have the commercial responsibility for the task in hand. It was never satisfactory to focus within a single, centralized DP department the data processing responsibility for most of a corporation's systems when other line staff continued, nominally at least, to hold the responsibility for executing the commercial task and providing the service. With micros, authority and control can once again be matched with responsibility.

Computers have undoubtedly become easier to use, and the expression 'user-friendly' sums up the trend. With a persistent shortage of computer professionals it is fortunate that unskilled personnel can now operate these computers; it is also fortunate that packaged software is being developed to such a large extent, as this obviates much of the traditional need for every organization to have its own full complement of professional computer programmers, and may improve control by reducing the amount of on-site programming.

A vast and growing range of packaged software (of varying quality) is available so that user-programming is often not required in order to make effective use of a micro. Another aspect of the ease of use of micros is that they may readily be moved from one place to another, and briefcase-size or smaller micros with flat screens will shortly enhance portability.

Within a wide range of operating conditions there is no need for air conditioning in order to operate a microcomputer.

Technical strengths

Being compact and cheap, micros are making it economic to computerize new application areas and to computerize small companies' affairs. They are undoubtedly much more technically reliable than the mainframes of the 1960s, as well as being more powerful and versatile. Faulty equipment can readily be removed and substituted by stand-by equipment in a way which would not generally have been feasible with costly mainframe computers. Repairs may be completed at supplier workshops away from user locations thus avoiding disruption of work routines.

Planning and other managerial issues

While data processing capability has been put back into user departments—and is likely to be increasingly located in user departments in the future as micros become larger, faster and open to a greater range of tried, tested and constantly enhanced and improved software—this exacerbates the problems of retaining control over corporate data processing. It is, however, arguable that line management never had control over centralized mainframe data processing, as the mystique and elitism of DP staff discouraged managers from querying let alone controlling the service they were receiving. It is fundamentally a sound principle to locate microcomputers within user departments, as this restores to the users the control over data processing which they lost with the advent of computers. It was always less than satisfactory that a function within an enterprise with responsibility for a particular operation (such as accounting or production) should have lost authority over its essential data processing. Now that often no longer need be the case.

Management must appreciate that while micro hardware and software is amazingly cheap, training costs may well now exceed total hardware and software costs.

A matter of managerial planning is to ensure there are controlled procedures governing the acquisition of hardware so that an organization has satisfactory back-up arrangements and acquires reliable equipment. While it is often justifiable for user departments to acquire their own machines, it is usually essential for the data processing department to establish and co-ordinate a coherent group acquisition policy. A frequently reported loophole in practice is that microcomputing equipment is so cheap that it avoids established capital acquisition procedures with the result that it is purchased in an *ad hoc* way making the organization much more vulnerable.

It is advisable never to be the first to purchase a particular type of computer. Talk to other users about their experiences. Check out the credentials of the supplier. It is preferable to buy from the manufacturer rather than from a dealer. Be particularly wary of doing business with a one person dealer, even if he or she belongs to a dealer network. Be wary of purchasing a computer imported directly from the USA or elsewhere by a dealer or a network of dealers—particularly if it has subsequently been cobbled in some way, perhaps to convert it to be suitable for UK electrical supply, or to add an additional chip to raise the memory size. It is preferable to buy direct from a manufacturer who is represented in the UK by his own workshops and retail outlets as this provides much more reassurance of after sales support—which is generally very important.

Try to avoid the typical 12-week US warranty period: although it is doubtful if such a short period could be enforced in law within the UK, in practice it may make it more difficult to effect repairs at reasonable cost thereafter. Do not place much reliance on a maintenance contract, as it is unlikely that one will be on offer which guarantees to keep your machine working at a guaranteed cost in the long term. Maintenance contracts are expensive and not very convincing in terms of long-term support. It is much better to have a close relationship with the computer manufacturer present within the UK. Where a maintenance contract is entered into, in practice it will be found that a quick turn-round is its most important feature, such as a guaranteed repair within 24 hours. In practice many users will protect themselves against the consequences of machine malfunction by duplicating essential items of hardware.

The careful buyer will also consider the expected model life: even 'state of the art' micros on sale today are unlikely to be current models within two or three years' time although they will normally still be able to be used for several years thereafter. Microcomputer manufacturers vary in their policy with respect to the compatibility of new and old versions of hardware and software. This is an important issue, as the major investment quickly becomes the time and effort the users have devoted to creating the files of data rather than the value of the hardware itself.

In general it is best to steer clear of a machine which is known to be coming to the end of its model life, and wise to weigh up the likelihood of new generations of micros from the same manufacturer being compatible with the software and files used and created on the first machine. In a short period of time the investment that must be safeguarded becomes not the investment in the hardware but the value of the information and software held on disks and the know-how of staff: it is absolutely imperative that these should be transferable to new generations of equipment. It is easy to overlook this point as it is not until a computer is in use that an enterprise starts to build up its information base to any great extent. The status of the manufacturer in the market is significant here: the market leaders of today are perhaps more likely to be around in the future.

Impacts upon equipment, files, software and output

Effective control depends to a great extent upon appropriate protocols over input, operations and output. One reason why this is true is that secure operations of microcomputers depend heavily upon operator disciplines—especially in order to avoid losing data.

Equipment

Machines are at risk of theft. Insurance must be adequate. Serial numbers should be recorded. The micros may be fastened to desks. Doors may be locked.

Files

Incompatibility of hardware and software restricts the sharing of data, increases duplication and will tend to lead to more data discrepancies. The objective should be that everyone in the organization should be using the same data.

It should be acknowledged that it is much easier to modify, destroy or remove sensitive data if it is computerized rather than held manually. Potentially it is even easier to tamper with the data if it is terminal-linked. Many more users now potentially have direct access to mainframe data via micro networks, and so the risks are magnified. It is preferable to allow microcomputer users to manipulate downloaded data only and not the 'live' mainframe data.

There is an obvious requirement for micro users to identify themselves when they are linked to a mainframe or into a network. Terminal identification will restrict access to authorized hardware; a 'time-out' facility may disconnect the micro after a specified period of time if it has not been used, thereby preventing an unauthorized person availing him or herself of a machine which has been logged on; an 'access attempt' facility will disconnect a terminal after a prescribed number of unauthorized attempts to use it, reporting the disconnection to supervisory staff; a call-back facility from a mainframe to a micro improves security when micro users have a dial-up capability; data to be transmitted should be encrypted; finally, communication lines should be disconnected outside normal working hours.

There is a risk of 'data obsolescence' if microcomputer users download and subsequently make considerable use of data from a mainframe computer. Regular updating or deletion of downloaded data may be imperative. Perhaps a practice should be established whereby all microcomputer reports and screen displays indicate the date on which the data was downloaded.

There are also risks of alteration or destruction of data during transmission without the knowledge of the sender or the receiver: high quality communications software will help to ensure reliability of data transmission.

Software

We may be able generally to rely upon employee knowledge of program coding within microcomputer application packages being minimal. On the other hand our opportunity to modify that coding, in order to incorporate our own programmed routines to achieve satisfactory internal control, may also be minimal in the absence of adequate system documentation.

Packages may reduce the need and opportunity for on-site programming, but many microcomputer packages are so flexible that they represent almost a high-level programming language with substantial tailoring features available to the micro user to adapt as he or she chooses. While on-site programming may not be required, learning to program a micro is very straightforward and the risk of program changes is much increased compared with systems which do not use intelligent terminals.

Output

Controlling the security of output becomes a software problem rather than simply a matter of physical control over the secure distribution of computer listings. Potentially a large number of microcomputer users may have access to all the data held within the database. It is necessary to ensure that access codes to common databases are not too widely known.

Conversely with electronic access and visual display of computer output it is harder to ensure that output has come to the attention of the authorized user. Likewise it is hard to ensure that users of an electronic mail system have called-off all the mail sent to them.

Countermeasures and controls

The control problem is, fundamentally, the difficulty of persuading people that a machine which costs so little should be effectively controlled. As a consequence the control procedures which were developed and applied quite effectively to the expensive computers of a few years ago have often fallen into disuse. This is an error of principle. The extent to which computer operations should be controlled should be a function of what the computer is asked to do, not of how much it costs.

While effective control may not necessarily use additional resources, sometimes it will. Incongruous though it may seem it may be necessary to spend thousands of pounds on an effective control system even though the hardware and software cost only some £3000.

Control advantages

On the face of it, it is an attractive control proposition to put the means of processing back into the user department. It has always been a sound principle that computer systems are *user* department systems, but it has been hard to enforce this principle when user departments have been saddled with computer systems which they did not want and for which they have had to abdicate the processing task to the computer department. Now that data processing capability is often located back in the user departments these departments can exercise greater control over the data for which they are held responsible. Further, accounting departments, where many of these minis and micros are located, should understand the principles of internal control and internal check and be in a good position to apply them to their new minis and micros. Unfortunately it often appears that they have forgotten what these principles are.

'Control' by one person?

It is not unusual to find that the choice of computer was made by one key person in the accounts department. He may be the person who learnt to program the machine and wrote many of the programs which his department uses. It should be pointed out that it may not be necessary for anyone within the organization to write any of the programs for the mini or micro: in many cases standard proprietary packages will be adequate, and in other cases the programs might be written by contract software houses. If this can be achieved, then control may be improved. Some advisors counsel that mini and micro programming know-how should not be available in-house for control reasons, but this is rather impractical as it may deprive the department of the capability to recover from processing failure due to program defects. But it remains a problem that programming know-how may be vested in one person within the department, with no independent checking of his work.

It is not unusual for the same person who acquired the computer and designed and programmed its systems to be the person who operates the computer, maintains and stores the data files (perhaps on floppy disk or cassette tape) and distributes the output. It is often the case that the justification for using a mini or micro rather than the concern's central computer is the special sensitivity of the processing that is to be done. It is therefore ironic that this often leads to an inferior control over processing than would be likely to occur at the main computer centre. Payroll, which should always be processed with two operators within the computer room, may now be processed by one accountant within the accounts department. The accepted segregation between operators and programmers may have been broken down and there may be no control section or tape and disk librarian.

It is essential that satisfactory controls exist over small-scale computers to cover these control points and achieve the same standards of control that are insisted upon for main computer centres. It is worth reiterating that control should be matched to the requirements of the work being done, not to the relative cost of the equipment in use. If the control objectives cannot be met by satisfactory segregation of duties then the only alternative is supervision. Supervision in the area of computerized systems often makes use of programmed controls: these program controls 'supervise' to the extent that they watch out for specified exceptional conditions and report them to a third party for management action.

It will be apparent that supervision cannot compensate for a complete lack of segregation. Where there is no segregation the programmed controls within the computer system cannot be relied upon and so the supervision control fails. In practice one of the costs of setting up a well-controlled mini or micro processing facility may be the investment in suitable staff resources to make segregation feasible. However, in large departments it will be a matter of designing the system of controls using existing staff resources, with some retraining.

A further disadvantage of vesting all know-how within one or two key personnel is the development of excessive dependence upon these staff; this may lead to a breakdown of the computer system in the event of the staff leaving or being dismissed. The consequences of breakdown will vary depending upon the nature of the systems. These consequences should be anticipated and appropriate fall-back arrangements should exist and preferably be tested.

Equipment

Microcomputer locations should be selected carefully having regard to dust, humidity, temperature and vibration levels, as well as risks of flood, being knocked while in or out of use, or being a temptation to the light-fingered.

Many micros come protected against voltage fluctuations, but an additional precaution is to insulate the micro by placing a suitable 'black box' between it and the power supply.

With a large number of microcomputer centres, computer centre controls are perhaps no less necessary but are much harder to establish and enforce. It used to be possible to argue that satisfactory computer centre controls benefited all the computer applications of an enterprise as they were all processed perhaps at one computer centre.

Certainly no application can be said to be well controlled if the computer centre's administrative controls are deficient, and it is likely that these administrative controls will be applied equally effectively to all the applications processed at the computer centre.

Segregation of duties

Suitable controls over input, operations and output involve ensuring that 'control' is not vested in one person. At the very least it is essential that every department which uses a micro ensures as a matter of routine that at least two persons are completely familiar with each application processed on the micro. Ignorance of systems is often a consequence of knowledge being vested in only one member of staff. The 'one-person syndrome' leads to excessive corporate dependence upon a key employee. There will be a problem of continuity if that employee leaves. The 'one-person syndrome' does of course also exacerbate the risk of loss due to fraud or accident. To guard against this it is wise to establish thorough segregation of duties so that control is not vested in one person.

The ease of use of micros puts a premium on preventing unauthorized use. At present it is less important that the micro itself should be secure against unauthorized use (this could be achieved if it were lockable, which most are not, or if it were located in a lockable room) than that the files of data on floppy disk are kept securely locked. This is because, in the case of floppy disks, files of data are not left within the computer itself after processing, so long as administrative controls are satisfactory. It is not adequate to lock up these floppy disks in lockable cabinets as the cabinets themselves are readily portable.

Good file practices

Personnel should be formally designated to particular micros so that responsibility for what occurs at that micro can be clearly established.

An essential user discipline is to copy updated floppy disks onto back-up disks, and this is done much more quickly if the computer has more than one floppy disk drive.

In fact, the most important controls with respect to micros relate to good diskette practices. There will be many occasions when a diskette is corrupted accidentally so it is essential that, before switch-off (corruption is a special risk when the computer is being switched on or off) the updated data on one diskette is copied onto another (back-up) diskette. This copying should ideally be done immediately after the file has been updated. Before this back-up diskette is ever subsequently used for any other purpose it should, itself, be copied in case it is corrupted in use.

We have referred to three copies of each data diskette—the operational copy, the back-up copy and the security copy. Many floppy disks are used to hold both software and data: in the case of a diskette with software on it, it is wise to take a copy of the diskette immediately upon purchase: this allows the original diskette to be thereafter retained unused in the form in which it was supplied by the software house: this represents a fourth necessary copy to be kept.

Periodically copies must be recopied in order to retain their freshness, before they become unreadable.

It will be apparent that copying files is an important discipline. We must add that every copied diskette or copied file should be tested before it is assumed that the copy is satisfactory.

So far we have referred to corruption in normal operational use, but there is also the risk that data will be lost through theft, fire, flood, etc. To guard against this, as with mainframe computers, a security copy of each file should be stored in a remote location with adequate security. Fortunately floppy disks are compact so this operation does not require much space.

In the case of hard disks broadly the same disciplines apply except that, in view of the high volumes of data, it may be best to copy these files onto cartridge tapes, rather than onto a large number of floppy disks. The erasure risk, of data and programs, may be twenty times greater with a hard disk if only because it may hold twenty times as much data as a floppy disk. If hard disks are in use, the data on hard disk files is likely to be left on those files within the hard disk drive after processing has ended. Unauthorized access to the computer would therefore provide unauthorized access to this data. Make sure that the hard disk drive being considered for purchase is lockable.

A designated employee should have a defined responsibility for regularly backing up the hard disk of a local area network. Highly sensitive data should not be stored on a LAN as the security available is not on a par with that of mainframe machines.

Software

One of the first actions the user of a package will take is to copy the package from one floppy disk to another for security purposes. Some packages come 'hard wired' into a module of ROM (Read Only Memory): since they cannot be overwritten they are much more secure and are unlikely to be corrupted in use. Whether or not ROM packages are appropriate depends partly upon whether the microcomputer has a ROM facility—most do not.

Much microcomputer software contains the facility of password protection against unauthorized access to data. Because of the difficulty of remembering and maintaining passwords, this feature is often not used. It is very common to find that, where a password is an unavoidable feature, the word 'PASSWORD' is itself used as the password.

The reliability of the software supplier should be investigated: there is much hobbyist software around which is being sold for commercial purposes but is likely to be of poor quality and inadequately supported after sale. It may have been developed for a specific purpose and be too specialized to be sold as a general purpose package. Make enquiries of other users—never be the first.

Check that the software is supported after sale by the issue of patches to customers. Ideally the user should acquire, as part of the purchase, a listing of program coding so that he is in a position to maintain the package himself—particularly if the software supplier goes out of business—but this is unlikely to be offered by the software house to most users.

One of the greatest problems is to evaluate alternative packages prior to making a decision to purchase. The only really effective evaluation is an extended period of use—and this is impractical when several different packages are in contention. In practice one has to rely mainly on the issues mentioned above to settle on a package to be acquired. Of course, in addition, care should be taken to establish that the package contains all the features the user requires. It is often possible to acquire the user manual at nominal cost and this may be the best way to determine what features are contained in the package.

Some security consultants recommend that no programming should be done at micro locations in user departments: instead any necessary programming could be done centrally. This does, however, seem a rather negative way of achieving security.

Leading firms and institutes of public accountants may under well-defined conditions be prepared to associate their names with microcomputer software, indicating that to their satisfaction it does what it claims to do. However, in view of the potential for litigation which this procedure might stimulate, it is unlikely to be adopted without a great deal of justifiable caution.

Contingency planning and monitoring

Detailed management policies relating to micros and micro networks should be contained within the corporation's 'management guide' or 'manual'.

Corporations are strongly advised to set up a working party represented by DP, internal audit and key users, to design a contingency plan to cope with microcomputer risks.

An early part of this study will be to establish an inventory of microcomputer equipment and uses. The study then moves on to anticipate the possible unwanted consequences which the corporation faces through any sort of possible abuse which may occur. Whenever possible the size of these risks should be assessed in money terms to allow for ranking of the risks.

The team then determines the most cost-effective ways of handling these risks. It may be a matter of investing in order to reduce or eliminate the chances of a disaster occurring. On the other hand it may be a matter of ensuring that the business can continue to function if the disaster does occur, and that recovery will then be expeditious.

Unfortunately most corporations have no clear idea of the risks they face from data processing calamities. The risks are as real in the field of microcomputing as they are with mainframe computers.

Monitoring

The contingency plan, when drawn up and agreed with top management, must be implemented, tested and maintained. The continued applicability of the plan should be monitored regularly.

Internal audit has a role in independent monitoring. Most of the audit interest relates to appraising policy and practice with respect to the acquisition and use of microcomputers, in order to conclude on the strength of control and to make appropriate recommendations. The issues discussed above are therefore relevant. Apart from this, there are special issues relating to the application of audit techniques to systems which are processed on microcomputers.

Audit and management trail is likely to be deficient when microcomputers are in use as on-line updating (without after the event evidence) is commonplace. Audit and management trail is needed in enough detail for adequate review and approval by supervisory personnel and this means that summary output is unlikely to be sufficient. Logs of transactions, transaction counts and a balancing of daily transactions to independently produced totals are all possibilities.

The auditor will find it difficult to interrogate the files created by packaged software, as the file layouts will not be available to him. Neither is there, to the author's knowledge, an audit interrogation package designed to operate on a micro, though this is a feasible proposition to be used on files created by tailor-made software written in a standard programming language.

On the other hand the auditor has an ideal opportunity to take copies of files and also of the application software and then to interrogate the files to his heart's content using the application software to do so—possibly using his own microcomputer (which he may also be using as a word processor to write his audit reports): he can maintain custody over the software and the files until he has completed his audit work. This provides him with a great opportunity though it has to be said that it is a pity he is dependent upon the application programs to conduct his interrogations: management expects the auditor to be in a position to reassure management that the application programs themselves are reliable, and that the files created by the application programs are accurate and complete. If the auditor depends upon the application programs to obtain his reassurance he is likely to overlook some defects within the programs.

Auditors would want to see that password protection is available when it is needed, and that it is used. It must be recognized that this is only of value against unauthorized access by the uninitiated: as the data remains on file it will always be possible for a computer buff to read that data.

Now, instead of having perhaps just one computer centre, there are a multiplicity of them, and a much greater proportion of the auditor's effort must be expended on computer centre audits.

Discussion topics

1 On what grounds should a decision be made to process a system on a mini- or microcomputer located within the user department rather than on the central computer administered by the data processing department?

2 What are the special control problems associated with mini- and microcomputers?

Part 3 **Computer Auditing Techniques**

9 An Introduction to Computer Auditing Techniques

Summary

Using the computer as a powerful audit tool. Why the auditor needs techniques which are independent of management's techniques. The distinction between audit techniques which are used to review real data and audit techniques which are used to review systems controls. An introduction to computer audit enquiry packages, one-off audit programs, audit program modules, the test data method, program comparison—and other computer auditing techniques.

Now that systems are computerized three things have changed. First, the methods by which data is processed have altered. Secondly, the techniques used to achieve effective control are vastly different: these include controls built into computer applications, as well as general controls over the computer centre and over the development of new systems. Thirdly, audit techniques must change as well. In part they must change in order to be equal to the task of auditing new processing methods and new control techniques; and in part they must change to make full use of the new possibilities the computer offers the auditor. He can use the computer as a most effective audit tool, harnessing its own properties of speed, accuracy, centralization (in particular of records) and reliability.

It is not strictly true to say that he can also use the computer to compensate for deficient audit trail for, if it is possible for the auditor to obtain data from computer files using computerized audit techniques, then the data is available in a *reasonably accessible form* and audit trail can be said to exist. However, in these situations it is the auditor who is making the trail visible.

There is a view that suggests that computerized auditing techniques should never be used by the internal auditor. This view goes on to say that, if the auditor needs information for audit purposes, then management also needs it for control purposes: the internal auditor should be able to depend upon management to provide that information.

However true it may be that management needs the information, the auditor will frequently encounter situations where information is not present even when it should be, and he may need to use his own computerized audit techniques to obtain it. It is quite possible that management has made a decision to manage without the information on cost-benefit grounds and that decision is not necessarily shown to be wrong when the auditor, using his own methods, finds the missing information is most revealing. Apart from these considerations an auditor sometimes needs to use independent means to obtain information or independent methods of testing the system: this is in keeping with management's view that internal audit is the *independent* appraisal of internal control. He can never be completely independent, but his audit work is likely to be more valuable if he can maintain a reasonable degree of independence.

Without independent methods of working, the internal auditor would be badly placed to pick up instances where the control techniques established by management were failing to work. If the auditor depended upon control reports produced by the system, he and management between them might both be depending upon unreliable reports. To a large extent the auditor will of course use internally produced management reports but it is at least useful for him to obtain reassurance that these reports are reliable. Without his own independent means he would also be very lucky to discover well-concealed frauds.

The auditor is now in a position to harness the computer so that it will vouch for him like an 'audit slave'. One of the reasons for the shift in audit emphasis (from the vouching and verification approaches to the systems approach, with vouching and verification in supportive roles) was that it was no longer possible to obtain adequate audit reassurance by vouching and verification in view of the immense volumes of data that the auditor would have to examine and the fact that there might no longer be adequate hard copy audit trail to look at. Yet now the auditor can use a computer audit enquiry program to conduct a one hundred per cent vouch of an entire file of perhaps hundreds of thousands of customers—even when all the data to be looked at is stored on magnetic tapes or disks. Or he can use his enquiry program as an aid in verification work by printing out certain balances for further audit work—or even to the extent of instructing his program to print accounts receivable circularization letters. For the external auditor this may indicate the validity of greater emphasis on more pedestrian vouching and verification approaches rather than systems audit work—for the principal interest of the external auditor is that year-end *results* are correctly stated. It may now be easier for the external auditor to obtain this reassurance by maximizing vouching and verification and minimizing systems review—particularly in complicated computer systems which are difficult to understand but amenable to computerized auditing methods. However, the view of all competent external auditors would be that system review skills are an indispensable weapon in the armoury of any auditor, internal or external, who wishes to be capable of doing a proper job.

Although the internal auditor will do some vouching and verification he will never be able to relegate the systems approach from its pre-eminent position. He is not particularly interested in year-end financial results; he will always be interested in the efficiency of systems, whether financial or otherwise, and the strength of their controls.

It should be mentioned that not all computer auditing techniques are *computerized*. For instance, one technique is 'program auditing' which may involve the auditor in a manual review of program code.

We have referred to the speed of the computer which allows it to be used to conduct an audit test of a complete file in quick time. The computer can also be trusted to work accurately—as accurately at the end of a tedious job as at the start of it. Not only will it work accurately but it can be relied upon to do what it has been told to do. It has vastly superior powers of comparison and correlation which allow it to take full advantage of the centralization of records within the computer centre.

The selection of the appropriate computer auditing technique should always follow, not precede, the determination of the audit objectives. There is a danger that these methods become a set of techniques look for problems, which of course is the wrong way round.

Computerized audit techniques can be subdivided between those which are used to review real (production) data and those which are used to review systems controls. The division is not perfect as the former can also, by implication, tell the auditor a lot about the system, and vice versa.

Techniques for the review of real data

These techniques use the computer to examine, retrieve, manipulate and report on real, processed data. They are suited to situations where audit independence, audit assurance (i.e. confidence) and fraud detection are of significant importance. These techniques all use computer programs, the commonest being:

1 General computer software, not written with the auditor in mind, but useful to him. A wide variety of general-purpose data retrieval packages is available in conjunction with the use of a wide spectrum of different types of computer.
2 Computer audit enquiry packages, similar to the above but written for auditors and capable of analysing and testing data in much greater depth. Often known as 'generalized audit software' or 'audit enquiry programs'.
3 'On-off' tailored audit programs specially written at the time to do a particular audit task—unlike computer audit enquiry packages, which are adaptable to undertake a variety of audit tasks from time to time.
4 Integrated audit monitor modules, which are programmed routines built into normal production programs. They act as continuous monitors of

the real data and processing conditions which occur during routine processing, reporting items of the nature specified by the auditor in advance. Alternatively these audit modules may not work continuously: they may lie dormant until activated by the auditor, or by a particular condition when it occurs.

Techniques for the review of systems controls

As all the above methods interrogate real data they are techniques which can be used in audit verification and vouching of real data. The second category of computerized audit techniques uses *dummy* data to review systems controls and does not examine real data, so this category is limited to telling the auditor whether or not controls exist and are functioning. It should be said that the techniques for the review of real data can also tell the auditor, by *implication*, that controls are not working if data is encountered which indicates this (for instance, customers whose overdraft limits have been exceeded). It is also true that the techniques for the review of systems controls may lead the auditor to suspect that data may be incorrectly recorded, if they highlight a control which is not functioning.

The most common of these techniques for the review of systems controls are:

1 The test data method (formerly known as the test pack method), where the auditor processes through the system dummy data containing all the conditions he wishes to confirm that the system can handle.
2 The integrated test facility, where the production system has been designed specially to allow dummy audit test data to be processed alongside production data without corrupting the business activities.
3 Code comparison programs, where the internal auditor keeps an authorized copy of each important computer program and periodically uses his comparison program to compare the authorized copy with the current operational version in order to report any discrepancies. This may work on source or object code and may not be designed exclusively for audit use.
4 Logic path analysis programs, which convert a program into a structure diagram or flowchart which is printed out for audit review.

It is interesting that each of the techniques for the review of systems controls is a technique which systems analysts and others might use in addition to the auditor. Although the techniques for the review of real data might appear to be designed specifically for the auditor, computer people themselves use similar techniques for their own purposes.

External auditors probably tend to make more use of techniques for the review of real data than techniques for the review of systems controls. From the external auditor's viewpoint this may be sound. He is giving an opinion on actual year-end results. He is much more interested in the data from which the results have been prepared than in control weaknesses which have not been exploited. Skilful use of a computer audit enquiry package will disclose to him data conditions of audit interest which may indicate that controls have actually failed to work. There could be a weakness in this reasoning, in that the computer audit enquiry package takes a snapshot view as of the date or dates of the files which are interrogated: unusual data conditions may have occurred earlier in the year which are no longer shown up on this snapshot. The external auditor is not only giving an opinion on the state of affairs at the end of the year but also of the results of operations during the year.

One of the internal auditor's responsibilities is to conduct a protective audit. He is as concerned to detect a control weakness which has not yet been violated as he is one that has. There is therefore perhaps more reason for him to use the test data method than for the external auditor to do so. There is also every reason for him to use the computer audit enquiry method.

Whatever techniques are used it is as well to be aware that they consume scarce audit resources. They take time to install before they can be used for the first time.

Thereafter they consume resources whenever they are used and the various techniques vary in their value to the auditor. The techniques may be evaluated under the following headings;

1 Set-up time and cost.
2 Running and maintenance cost.
3 Degree of expertise required.
4 Level of audit independence achievable.
5 Scope of audit assurance obtainable.

Table 8 summarizes the common computer audit techniques.

Table 8. Summary of common computer audit techniques

	Direct	Indirect
Techniques for the review of real data:		
Generalized computer software Generalized computer audit software 'One-off' tailored audit programs Integrated audit monitors	→ *Verify* data* not controls →	*Imply* control strengths and weaknesses
Techniques for the review of systems controls:		
Test data method Integrated test facility Code comparison programs Logic path analysis programs	→ *Verify* controls* not data →	*Imply* possible errors in data

* N.B. The auditor should make sure as far as possible that the data or the controls which are being verified are the *real* data or controls which would be applicable even if auditing were not being performed. Auditors have been known to review wrong and even dummy *data* files, or the operation of controls contained in outdated or even dummy computer *programs*.

10 The Test Data Method

Summary

What is the test data method and what can it do for the auditor? How should it be used? What are the advantages and drawbacks of this method? What has the integrated test facility to offer?

The test data method is one of the techniques for the review of system controls and other system procedures. It is test data processed by the normal, operational programs. It is very little different from the testing done by systems designers and user departments during the development of systems—except that it is done by the auditor for his own purposes and in his own way. The technique is of use in the review not only of the *computerized* controls but also of the *manual* controls over input preparation. The test may be carried through to test output controls of a manual nature as well. Examples of the use of this test to examine manual controls are the batching of source documents, the verification of data conversion, and even the suitability of output forms design.

The scope of the test data method

The test data may be constructed to test the processing of normal, unusual or even seemingly ridiculous data—errors are perhaps most frequently found in the latter, which are most likely to have been overlooked as possibilities when the system was tested during its development. The test data method may test program processes such as the validation or editing of data, calculations, treatment of conditions and the accuracy of exception reports.

It is a useful technique to be used by the internal auditor when he is engaged in pre-event auditing of a system prior to its initial implementation. It may also be used by him when he is auditing modifications to the system. If he is conducting an efficiency audit he may use this technique as an aid to establishing the performance characteristics of the computer system—for instance, by measuring the processing time taken to deal with a sample of transactions of similar type. It also has an application for the routine, continuous type of systems audit: the auditor can use his test data from time to time to gain reassurance that at least the system has not been modified since his last audit visit with respect to the conditions tested by his data.

Using live data

At its most basic, the auditor is using the test data method when he finds, amongst the real data of the system, items which are examples of the conditions he wants to test. He then manually predetermines the results he would expect from the processing of his data and later checks that the actual processing has been done in the way he expected it to be done. The prediction of results is an essential step: without it, experience shows that the auditor too easily overlooks errors in the actual results of processing. By using the method in this way he has avoided preparing his own test of dummy data. But this way is usually not feasible; in practice it is not easy to sort through genuine input data and amongst it find all the input types which the auditor is interested in testing. The vast bulk of day-to-day input contains few exceptions and it is unlikely that a day's input contains all the exceptions (including the nonsense conditions) that the auditor wants to test. Even if it did, it would take him a long time to find them.

Dummy data in the production run

The second way is for the auditor to construct a batch of dummy data which contains the conditions he intends to test and to process this as part of the normal production run of the system. Unless an integrated test facility is in use (we discuss this later) the risks associated with entangling audit test data amongst the live data in this way are considerable. There have been stories of auditors quite innocently inducing the delivery of lorry loads of furniture to their apartments because they used their own names and addresses on some of their dummy test data of orders. On another occasion a fleet of road tankers went abroad looking for a garage which did not exist.

If the auditor uses test data in this way he must prevent the unwanted physical side-effects. This may even require unpopular program amendments, and is getting very close to the integrated test method. Or it may entail the interception of computer-produced documentation before it is released. One further possibility in some situations is for the auditor to reverse out the effects of his test by feeding through reversing entries. This has the added disadvantage of involving the auditor in work which is of no direct interest to him in order to meet his audit objective; it may also distort management reports—for instance, it may swell the number of cancelled orders or the number of credit notes. The interfaces of the computer system with other systems also need to be borne in mind: for instance, the sales order processing system may provide data which is used in the production scheduling system. Management reports and computer-produced financial accounts may both be corrupted by the effects of the auditor's test. Sometimes the auditor will want to use the test data method to check on whether the system can handle large quantities properly—if so, the scope for damage and distortion by the auditor is correspondingly greater. In practice it is often extremely difficult indeed to anticipate all the possible physical and accounting consequences, and this way of using the test data method is very risky.

Test data in a special run

Many of the problems associated with inserting the auditor's test data into the live job stream may be overcome by setting up a special run for the auditor's test, using copy computer files. This may perhaps be a repeat of an earlier production run, but with the auditor's test data added and using generations of master files which are no longer needed for security purposes. Using the test data method on copies of master files is the commonest way. Care must still be taken to suppress unwanted consequences. For instance, invoices might still be produced. Files of other systems (such as the production scheduling system or the sales analysis system) might still be updated unless the media librarian is fully aware of the nature of this special run.

The first cardinal rule is therefore that the client must be consulted before the auditor uses the test data method—which unfortunately reduces the independence of the test and the amount of reassurance the auditor gets from it. The only exception to this would be with the integrated test facility which, once set up, can be used by the auditor without consultation. Using the test data method on copy master files does have the disadvantage that it entails a special computer run set up for the auditor, so the auditor must take steps to satisfy himself that programs used to run his data are the same programs which are used in day-to-day operations. Auditors still recount the example of a client who kept a version of a program specially for periodic use by the auditor. The client did this to be obliging, as he remembered the time and effort it took the auditor to set up his test pack, and when, later, the system was amended he did not wish to upset the auditor. The client did not understand the purpose of the auditor's test—presumably the auditor had maintained a degree of secretiveness about his methods in order to improve the degree of assurance he would obtain from his test—and the client had not appreciated that his action had invalidated what the auditor was trying to do.

Integrated test facility

The remaining way in which the test data method can be used is the integrated test facility. With this method the system is designed at the outset to handle audit test data and avoid any unwanted consequences occurring. A concern might divide its sales ledger into a number of sales areas and have an additional area for audit testing purposes. Any data input to the computer which is coded for this area is identified by the programs as the auditor's test data. All the routine processing of the auditor's data should be identical to the processing of real data, except that orders would not be delivered, invoices would not be dispatched, management reports would not be corrupted (the auditor's data would be shown separately if at all) and systems which integrated with the system being tested would not receive dummy data as a consequence of the auditor's test. Of course the weakness of this method is that the system has been designed to identify audit test data and consequently the auditor has less assurance that his data is being treated in the same way as other data.

Nevertheless the integrated test facility has advantages. The client does not have to be involved each time a test is done. The auditor can set up dummy accounts and then maintain them with dummy data on a continuous basis—which extends the scope of the test considerably.

Usually the auditor shares an integrated test facility with other interested parties who wish to test the system from time to time—systems designers and programmers who want to test modifications, and the user department. This department will also want to test modifications, and may wish to test features of the system which had not been adequately tested before, or to test whether the system can handle new commercial developments unrecognized when the original application was designed and tested. Sharing the test facility in this way once again weakens the independence of the test and the assurance the auditor can obtain from it: some other party with legitimate access to the test area might be tampering with the auditor's data.

Audit steps

Standard audit steps for the use of the test data method are:

1 Define the audit objectives.
2 Determine which auditing technique(s) will assist in meeting these objectives.
3 If the test data method is to be used, budget audit time for the test.
4 Discuss the test requirement with management.
5 Learn about the system: obtain computer documentation and conduct interviews.
6 Open audit working papers, and set up an audit test sub-file.
7 Construct the test data—on source documents or computer input forms, depending upon what the auditor is interested in testing.
8 Control the test data.

9 Manually predetermine results.
10 Have the data keyed in for the test.
11 Attend the computer run.
12 Check and summarize the results.
13 Draw audit conclusions.

Costs and benefits

To summarize, the test data method may be used with good effect in the following audit situations:

1 To test controls over input data, including the data validation procedures.
2 To test processing logic and controls in order to obtain assurance that the master files are valid.
3 To test computation done within computer programs—such as the calculation of interest, discounts, commissions, payroll or depreciation.
4 To test manual procedures and controls which relate to the computer system—especially procedures over input and output.

Table 9 provides a summary of the relative costs and benefits of the test data methods, showing the integrated test facility separately for comparison.

Table 9. Relative values for the test data method

(See also Table 10.)	Test data	Integrated Test Facility (ITF)
Set-up time and cost	5	3
Running and maintenance cost	4	2
Degree of expertise required	3	5
Level of audit independence	3	2
Scope of audit assurance	3	1
Potential for the detection of fraud	2	2

(With grateful acknowledgement to B. M. Matthews of Deloitte Haskins and Sells).

There is a low rating for the integrated test facility with respect to the level of audit independence and assurance achieved by the test: this may be improved if one or both of the following apply:

1 There are strong software controls over program amendments (this would reassure the auditor that it was less likely that illicit routines had been built into the programs which would result in the auditor's test data being processed in a way which was different from the processing of real data).
2 Code comparison is in use in order to compare versions of programs as a means of ensuring that the operational versions have no unauthorized amendments.

The integrated test facility does not involve so much set-up time and cost for the auditor as it is a feature which is built in for him by others at the development stage. However, the overhead at the systems development stage may be considerable as most of the programs will have to allow for two types of data—audit data and real data. Set up for the other ways of using the audit test data method, apart from the integrated test facility, may be reduced if:

1 Systems test data originally produced by analysts or users to test the system at the development stage, is taken over and adapted by the auditor to do subsequent audit tests.
2 The auditor uses a test data generating program.

The test data method may be a good test of specific controls, providing evidence which is quite objective. It tests controls which may not have been tested by real data and it therefore has a function which cannot be fulfilled by audit enquiry programs. To use this method the auditor only needs the average amount of skill that a computer user should have, whereas a computer enquiry package calls for a measure of data processing skill. Once the test is set up it is fairly cheap to run again and again, with variations as appropriate, although the prediction and analysis of results can be time-consuming. It is portable, comprising a sheaf of documents or a magnetic tape, and is therefore easy for the auditor to maintain control over—which improves the independence of the method. Not being a computer program there is less risk of serious damage to the files of an application than there would be from indiscriminate, unskilled development of computer audit enquiry programs. However, as we have discussed, there may still be a risk of computer files being corrupted to the extent that they have been modified by audit test data. As with some audit enquiry programs, the auditor who is using the test data method is himself in a position to tamper with the system by modifying master file records. This method should only be used if the work of the auditor is controlled to the satisfaction of the user department.

Drawbacks and limitations

The test data method has a number of drawbacks which do not, however, disqualify it as a useful audit tool. Experience has shown that it is a very time-consuming technique, especially to set up. It becomes more practical if the test is to be used again and again. It is also only a snapshot of the system at a specific time, although it may be used repeatedly to provide assurance on the continuity of processing; the integrated test method is ideally suited to this. To use the test data method a detailed knowledge of the system is needed, at least from a user point of view, and a prerequisite of this is usually that the system must have been well documented.

To set up the test there may be a need to do some basic housekeeping which is of no direct interest to the auditor. For instance, it may be necessary to set up some dummy customer accounts in order to use a set of dummy transactions against these accounts. The process of filling in the coding sheets for the dummy master file records, batching them, encoding them, coping with validity errors on input and so forth, may be of no interest to the auditor but this has to be done before the auditor can start his test.

The fact that the method takes computer time is perhaps less important than it was when computer time was more costly. In particular circumstances it may still be an embarrassment: even if there is no shortage of computer time there may be a shortage of computer operating staff. If the test is set up as a special audit run on copy files, then this time consideration is greater than if the audit test is done as part of the usual production job—as would usually be the case if the integrated test facility were in use. Of course, if any program modifications have to be made in order to prevent unwanted consequences occurring as a result of the auditor's test, then programmer time has to be budgeted as well.

The test data method is a useful procedural test but as it deals with dummy data only it cannot be said to directly contribute to the *verification* of balance sheet and operating statement items, or any other items. Since the external auditor is primarily interested in such verification it is not surprising that he favours the enquiry program method which looks at real data and can, therefore, contribute directly to verification work as well as indirectly providing information about the controls and other procedures of the system. But the internal auditor is as concerned with security and control of systems as he is with the verification of amounts: he will find the test data method useful for this purpose.

Even an exhaustive application of the test data method cannot be expected to test every combination of data. This technique should not be interpreted as a means of gaining complete reassurance that the computerized system can handle anything and everything correctly.

Not even the auditor can anticipate everything which might occur. This is the same problem which faces systems analysts, programmers and user departments when they test a system prior to implementation. It is much more sensible to use this technique to test for specific conditions which the auditor needs to know whether or not the system can handle rather than apply it in a sweeping, all-embracing attempt to test every aspect.

Discussion topics

1 Consider the proposition that as the test data method uses dummy data it does not verify 'live' data but is a procedural test only.

2 What are the risks associated with the use of the test data method and

how can these be avoided?

3 What are the advantages and disadvantages of the test data method?

4 Do you consider the relative values shown in Table 9 are reasonable when considered in comparison with the values given in other tables for other computer auditing techniques (*vide* Table 10)?

11 Audit Enquiry Programs

Summary

What these programs are. The types of test the auditor can use them for and the confidence he can place in the results. The technical features of enquiry packages. The relative merits of enquiry packages and specially written 'one-off' audit programs.

In this chapter we seek to show that audit enquiry programs are indispensable aids to auditing in a computerized environment and also to explain their use. We will cover the following in turn:

1 A brief résumé of what they can achieve for the auditor.
2 A description of the technical features of enquiry packages.
3 A discussion of the tests that the auditor can design.
4 General advice on their use.
5 Selecting an audit enquiry package.

The audit purpose of audit enquiry packages

Audit enquiry packages aid the auditor in five ways:

1 They may solve many of the problems caused by loss of visible evidence by enabling the auditor to interrogate computer files and extract the required information—so long as it is there.
2 The auditor may extract details from files for further audit work—such as the detailed testing of transactions, the confirmation of accounts receivable or payable, or the physical checking of the existence of employees, stock or plant.
3 They provide a means of verifying *independently* the values, details and analyses provided by the computer application for management control purposes. The verification is independent for two reasons:
(a) It does not rely upon management, who may have modified the control

information provided by the computer system prior to showing it to the auditor (by insertion, suppression, alteration or by the withholding of entire reports or sections of reports).

(b) It does not rely upon the application programs to extract the requisite data, as with this method the auditor uses his own program over which he maintains security. The application programs may be deficient in certain respects and one of the values of this audit method is that it reassures the auditor as to the extent to which the application programs can be depended upon.

4 They provide the opportunity to conduct complex calculations faster, more accurately and more comprehensively than is possible with clerical audit methods, opening up new possibilities in audit work. Correlation analysis is just one example amongst many.

5 They allow identification of items which do not comply with the laid down system rules or which, while complying, seem unreasonable.

Technical features of generalized audit packages

The architecture of these packages falls into the categories of 'load-and-go' packages or 'source program generator packages'. With a load-and-go package the package is a ready-written computer program which is defined for a particular audit task by the submission of audit instructions in the form of a data file. The program logic remains unaltered whatever the audit work it is instructed to do. For a particular use this means that there is likely to be redundant coding within the program which is not being used for this enquiry. Source program generator packages use the auditor's specification of the work to be done in order to produce a source program which is tailor-made for this particular task.

In order to use a package of either type the auditor must specify the files to be interrogated, the layout and character of the relevant records on those files, what processing he wants done and the format of the reports to be produced. A package is said to be 'parameter-driven' if the auditor is only required to give a limited amount of information (i.e. 'parameters') in labelled boxes or columns on the input forms. This is the equivalent of writing in a very high-level programming language unique to the particular package—each item of information given by the auditor is converted into a series of program code instructions by the package. The programs in the package itself must have been written in a common programming language that the computer supports. This means that the computer manufacturer must have produced a software compiler for that language which works on that computer, and the computer department must have invested in this compiler. As it is often useful for these audit enquiry packages to be machine-interdependent, i.e. able to work on a variety of different computers sold by most of the computer manufacturers, it is incumbent upon the designers of the package to develop it using a widely supported programming language. Low-level languages are technically more efficient and allow better manipulation of data but they tend to be unique to a particular computer manufacturer. High-level languages such as COBOL (*CO*mmon *B*usiness *O*riented *L*anguage) or Fortran (a scientific language) or RPG Report Program Generators), are generally supported by most computer manufacturers and the package is likely to have been written in one of these languages. Alternatively the package may have been written in a low-level language and a different version made available to function on each of the major manufacturers' computers. A midway position is for the package to be written in a high-level language, with certain subroutines written in a low-level language.

A source program generator package must generate a source program in one of the languages for which the computer centre maintains a compiler, which is a special manufacturer-provided program which converts programs coded in source code (by programmers or by the audit package) into object code (the language the computer itself understands).

An auditor can learn to use an enquiry package in quite a short time. Estimates of the training period needed vary widely (no doubt it depends on the individual auditor and the complexity of the package) and in any case, of course, the user becomes more competent with experience. It is wise to attend the appropriate training course to learn to use the package.

Packages vary widely in the facilities they offer. If a required facility is missing it may be possible to compensate if the package allows for 'user exits', i.e. the opportunity for user coding to be inserted. The packages are used principally to examine files, retrieve data from them, compare files and produce reports. The chosen packages should be capable of looking at as many input files as the auditor is likely to wish to specify: a typical audit test would be to conduct a comparison between two files, so a package should be able to handle at least two files for this purpose. The two files may have identical layouts (such as this week's payroll file being compared with an earlier one), or one may be a transactions file and the other a master or reference file with a different layout though with the same keys (an example would be a comparison between a priced orders file and the stock file from which the unit prices had been obtained). It would not be unusual for the auditor to wish to conduct comparisons between three files—two master files of identical layouts but of different generations and also a reference file—so he should be sure that his package would allow comparisons between a number of files, including files with differing record layouts but the same key.

The package should also be able to handle all the different file types likely to be encountered such as sequential, indexed sequential and random, as well as the various types of data, such as character, packed-decimal, binary and bits. If a database is in use it is important to make sure that the package can examine the database information via linked modules, or directly.

There are many other technical features which are also important but are too detailed to be covered here. The Evaluation Check List in Chapter 12 covers many of them.

Audit packages are designed to incorporate routines which allow the automation of work which the internal auditor might otherwise do manually, and also incorporate additional techniques which are valuable though beyond the scope of manual auditing. The package should be able to sample data, and packages vary as to the sampling methods they support—whether interval, random (using an internal random number generator) or monetary unit. The auditor also wants to be able to check the sequence of records on files and to look for duplicates and records on one file which do not match those on other files. He may wish a stratification of a file to be done, depending upon value or quantity with the provision of totals for each stratum as a prelude to stratified sampling. Different packages allow a different number of strata to be handled. He will sometimes want to sort and merge data prior to other audit tests. A common requirement is to conduct an age analysis: many audit packages have the appropriate routine built in. Routines to conduct correlation analysis and to compute means and standard deviations may also be useful to the internal auditor.

Finally, the auditor should pay attention to output requirements. Packages vary as to whether the format of the output is fixed by the package or free format to be determined by the auditor, whether page numbering is provided, whether the user can specify titles and headings, and what will be printed and what will be suppressed. It should allow the printing of several different reports from just one entry phase of the package. Output may also be required on other computer media apart from paper—such as CRT at the auditor's terminal, tape or cards.

One feature of audit enquiry packages occasionally found is the facility to replace on the files the examined data by data specified by the auditor. This is a dangerous facility which can never be justified and should not be wanted by, or made available to, any auditor—either internal or external. An auditor should subscribe to the view that only the appropriate purpose-designed application programs should be permitted to amend data on application files, and the use of these programs should be strictly under user department control and supervision. There is no justification for the use of other programs, whether by the auditor or by data processing staff, for tampering with application files. The enquiry program should be used to *read* application files only, not to *write* data onto them. If this feature is available on the selected audit package it should be rendered inoperative. It would be difficult for the auditor to convince others of the need for tight control if he were not to apply this principle to himself.

Audit tests

We have already introduced the ways in which enquiry packages can aid the auditor, and now we shall consider typical audit tests in more detail.

Compensating for loss of visible audit trail

This is a straightforward use of the package to provide information for audit purposes when it is not provided as a matter of routine. It could be, for instance, that there are no management reports which allow the auditor to confirm that business was not done with a new customer prior to the opening of his account being properly authorized: after the event it is possible that the only record of this authorization might be held on a computer file.

In an on-line system using terminals for the entry of transactions, a log of the work done on each terminal may be maintained on backing store. It is quite likely that the auditor might wish to interrogate this data to extract information which has not been provided in any management abstracts.

Selection of items for audit work

In this case it is not that the audit trail is inadequate, just that the package is better suited to do this tedious work. In addition, by using the auditor's own program to access the files directly he is not basing his selection upon a management report which may be inaccurate or incomplete. Under this heading we include the selection of *samples* for further audit work or the listing of all items which have a particular profile, such as slow-moving stock items, items for which the stock holding is larger than a certain amount, stock items which are large *and* in excess of a stated number of weeks' usage (this would require the package to do some analysis and deduction), or customers whose accounts are in credit or whose credit is above a certain amount. The selection of customers for an accounts receivable circularization together with the printing of the circulars may also be handled by some audit packages.

Verification

This involves the audit package duplicating the processing performed by the application programs, then comparing its own results with the results produced by the application. It is normally used to duplicate the production of control reports upon which the auditor would wish to rely, but it can also be used to duplicate the production of transactions documentation, such as bank statements or invoices.

Conducting complex calculations

Were the auditor to try to do these manually he might be limited at best to working with a small sample, whereas the enquiry package can work with the total population. Our earlier category of verification of management control data may, of course, involve the package in conducting large calculations, in particular totalling records by number or value. Calculations which the internal auditor might like to perform may be much more complex than that. He may wish to carry out several forms of statistical analysis on available data. He may wish to use his package to apply complex formulae already in use by his concern, perhaps to determine reorder qualities and reorder levels or to arrive at production schedules. If he is applying formulae already in use he is seeking to confirm that these formulae are in fact being applied correctly by the computer system; he may however use different formulae from those already in use as a means of testing whether efficiencies can be recommended to management.

Detecting violation of rules

The auditor's use of the package in this way tells him indirectly by implication when controls are not functioning as they should or are inadequate. It also tells him *directly* about transactions, accounts or other aspects of business which, being unauthorized or improperly authorized, may result in a misstatement in the accounts or a possible fraud—or both. For instance, an unreasonable credit limit may put doubt upon whether the account is collectable. Airline tickets sold off at a huge discount may indicate a collusive fraud between computer programmers and the travel agency in receipt of these bargain tickets. Note that the auditor is not only looking for items which violate the rules; he is also looking for items which, though in keeping with the rules, do not appear to be justified.

Practical use

The sequence of steps that the auditor should follow when he uses an enquiry package are as follows:

1 Define the audit objectives.
2 Identify the tests that the package will be required to do in order to assist the meeting of the audit objectives.
3 Make out the package input forms for these tests.
4 Compile the package on the computer, clearing reported edit errors. There should be a full edit of the parameter cards prior to execution (step 7). Maintain security over the package and the audit tests at all times.

5 If a programmer was used to add coded routines to the package, to fill out the input forms or to advise generally, his work must be tested.
6 Obtain copies of the application files to be tested.
7 Attend the execution of the package against the copy files.
8 Maintain security of the copy files and output until the tests have been fully checked out.
9 Check results of the test and draw audit conclusions.
10 Interface the test results with whatever subsequent manual audit work has to be done.

One problem to be guarded against is the fact that an enquiry may produce huge quantities of unexpected output at considerable expense and loss of audit face. This may be because the system is wrong or is badly programmed, so that there are many more discrepancies on the files than the auditor expected. Alternatively the input to the system may have been invalid in certain ways which the system had not been designed to detect. It is also possible that the auditor may not have understood the rules of the system, in which case it is the auditor who is wrong. Whatever the reasons it is wise to avoid this sort of thing occurring—at least on the first occasion that the enquiry is made. There may be several ways to prevent it, depending upon the package in use. Some packages can be set to terminate after a defined number of errors have been detected. Others can be instructed to print out a sample limited to a certain number. Alternatively, enquiries may be made on a 'count basis' without a detailed printout of the items included in the count; and, related to this, total-only reports can be provided.

It is important that the auditor takes care in constructing his test. There is a story, probably apocryphal, of the auditor who asked his client to write a special program to print 200 000 customer accounts, double spaced at twenty five to the page. He forgot to ask for subtotals, so his printout—almost two miles long—was of little value as he could never check that the grand total at the end of the listing was an accurate sum of the detailed accounts!

Table 10 summarizes the audit value of three types of audit enquiry program, including the specially written 'on-off' audit program tailored to a particular task. It will be noted that it takes longer and costs more to set up a program generator package and to get it to work than it does a 'load-and-go' package, but the time and cost is significantly less than that for a tailor-made program. If set-up can be done on VDU terminals, time will usually be saved. There is nothing to chose between 'load-and-go' and 'program generator' packages with respect to subsequent maintenance and running costs: once they have been set up they are little trouble to use from time to time, and the output they produce is easily understood by auditors who are familiar with the package. Again, VDU terminals are helpful here; there is a case for the internal audit department to have its own secure terminal. Enquiries can also be more quickly specified if the package is 'parameter

Table 10. Relative values for three types of audit program
(Low values are 'good' for 1, 2 and 3; high values are good for 4, 5 and 6).

	Generalized computer audit enquiry packages		
	'load & go'	program generators	Specially-written audit programs
1 Set-up time and cost, including programming if applicable	2	3	5
2 Running and maintenance costs, including audit work done on output and assuming a normal number of systems changes between audit visits	1	1	3
3 Degree of expertise required to use this technique	1	2	5
4 Level of audit independence achieved	5	4*	4*
5 Scope of audit assurance	5	5	5
6 Potential for the detection of fraud (e.g. ability to detect programmed manipulation or falsification of data)	5	5	5

* Assumes program compilation, development and testing is carried out 'off-site' or in a very carefully controlled environment.

(With grateful acknowledgement to B. M. Matthews of Deloitte Haskins and Sells.)

driven'—that is, instructions made in parameter form. Once again, specially written programs fare much worse as they have to be written from scratch for every new audit enquiry. The added complexity of a program generator package is reflected in the additional expertise needed in order to use it, but as they do not require programming knowledge (unless user coding is added), such packages require much less computer expertise to use than a specially written program.

All these methods provide high levels of audit reassurance, because the auditor is using a thorough and accurate technique which gives him considerable independence. It follows that the techniques are very good, in comparison with other audit techniques such as the test data method, for detecting fraud by programmed manipulation or falsification of data. If user program coding has been introduced—perhaps to solve file handling problems when a database is in use—the degree of audit reassurance, while still likely to be high, may be less. Table 10 assumes that any specially written coding or program is developed in a tightly controlled way—written by computer audit staff and compiled and tested in a secure way—preferably off-site.

12 Evaluation and Selection of Enquiry Programs

Summary

With dozens of enquiry packages available on the market today, it is not easy to select the best one for a particular audit department. This chapter considers the general features of these packages and goes on to examine hardware restrictions, package structure, input features, data-handling capabilities, analysis facilities and output options.

Selection of a package

We have already covered many points which are germane to the selection of a package. The Evaluation Checklist in this chapter should also be consulted. There is a variety to choose from and may be found helpful. Internal auditors are advised to consult their external auditors first. Several firms of public accountants have developed their own enquiry packages. Others use commercially available ones. Because of the set-up problems it is helpful if both auditors use the same package so the external auditor's packages should be considered seriously. By using the same package there is more opportunity for both groups of auditor to exchange experiences and to assist each other in their work, and this in itself is valuable.

Apart from the external auditors, packages are available from some software houses and computer manufacturers. Some of the software houses' packages are amongst the best: some leading firms of public accountants have opted to use these and discard their own. On the other hand, other software houses' packages are very poor. The age of the packages sold or rented out, and whether a trial period is allowed, are all points to be investigated. The user does not want to be saddled with a package with inadequate maintenance provision and which proves unreliable.

External auditors are unlikely to use enquiry packages provided by computer manufacturers as their requirement is for a portable package to be used at many clients' locations on a variety of machines. Manufacturer packages are not machine-interdependent. If the internal auditor's company or concern is a dedicated user of equipment from only one manufacturer he should seriously consider the virtues of that one manufacturer's audit package: it may have enough good points for the auditor to opt for it rather than for the one that the external auditor uses.

It should be remembered that the objectives of the two audits are different. External auditors develop their own packages for their own purposes. They are also the strongest lobby group in influencing the way that software houses develop their packages. The external auditor is more interested in achieving high levels of independence and reassurance than is the internal auditor. On the other hand, the internal auditor is concerned with efficiency aspects of systems, financial as well as non-financial. It is, for instance, difficult to visualize an instance when the external auditor would want to use a package's linear programming facilities but the internal auditor might wish to do so. Few packages offer this facility and it is one example of a complex mathematical routine which would be beyond the capacity of a quick piece of user coding.

Audit enquiry programs evaluation checklist

(Based on a list designed by P. W. Morriss of Thomson McLintock and Co., to whom grateful acknowledgement is made).

Introduction

(a) The accompanying checklist is designed to assist in the specification of the requirements for an enquiry package and as a comparison schedule for evaluation purposes.
(b) The features described on the checklist can be rated as 'Essential', 'Desirable', or 'Not necessary' and the features of a package can be noted and measured against this 'model'.
(c) The checklist does not purport to be exhaustive but does perhaps show the extent of research needed before a commitment is made to acquire a package.

1 General.
2 Hardware restrictions.
3 Package structure.
4 Input validation.
5 Input files.
6 Data handling.
7 Data manipulation.

8 Record selection.
9 Totals and analyses.
10 Output.

1 General

(a) Is the package available on trial, and if so for how much and for how long?
(b) Is the package available to buy? How much?
(c) Is the package available on lease or rent terms?
(d) Is there an additional price for installation?
(e) Does the supplier of the package maintain it?
(f) Are subsequent releases of new versions or enhancements automatically made available to existing users? For extra cost?
(g) Is the package portable per the terms of the contract?
(h) Is any estimate available of the amount of training required to make effective use of the package?
How much?
(i) What degree of programming knowledge is needed?
(j) Is this training available:
  (i) within the cost of the package?
  (ii) on a 'pay for' basis?
(k) Is a comprehensive user manual included in the cost of the package?
How many?
(l) Are forms supplied and how many would be used in a typical enquiry?
(m) Is any technical help available from the supplier for users?
(n) Are any representative performance figures available to the prospective user?
(o) For how many years has the package been in use?
(p) What is the age of the supplier?
(q) What is the accessibility of the supplier?
(r) Are there users' group meetings?

Any other questions:

2 Hardware restrictions

(a) On what computer does the package (or versions of it) run?
(b) Can the single package easily be modified to run on the given range of computers?
(c) Within which operating system can the package operate?
(d) What is the minimum configuration which will accept the package?
  (i) Memory size?

(ii) Disks?
(iii) Tapes?
(iv) VDU's?
(v) Other?

Any other questions:

3 *Package structure*

(a) Does the package generate a specific program to perform the enquiry?
(b) If so, in what source language is the generated program written (if any)?
(c) Is the package parameter driven?
(d) Are *all* instructions to the package by parameter?
(e) Are parameters coded on fixed format or free format sheets?
(f) In what language(s) is this package written?
(g) Are any modifications required to source code prior to running the package to define:
  (i) Computer identity?
  (ii) Computer configuration?
  (iii) File descriptions?
  (iv) Output requirements?
(h) Does the package allow entry points for user's own coding to solve problems outside the capability of the parameter driven facilities?

Any other questions:

4 *Input validation*

(It is assumed that all source code used, whether generated or user coded, is subjected to the normal compilation checks of the language/computer concerned).

(a) Are all parameters fully edited prior to the execution of the program?
(b) Are clear messages produced describing the errors?
(c) Do errors automatically abort the run?
(d) Is there an option to terminate the program after the edit run?
(e) Can parameters be developed and validated via VDU?

Any other questions:

5 *Input files*

(a) What devices will the program accept for reading files:

(i) Tapes?
(ii) Disks?
(iii) Other?

(b) How many input files will the program accept:
(i) Main input file(s) (minimum and maximum)?
(ii) Reference files?

(c) Will the program allow two files to be compared:
(i) Two versions of identical files?
(ii) Two different files with common key information?

(d) Will the program report any erroneous formats/organization found on input file(s)?

(e) Does the program have any facilities for dealing with 'data exceptions'? (e.g. zeroizing erroneous data in packed fields)

(f) Can the program be set to terminate after a defined number of data errors?

(g) What file organizations will the program access:
(i) Sequential?
(ii) Random?
(iii) Indexed sequential?
(iv) Other?

(h) Does the program allow the linkage to special modules to read complex file structures?

(i) Can the program handle database structures, and if so, how?

(j) Can the program handle 'open item' files and create 'balance records'?

(k) Can the program handle variable length records:
(i) Fixed portions only?
(ii) All fields?

(l) Can the program cope with different record layouts on the same file (of either equal or unequal length)?

(m) What is the maximum number of fields which can be defined on, and extracted from, an input record?

Any other questions:

6 *Data handling*

(a) What types of data storage will the program accept:
(i) Character?
(ii) Packed decimal (signed and/or unsigned)?
(iii) Binary?
(iv) Other?

(b) Will the program access binary digits (bits)?

(c) Will the program replace one specified constant with another?

(d) What types of 'date' representation will the program accept:

(i) DDMMYY?
(ii) YYMMDD?
(iii) YYDDD?
(iv) Other? (e.g., number od ays since 1900 as with ICL)

Any other questions:

7 *Data manipulation*

(a) Does the program allow for the following arithmetical functions:
   (i) +, −, ×, ÷?
   (ii) Roots?
   (iii) Exponents?
   (iv) %?
   (v) Other?
(b) Are arithmetic functions available limited to fields on the input records?
(c) Are arithmetic functions available for created fields and/or created constants?
(d) Can the program accept constants:
   (i) Numeric?
   (ii) Alphanumeric (descriptive constants)?
(e) Does the program provide for intermediate storage, or calculate results for subsequent access:
   (i) Within the same record?
   (ii) Within a later record?
(f) Does the program allow different processing of records at differing levels of organizational significance?
(g) Does the program allow an internal sort and/or merge, and if so what is the maximum sort key size?

Any other questions:

8 *Record selection*

(a) What methods of selection are available: (indicate also any limits on selection method)
   (i) Decision table?
   (ii) Field-to-field comparisons? }
   (iii) Field-to-constant comparisons? } <, >, =, (NOT)
   (iv) Tolerance tests (one field varying from another by more than a given percentage)?
   (v) Boolean algebra expressions?
   (vi) Compount tests linked by AND/OR?

(b) Can the file be 'stratified'? (That is, divided into logical sub-files with different tests defined for each sub-file).
(c) What sampling methods are available?
   (i) Interval?
   (ii) Random (via internal random number generator)?
   (iii) Monetary unit?
   (iv) Attributes?
   (v) Other?
   (vi) Any of the above populations restricted by other tests?
(d) (i) By limiting the number of records selected for any given condition?—with a count of non-slected?
   (ii) By production of intermediate 'hit' counts (e.g., statement of selected records after every 5000 input records)?
   (iii) By limiting the number of input records read?
(e) Can enquiries be made on a 'count' basis without selecting records?
(f) Can the program perform sequence, duplicate, or matching tests?

Any other questions:

9 *Totals and anlyses*

(a) Will the program provide:
   (i) Sub-totals on change of control fields?
   (ii) Totals or records selected for a given reason?
   (iii) Totals only reports?
   (iv) Input file record counts?
   (v) Input file counts and numeric totals of designated fields?
   (vi) Analysis by value?
   (vii) Percentages of selected items to the whole population:
      by number?
      by value?
(b) Does the program have a built-in facility for correlation analysis?
(c) Does the program have a built-in age analysis routine?
(d) Does the program handle the calculation and printing of means and standard deviations?
(e) What are the maximum number of accumulations that can be made simultaneously?

Any other questions:

10 *Output*

(a) What are the possible forms of output?

- (i) Print?
- (ii) Tape?
- (iii) Disk?
- (iv) VDU?

(b) Will the program write files for further processing, and if so how many?
- (i) Fixed format?
- (ii) Free format?

(c) Does the program produce a fixed format print out?
(d) Does the program have the facility to produce a standard report in the absence of other instructions?
(e) Does the program produce free format print out?
(f) Is there any restriction on the size of an output record?
(g) Can titles for reports be specified by the user?
(h) Can headings for each page be specified by the user?
(i) Are pages automatically numbered?
(j) Can the program produce complex output such as confirmation requests?
(k) Can the program produce both output files and print reports at the same time?
(l) Can output reports be produced restricted to selections for each or a group of given reasons? (This presupposes one enquiry phase and several subsequent reports)
(m) What are the maximum number of reports that can be produced on one pass of the file(s)?
(n) Are reasons for selection produced automatically?
(o) Can they be suppressed?
(p) Can different reports be produced on a change of control field?
(q) Are standard edits available?
(r) Are user-edit facilities available?
(s) Can the program produce bar graphs?
(t) Can the program produce histograms?

Any other questions:

13 Enquiry Program Case Study

Introduction

This is an introductory case study on specifying the tests to be performed by an enquiry program. The file to be interrogated is a fictionalized, simplified FIXED ASSETS FILE designed for training purposes. Details of the file are set out here. The exercise excludes any consideration of file comparison techniques.
(This case study was provided by P. W. Morriss of Thomson McLintock & Co., to whom grateful acknowledgement is made.)

Suggested approach

Participants are advised to make a schedule of tests, analysed by class of test under the headings shown in Table 11.

Suggested solution

A suggested solution is given in Appendix 1.

Fixed assets master file

1 The file is maintained on an annual basis and keeps all records for sold or scrapped goods until the end of the year of scrapping. For the purpose of simplicity, in this case study participants are to assume that all additions are created as new, discrete records.
2 In reality the contents of such a file would be considerably more complex but the file described in Table 12 is sufficient to demonstrate the principles involved in specifying an enquiry within the classification of tests discussed in Chapter 11.

Accounting policies

1 Depreciation is calculated each accounting period on the status of the

Table 11. Classification of test

Field name	Audit samples	Reperformance of calculations	Items not conforming to system rules	Items conforming but of audit interest	Totals and analyses	Comments

Some tests will involve a combination of fields on the file.

Table 12. Fixed-assets master file

Field name	Mnemonic	Comment
STATUS INDICATOR	SI	A = addition this year, E = existing asset S = scrapped asset
ASSET NUMBER	AN	6 digits, plus a check digit
ASSET DESCRIPTION	AD	
ASSET LOCATION	AL	3 digits, (location code = cost centre)
ASSET CLASSIFICATION	AC	FH = Freehold property LL = Long leasehold (over 50 years) SL = Short leasehold (under 50 years) PM = Plant and machinery FF = Fixtures and fittings MV = Motor vehicles
DEPRECIATION RATE	DR	5 digits nn.nnn%
DEPRECIATION BASIS	DB	N = not depreciated S = straight line R = reducing balance
DATE IN USE	DU	6 digits, ddmmyy (mm = accounting period number)
ORIGINAL COST	OC	9 digits, n,nnn,nnn.nn
REVALUED COST	RC	9 digits, n,nnn,nnn.nn
DATE OF REVALUATION	RD	6 digits, ddmmyy (only made at period 01)
DATE OF DISPOSAL	DD	6 digits, ddmmyy (mm = accounting period number)
DISPOSAL PROCEEDS	DP	9 digits, n,nnn,nnn.nn
CUMULATIVE DEPRECIATION BROUGHT FORWARD	CD	9 digits, n,nnn,nnn.nn
DEPRECIATION CHARGE THIS YEAR	DC	9 digits, n,nnn,nnn.nn

asset as at the end of that period (i.e. no depreciation in period of disposal).

2 Monthly depreciation is accumulated in the 'depreciation charge this year' field.

3 Table 13 shows rates and bases.

4 Depreciation is calculated until residual value is $0.

Table 13. Rates and bases

Asset classification	Depreciation rate(s) (per cent)	Basis
FH	Nil	—
LL	Nil	—
SL	2	S
PM	20	R
FF	25	S
MV	33.333	R

14 Other Computer Audit Techniques

Summary

The use of computerized audit techniques other than audit enquiry programs and the test data method. A description of the audit use of general computer software, integrated audit monitors, parallel simulation and normative auditing, program auditing, code comparison programs, logic path analysis programs, tracing and mapping.

Introduction

The purpose of this chapter is to explain the use of computer auditing techniques other than (a) computer audit enquiry programs and packages, and (b) the test data method including the integrated test facility. Table 14 provides a list of all the most common techniques and we shall be dealing with those which are asterisked.

The division between techniques which review real data and those which review systems controls is not a perfect distinction. Apart from the fact that audit techniques which examine real data also provide reassurance *by implication* that controls either are, or are not, satisfactory (and vice versa), some categories of computer audit technique include methods which review real data and others which review systems controls. For instance, general computer software includes file interrogation routines which review real data, as well as trace and mapping routines which review the functioning of the system. Parallel simulation and normative auditing will be shown to be techniques which are effective in giving audit reassurance on both the integrity of the real data and the adequacy of controls within the system—and it is difficult to know where to classify this category of audit techniques.

As he considers each technique, the reader is advised to consult Table 15, which provides a comparative analysis of the strengths and weaknesses of all the techniques, including those not specifically covered in this section.

Table 14. Computer-audit techniques

Techniques for the review of real data	Techniques for the review of systems controls
1 *General computer software	1 Test data method
2 Generalized computer audit enquiry packages;	2 Integrated test facility
	3 *Program auditing
'load-and-go' packages	4 *Code comparison programs
program-generator packages:	5 *Logic path analysis programs
	6 *Tracing and mapping
3 'One-off' tailored programs, i.e. 'specially written' audit programs	
4 *Integrated audit monitors:	
—general	
—tagging	
—Cusum	
5 *Parallel simulation and normative auditing	

* The technique is described in this section.

In general it can be said that audit software for the analysis of *operational software* is in its infancy and is likely to be developed in the future. Audit software for the analysis of *real data* on client files is better developed—thanks, in the main, to the needs of external auditors.

One criticism of many of the techniques we shall examine is that they only provide a snapshot at a given instant. This is not necessarily a valid criticism. A computer audit enquiry program may take a snapshot of a master file at a specific time, but that master file reflects the results of processing over a long period. Some techniques such as the resident audit monitor are specifically designed to take a snapshot when particular conditions exist which trigger it: this technique may also be used to take regular snapshots at quick intervals which gives it the advantages of a continuous audit monitor.

Unfortunately many of these techniques have a variety of terms which are used to describe them. Where more than one term is in use we shall mention each.

General or generalized computer software

These are software packages such as manufacturer-provided utility programs which, although not written with the auditor in mind, may be found useful by him. Some facilitate file handling and interrogation and may be useful

Table 15. Summary of computer-audit techniques

	Low values: 'good'			High values: 'good'		
Technique	Set-up cost	Running cost	Expertise required	Audit independence	Audit assurance	Fraud detection
Generalized software	1	2	2	2	3	2
Generalized computer audit enquiry packages:						
(i) load and go	2*	1	1	5	5	5
(ii) program generators	3*	1	2	4†	5	5
'One-off' tailored, (i.e. specially written) audit programs	5	3	5	4†	5	5
Integrated audit monitors	4‡	3	5	2	3	3
Parallel simulation and normative auditing	4	4	5	4†	5	5
The test data method	5	4	3	3	3	2
Integrated-test facility	3	2	5	2	1	2
Program auditing¶	1	5	5	3	1	2
Code comparison programs	1	3	4	4§	5§	4
Logic path analysis programs	1	5	4	1	1	1
Tracing and mapping	1	3	4	1	1	1

* Set-up time and cost increases with the complexity of the files to be handled by the program.
† Assume program compilation, development and testing is carried out 'off-site' or in a very carefully controlled environment.
‡ The cost may be higher depending upon the sophistication of the monitor. For instance, an on-line audit tagging facility protected by the operating system will be very costly.
¶ Not strictly a computer technique as this is a *manual* check.
§ The degree of audit independence and assurance attained depends upon whether the code comparison program is used as part of an effective system of program change monitoring under the control of the auditor.

(Acknowledgement: Much of the data in this Table was originally developed by Mr B. M. Matthews of Deloitte Haskins and Sells, London, and is used with his kind permission. He should not be held accountable for any mistakes as his material has been altered and added to.)

in the auditor's examination of real data. For instance, the database management system may be used to 'front-end' with the auditor's computer audit enquiry package, in order to supply data and format it in a way that can be handled by the audit enquiry package. In the absence of an audit enquiry package a regular file interrogation package may be an adequate alternative in some circumstances.

The advantages of this software for audit are that it is cheap and easy to use. It may already be used by the concern, and there may be experienced users outside the audit department to advise on its use by audit. The disadvantages are that it rarely provides the tools for the auditor to conduct sophisticated audit work and it may not always give the auditor an adequate level of independence and therefore of assurance.

It is unfortunate if the auditor has to rely on general software to supply and format database entities; he then has no reassurance that the data on the database has been supplied to him accurately and completely, unless he can develop other techniques to satisfy himself on these points. If the general software cannot be controlled by the auditor he will have less confidence in its use: not only might it be unreliable, it might be altered deliberately to hoodwink the auditor. Being generally available within the concern it also has the disadvantage that the specification of the software will be available knowledge for non-audit staff who may be able to circumvent the effect of the auditor's test.

Apart from its use in auditing real data, general computer software is also available to assist the auditor in his review of the system and in particular of the systems controls. Examples are code comparison programs, logic path analysis programs, tracing and mapping. We shall discuss these later.

Integrated audit monitors

A wide variety of terms is in use to describe this technique including: resident audit programs; resident auditor; resident file monitor programs; resident audit software; integrated audit modules; integrated file monitor programs.

In addition, 'on-line audit monitoring' is sometimes used to describe this technique in use on on-line systems. Certain audit techniques which are usually considered separately may be in essence examples on integrated audit monitors. These include tagging, tracing, mapping and the integrated test facility.

An integrated audit monitor is a module of computer program which is built into the operational system either temporarily or permanently, and is used either occasionally or continuously for audit purposes. The monitor may be a separate program which is incorporated into a computer application as if it were a regular operational program. Alternatively it may be just a part of an application program. It may also be part of the installation's operating system—sometimes known as the 'supervisor' or 'executive'—or inserted into the teleprocessing monitor in the case of a real-time system.

In concept this technique is marginally different from computer audit enquiry programs and packages (whether generalized or tailor-made) in that the audit module of programming functions as if it were part of the application which is being audited rather than as a separate run for audit purposes. It may also involve the generation of audit flags which are tagged onto user records—which would be unlikely with computer audit enquiry programs.

This technique allows the auditor to do some of his audit work *at the time that the data is being processed by the operational system* or very shortly afterwards. He need not be there at the time. It is ideally suited to situations where audit trail is deficient so that historical audit work is difficult. The integrated audit monitor may be programmed to print out items of audit interest (or write them onto magnetic tape or disk) as they occur, for subsequent audit work. It is necessary for the audit monitor to be designed so that it can accept the definitions of items of audit interest that the auditor is likely to wish to make in future. Of course it is necessary for the auditor to specify in advance to the monitor the nature of the work he wants it to do and the character of the items he wants reported. In some circumstances this may be a weakness of the method in that it does not spot a condition which is unexpected, unless it can be specified as an exception to a certain set of conditions.

As the technique can be used for continuous monitoring of transactions passing through a system it is particularly useful in distributed systems with on-line entry via a number of terminals. With these systems—and in particular with real-time systems—the architecture of the system is often suited to the incorporation of an audit module of programming, to which control is passed from time to time: the application itself may use similar modules for operational purposes.

The technique is commonly used to achieve three audit requirements:

1 To gather and store information relating to transactions which is available at the time of processing, for subsequent audit review to determine its correctness.
2 To check, at intervals, the integrity of the files which are being processed. In other words, to determine that the processing has not resulted in any defined discrepancies on the files. This use of the method is particularly appropriate for the audit of databases but it may also have its application in audits of systems with conventional file structures. It allows the spotting of the time and event when errors arise.
3 To spot and record for subsequent audit attention any items which are unusual or of special audit interest in some other way, as previously defined by the auditor.

Tagging

One derivation of the integrated audit monitor is the audit tagging method. This is particularly suited to on-line, real-time systems using a database. It involves the incorporation at the design stage of a system of a single-character field either physically within each entity of data to be monitored or logically associated with it. This field may be activated ('tagged') by the insertion of an auditor's flag or 'tag'. Activation will occur either on the demand of the auditor—perhaps he has selected the data entity for further audit work—or as a result of internal systems events occurring. When the system is operating, the software will test for audit flags in the data entities which are being processed, and record the data and any associated items of information when an active flag is detected.

It will be apparent that this method requires special audit software to activate the auditor's flag: this software must be capable of detecting the existence of conditions specified to it by the auditor. Subsequently, software must be capable of detecting active flags and reporting in a manner specified by the auditor. Reporting may entail writing the salient information onto magnetic tape or disk for subsequent printing.

Alternatively the auditor might obtain a display of the reported data on his audit terminal, at his convenience. The software should be sophisticated enough to respond in different ways when differing conditions are detected, and to report in a variety of ways. Total-only reports may, for instance, be adequate for the auditor in some circumstances.

The principal disadvantage of this method is that there is a considerable overhead at the systems development stage in terms of audit or analyst and programmer involvement. When the system is operational there is a constant overhead in terms of computer time (except when the audit tagging facility is not active) and program sizes. File sizes are also permanently larger. This operational overhead is becoming less significant as computer hardware becomes cheaper, which is one reason why this method is now becoming attractive.

Audit independence is best preserved if the tagging system can be protected by the computer manufacturer's operating system. Few computer staff are competent or able to tamper with the operating system, so this gives the auditor's technique a measure of protection from unauthorized scrutiny or amendment. Protection by the operating system also enables the tag to be invisible to the computer user or computer department staff: the operating system compensates for the existence of the additional character of data for each data entry and never prints it out except on the instructions of the auditor. User and computer staff can neither access the tag nor modify it. Likewise measures should be taken to ensure that only the auditor is able to examine the output from his tagging system. The converse of this is that the auditor does not need to change the user's record in order to operate this system.

The 'cusum' technique

A final example of integrated audit monitoring is the cusum ('cumulative sum') technique, where the auditor uses his own incorporated routines to accumulate cumulative sums or moving averages relating to the occurrence of particular conditions during processing. The auditor's module may be programmed to report significant variances from regular practice. Examples of the use of the cusum technique by the auditor include:

1 The incidence of specified processing conditions (such as credit limits exceeded).
2 The nature of output (such as the average number of lines per document or the average number of documents per run).
3 The inconsistency of related data items.

Apart from the need to provide protection by the operating system in order to improve independence, independence may also be improved if the audit monitor is developed off-site. Generally, audit monitors are high-cost facilities requiring a high level of technical computer expertise on the part of the auditors involved. They do, however, provide a continuous monitoring facility which has been described as a form of continuous exception reporting for the benefit of the auditor. Alternatively they may be triggered at the auditor's discretion. The auditor must take steps to ensure that the output produced by his monitor is protected, as in most cases the vulnerability of this output to unauthorized review or amendment may weaken the value of the test. The auditor should ensure that the monitor only does essential audit tasks in view of the computer time and space it constantly takes up.

Parallel simulation and normative auditing

This method involves the development under the control of the auditor of a, possibly simplified, duplicate or 'model' of the computer application to be audited. The model is also computerized and contains the essential features of the system from the auditor's viewpoint. The live data is processed both through the operational version of the application as well as through the auditor's model. In its fully developed state the auditor's computer system then compares the results of processing by the two methods (the user's system and the auditor's model) and classifies the differences in audit reports which may go as far as selecting items on a statistical basis for further audit tests. There may be nothing here that a good computer audit enquiry package could not be set up to do, but the use to which it is being put is more elaborate than usual.

This method is sometimes called normative auditing, which implies that the auditor's model of the system provides the 'norm' or 'standard' against which the production processing is assessed. The literature tends to use the term 'normative auditing' to imply that the entire computerized application is modelled by the auditor, albeit in a simplified way. 'Parallel simulation' is frequently used to refer to the modelling of only detailed parts of the system. The terms are interchangeable and were it not that 'normative auditing' is in use it would be better to drop the term in favour of 'parallel simulation' as the former seems to cause confusion.

This method both tests the correct operation of specific programs and programmed controls *and* verifies specific values included in computer records. It is therefore both a test of the system and a verification of real data.

The method has been used for a variety of computer systems. Early examples of its use for payroll and inventory systems using batch processing were published by Boutell ('Auditing through the Computer', *Journal of Accountancy* 41–47, November 1965; and 'Business-oriented Computers—a frame of reference', *Accounting Review* 305–311, November 1965). More recently (Aiken, Hulme and Grouse, *Normative Audit Control for On-line/Real-time Systems; a feasibility study*, University of New South Wales, October 1974) an example has been published of its use for auditing an on-line system for the processing of passbook transactions in a savings bank.

Program auditing

Program auditing is a rather grand title for the review by the auditor of program documentation. It is sometimes referred to as 'program review', 'review of program code' or 'documentation review'. Strictly, it is out of place in this section as it need not be a technique which uses the computer as an audit tool: rather, it is a manual technique. It is technical only in so far as it is quite an expert task to review the program code. On the other hand other techniques such as code comparison programs, tracing, mapping, and logic path analysis programs may all be regarded as computerized tools which assist in program auditing.

The affection for this technique amongst some auditors is probably due to the feeling that the systems auditor must review the actual system: the program listing of the program is about as close as the auditor can get to a computerized system. Unfortunately the auditor who is looking at a program listing may not be looking at what the system actually does—today's operational version may not be a facsimile of what he is reviewing. So it is essential that the auditor takes all reasonable steps to satisfy himself that he is reviewing the operational version.

It is not a technique to be used indiscriminately. Owing to the difficulties of reading program coding, it is really only a practical technique when the auditor wants to satisfy himself about a particular routine in the program over which he already has doubts. Guided by an experienced programmer, he may have the routine explained to him and he may in this way find that his suspicions are confirmed or denied. To use this technique to spot the unexpected error is like looking for a needle in a haystack. Even experienced programmers find it difficult to review other programmers' coding.

On the other hand this technique may be used to review programs for compliance with programming standards relating to coding conventions, modularization and general efficiency of coding. Efficient coding is less important now than it used to be as machine time is relatively cheap compared with the cost of programmer time.

In summary, this method may be used to follow up queries raised by other audit techniques, to audit programs whose sophistication makes inadequate other techniques available at the time, to verify complex and critical program functions such as control totalling and to confirm the efficiency of the programming.

Its disadvantages are that it is time-consuming and tedious. It cannot be a comprehensive review of the program code and, being tedious, it tends to be unreliable.

While it has been said that the program audit is the equivalent of the auditor's walk-through of a manual system, there are other ways to learn about a computer system, and better ways to gain audit reassurance that the controls are functioning effectively. Nevertheless, in a recent survey sixty-four per cent of internal auditors claimed to review program code as one of their audit procedures, although only ten per cent did so as a regular routine.

A checklist for testing the quality of programs has been produced by the UK National Computing Centre entitled 'Quality of Programming' in its *Guidelines for Computing Management* series (1979).

Code comparison programs

Programs are certainly key elements in a computer system and they must be tightly controlled. More and more internal auditors are using code comparison programs *as part of an organized procedure to control application programs.* Many concerns have charged internal audit with the responsibility of maintaining an authorized version of all important application programs in a master program library under separate lock and key. Periodically the auditor makes a snap check of the production version of a program by using a special computer program to compare his master copy with the production copy. A code comparison is therefore the comparing of two programs by a third.

Authorized amendments to an application program would be approved by the auditor, and the auditor would use the amendment to update his master version separately from its use to update the operational version. The amendment of an audit master version would be done under audit control. If this system is applied there should be no discrepancies reported by the code comparison program. Experience has shown that reported discrepancies are expensive in staff time to check out. One annoying tendency is for apparent discrepancies to turn out to be random differences of no significance.

This method may be used to compare either source or object versions of programs. The latter is the more common and is the better test, as it is the object version which is executed during production processing. The auditor must take great care to ensure that he is comparing his authorized version with the version which is actually being used, rather than with some other copy which might be maintained specifically to fool the auditor.

This method picks up many unauthorized program amendments. It would not however pick up the illicit routine which was part of an authorized amendment and had therefore been built into both the production version and the auditor's copy of the program. It is also a snapshot; it would not detect an amendment which had been reversed-out prior to the auditor's test. Control over program amendments must be rigid. The use by computer staff of standard programs for the modification of programs must also be tightly controlled.

Logic path analysis programs

These are programs which convert a source program into a logical path printout, sometimes in flowchart form. The available programs have severe limitations and will only interpret simple programs with adequate accuracy. Complex programs have so many possible logical paths that this technique is impractical in view of time constraints in interpreting the results. Once again it has the limitation that it interprets the program only at a point in time—the program may have been different yesterday and may be different again tomorrow.

Trace routines and mapping

Whereas the logical path analysis program analyses an application program as a special analysis run, tracing and mapping are routines built into the application program itself. Rather than reporting on the *possible* logical paths that the program may execute (as does the logic path analysis program) this method reports on the *actual* logical path executed on a particular production or test run of the application program (tracing) or it reports on the logical paths not so executed (mapping).

Tracing is frequently used during initial program development as an aid to 'debugging' programs where the reason for the error is not otherwise apparent. A COBOL program with a TRACE instruction inserted will print out the paragraph names within the procedure division of the program each time the coding in those paragraphs is executed. This allows the programmer or auditor to see exactly what program instructions were executed on particular items of data. The TRACE instruction can be set on selectively to avoid excessive printouts and delay.

The mapping routine is useful to detect illicit or redundant coding, or coding planted for later illicit modification.

Discussion topic

For each of the following computer audit techniques, explain what the auditor can achieve by its use and identify the factors which determine the level of independence that the auditor can achieve in its use:

(a) general computer software;
(b) integrated audit monitors;
(c) parallel simulation and normative auditing;
(d) program auditing;
(e) code comparison programs;
(f) logic path analysis programs;
(g) tracing and mapping.

15 Automating the Audit

Summary

The use of information technology by auditors. Use of micros. Automating the audit: categories of audit activity and the ways in which information technology can be applied to them currently. Current and continuing developments. Possibilities for the future.

Background

Much of the material in this chapter has been derived from:

1 discussions with a selection of practising accountancy firms;
2 the results of a study, partially funded by the Department of Trade and Industry, of smaller practising accountants' use of office automation;
3 surveys of hardware and software by practising accountants, published in the computing press;

We are going to concentrate, in this chapter, on those aspects of an audit where:

1 information technology is already being used;
2 the use of information technology, or its further use, is being actively considered;
3 there is still some way to go, but where such use is bound to come.

Other possible uses of information technology by auditors are also briefly considered.

Not all auditors give equal priority to different uses of information technology. This ought to be an advantage to the profession, as it will ensure that progress is made, across a wide spectrum of technology, by those most keen to make it.

By implication, there are aspects of an audit to which information technology is never likely to be applied. Explicitly, these are:

1 the *ultimate* exercise of audit judgement, however well fortified by programmed assistance, particularly about such matters as the relative degree of weight to be given to the different elements of an audit (compliance testing, substantive testing and analytical review);
2 verification of existence and ownership of fixed assets;
3 setting the legal and professional standards and criteria in accordance with which an audit ought to be performed.

Information technology *can*, however, assist the auditor to assess the degree of compliance with financial accounting standards, and the auditor's own compliance with auditing standards and guidelines.

Use of information technology by external auditors—non-audit areas

Certain uses of information technology, although not of direct relevance to automating audits, are so widely used, and so closely related to accountants' professional activities in general, that they ought to be mentioned at the outset in order to provide a proper perspective on the subject.

Bookkeeping

There is a large choice of systems to maintain sets of books, to produce accounts from incomplete records, and to manipulate trial balances and accounts (e.g. consolidations) once they have been produced. The basic use of such systems is not auditing, but uses of such systems to simulate the production of accounts, CCA and depreciation calculations and consolidation, (which *are* audit procedures) are quite widespread. Such systems are also used both to provide accounting services to clients and to maintain general accounting records for accounting practices themselves.

Practice office administration

The majority of larger firms of accountants, and many of the smaller ones, maintain computerized time recording and fee billing ledgers. This automates the records of the performance of an audit. It may enable the relative impact of the individual tasks to be evaluated. It may sometimes be used as the front end of a partnership accounting system. Although such systems do not help to ensure that an audit is satisfactorily conducted, they do help to ensure that it gets paid for. They may also enable the progress of an audit to be monitored.

Taxation

A number of tax packages currently exists, and there is a lot of experimentation with tailored software for tax purposes. Such systems are making money for a few and costing it for many others. Partnership accounting, as well as advice to clients, is again a likely growth area for the use of such systems.

Other applications

Computer applications are used for such things as portfolio valuation; cash flow projections (used by a number of bigger firms); vote-counting at company general meetings (mentioned by at least one firm); and financial planning and modelling (used very widely indeed). Use of graphics is not unknown, but is not yet widespread. Such systems provide ancillary audit capabilities, as well as management consultancy tools and aids to other forms of professional activity.

Use of micros

Although many firms use micros for the purposes mentioned above, some firms also use libraries of relevant software maintained on public networks so that their various offices can more readily use common approved methodologies.

The use of micros in audit staff training is fairly widespread in connection with learning about the micros themselves, and about BASIC programming, but not yet widespread in other contexts (e.g. as a medium for programmed learning).

Some companies actively encourage their staff to take micros and proprietary software away with them, on audits and elsewhere, and experiment with them. In the context of small companies certain individuals are also doing this for themselves, and are not being discouraged.

Many companies that use a lot of micros are tending to the view that a certain amount of hardware standardization is advantageous: this is particularly important if micros are to be used in, or to communicate between, offices which are heterogeneous in other respects (e.g. in different countries), or are to provide access to local area networks.

Micros are already sometimes used to communicate between the auditor, at a branch or at client's premises, and the auditor's own office.

There is extensive use of a variety of micros. Among the most popular are apparently Apple, IBM PC, DEC Rainbow, Wang, Commodore, Apricot, ICL and Olivetti.

Automating the audit—categories of audit activity

Major audit activities have been categorized, for the purposes of this chapter, as follows:

1 Understanding the business and system of accounting.
2 Recording the system of accounting.
3 Determining the audit approach.
4 Planning the audit.
5 Performing compliance and substantive audit tests.
6 Recording the work performed during the audit.
7 Analytical review of accounts (before or after other audit procedures).
8 Audit reporting.

Certain uses of information technology, however, cannot be confined to any single category of audit activity. This position will become even more prevalent as the ability to integrate different uses of technology improves.

Automating the audit—current uses of information technology

Current uses of information technology and office automation, in respect of each category of audit activity, are set out below. Certain instances where technology might in the abstract be thought useful, but where this has evidently not been borne out in practice, are also mentioned.

1 Understanding the business and system of accounting

This must still be achieved by the auditor unaided.

2 Recording the system of accounting

Word processing is used for the maintenance of indexes to, and text of, permanent audit files and internal control questionnaires.

N.B. The possibility of using software to derive control flowcharts has been considered by a number of large firms. It has not yet been extensively pursued, probably because it is not yet particularly efficient.

3 Determining the audit approach

There is no significant use of information technology in this context at present.

4 *Planning the audit*

Word processing is used:

(a) to maintain audit manuals;
(b) to record audit programs, detailed audit planning memoranda and budgeted time allocations.

5 *Performing compliance and substantive audit tests*

(a) Mainframe computers (and to a varying extent minis) are still extensively used (as they have been for very many years) for the performance of file interrogations based on the use of generalized audit software, together with occasional uses of test data and integrated test facilities, and various forms of program analysis. Indeed, because of the sheer number of computerized systems, the number of such techniques which are used continues to increase, although their proportion relative to all audit activities in a computer environment is probably falling.
(b) Micros are used for statistical sampling; estimation sampling; regression analysis. Firms whose audit philosophies are orientated in this direction inevitably use micros in the performance of the necessary mathematics.
(c) Direct communication is carried out between auditors' micros and other computers. Auditors' terminals, very often with their own independent processing capabilities, can also be put on-line to a large variety of different types of computer by the use of emulator programs. Internal auditors may thus have direct access to relevant computer files of their own organization, and the availability of terminals in the offices of external auditors provides the means whereby they too may have on-line access to the computer files of many of their clients, to carry out a wide range of computer audit techniques with greater frequency and facility. The potential benefits of this technique are high.
(d) Auditors' terminals may often give them access to publicly available time sharing systems, to enable them to carry out a variety of different procedures and calculations which may from time to time be useful in the performance of their audits and investigations, and which give them an opportunity to develop and maintain audit software in interactive mode.

6 *Recording the work performed during the audit*

Micros are used to produce audit schedules, including brought forward comparative figures. Such use is now quite widespread.

The direct preparation and immediate storage of 'working papers' on media other than paper was slow in coming, bearing in mind how technically straightforward it is. Finally, however, it has become quite widespread.

7 *Analytical review of accounts (before or after other audit procedures)*

Terminals are used to gain access to:
(a) news services;
(b) financial data;
(c) company information;
(d) legal cases and precedents.

These procedures assist auditors to obtain information of relevance to their audits (e.g. analysis of their clients' or company's performance relative to other companies in the same economic sector or the same line of business).

Micros are used for balance sheet and profit ratio analyses.

8 *Audit reporting*

Word processors are used for production of standard letters (debtors' circularization, etc.), reports by the auditors to management and standard audit report paragraphs.

Automating the audit—current and continuing developments

Use of all the procedures mentioned above is likely to increase.

In addition, the following developments are either taking place or being seriously considered. Companies with access to the results of overseas research, particularly in North America, have marked advantages, but the amount of actual development work being performed in Britain is still encouragingly high. The synergy which is currently being obtained from international exchanges of ideas is very strong.

Understanding the business and system of accounting

There is still no likelihood of the extensive use of information technology in this connection in the medium term.

Recording the system of accounting

Software already in existence will be modified to facilitate the preparation and subsequent amendment of audit flowcharts, and eventually to generate a flowchart from a specified set of facts and relationships.

Determining the audit approach and planning the audit

Bases of data will be maintained about clients, for the establishment of financial and audit history, financial trends, and the generation of initial audit strategies, initial accounts reviews and initial identification of possible areas of audit concern, as a result of:

1 the programmed examination of history and trends;
2 the programmed comparison of the current year's accounts with a projection of those accounts generated by program from an analysis of the history and the trends.

Such databases may include data which is essentially descriptive text: many firms are already building up such data. The generation of detailed audit strategies, however, requires data which is essentially numeric, and this is not being built up so fast. The full-scale use of both categories of data requires considerable front-end outlay of money. It also requires patience, because it needs some three to five years before a stable profile for a client can be built up.

Performing compliance and substantive audit tests

1 Interactive generalized audit software systems, enabling non-specialists with micros to develop audit interrogation programs, will increasingly be used from now on.
2 Audit software will tend to be developed to a greater extent than in the past, to carry out standard procedures in connection with particular categories of data and particular types of system. It is also possible that we will shortly see the development of a piece of audit hardware (an 'audit chip') incorporating standard data analysis facilities, for use in conjunction with a portable audit micro. (It is particularly difficult to estimate how close we are to the successful development of such a facility, but available technology certainly makes it theoretically possible).

Recording the work performed during the audit

Current trends are likely to continue and to be reinforced in the medium and long term.

Analytical review of accounts

The use of better-indexed data, and more sophisticated data retrieval systems, as outlined above, will provide facilities for the much more incisive and scientific analysis of accounts. This will, however, make the auditor's personal judgement (of what is really significant and what is not) more, not less, important.

Audit reporting

No material developments of current procedures are anticipated.

Automating the audit—longer-term developments

Understanding the business and system of accounting

The recent report of the Alvey Committee in the UK describes an intelligent knowledge-based system (IKBS) as 'a system which uses inference to apply knowledge to perform a task. Such systems can be envisaged handling knowledge in many cases of human thought and activity from medical diagnosis to complex engineering design, from oil technology to agriculture, from military strategy to citizen's advice. The development of such knowledge-based systems is widely regarded as the best means of expanding the application of IT to activities which today's computing technologies cannot approach.'

At the end of a five-year period of research, the Alvey Committee suggests that it should be possible to demonstrate a pilot medical system which would be able 'to make inferences in some depth from limited descriptive inputs'. If this can be done for one profession, it is not unreasonable to suppose that it might be done for another.

It is important to understand that an auditor's judgement would not be undermined by such systems; only that certain elements of it might be influenced (for the better) by them. Some auditors would regard us as nearer to this objective than others would suppose.

Recording the system of accounting

The facilities for recording systems of accounting, described above, will become even more sophisticated, and will provide the basis for the generation of draft audit programs for specific sections and tasks within an audit.

Determining the audit approach and planning the audit

Draft audit programs will be generated from the programmed evaluation of flowcharts, specified facts and relationships, and responses to internal control questionnaires.

Determining the audit approach, planning the audit and analytical review of accounts

The correlation of privately maintained data, about particular companies, with publicly available data about other major companies in the same industry or sector, including information about their degree of compliance or otherwise with accounting and reporting standards, and their conformity or otherwise with economic or other indicators of performance, already in principle provides useful input to the planning of audits and the analytical review of accounts. The programmed correlation of relevant items of such information would enable this to be done much more readily. This possibility, in respect of which a number of relevant public databases are available already, is currently being investigated in a number of different quarters. It is generally felt, however, that the full cross-referencing of such data, and the programmed framework for extensively correlating it, is likely to be developed later rather than sooner. This is because a good deal more research is still required before an appropriate system could be fully implemented. The development costs of such a system are high.

Performing compliance and substantive tests

Commentators have specifically noted that systems are needed, and will come, to prevent divergence from controlled audit quality. Thus, systems to monitor compliance with public auditing standards and guidelines, and/or adherence to a firm's own audit manual or other required procedures, and to report for executive attention on an exception basis, seem inevitable. Because this can already be done clerically, with only a limited number of apparent problems, some firms regard such a development as being of low priority. However, the clerical performance of these functions may sometimes be less than perfect, and less than fully consistent between different audits.

Such systems will therefore be a formidable instrument in the demonstration of adherence to rigorous standards of quality control. This will surely become more important, not less, as time goes on.

Recording the work performed during the audit and audit reporting

Use of information technology in these connections will be more or less fully exploited in the short and medium term, as already described.

Part 4 **Computer Audit Problem Areas**

16 Auditing Proprietary Software, Bureaux and Time-sharing Services

Summary

An explanation of the use of proprietary software, bureaux and time-sharing services. Packaged software evaluation and the user environment. The appropriate responses to the control problems which these facilities present. The audit approach.

Type of service

There is a wide variety of services which may be acquired. Software houses provide application packages for use by their customers on the customers' computers; this is known as proprietary software. Alternatively, computer bureaux will sell time for customers to run their own systems. Frequently a bureau has its own programmers and will provide both computer time and an application package for the customer, and this will often be a customer's first venture into computerized operations. Of course many bureaux offer application packages which were developed elsewhere by other software houses.

The traditional way of using a bureau is to deliver the input to the bureau and collect the output, or to use the bureau's services for delivery and return. It may be possible for the data to be prepared at the customer's location and fed down a telecommunications link to the bureau; such a method will give a new computer user his first experience of data preparation. Of course, it requires a terminal to be located at the customer end. Editing may be off-line or on-line. If it is on-line the customer will invariably be sharing the bureau computer with other simultaneous users: such a bureau is said to be a time-sharing service.

Time-sharing services

Time-sharing services are not just appropriate for some accounting and administrative data processing—they may be very useful for mathematical and scientific purposes: a time-sharing bureau may offer users hardware and software facilities beyond their own resources to develop perhaps in view of the rare occasions on which they are required. They make large computers available to 'small' users; they make complex mathematical packages, which took many man years to develop, available to users who could not justify an in-house development of the same system, even had they the competence. So time-sharing services are widely used by established computer users. By using the public switched telephone lines access can be made to a number of time-sharing services, each perhaps suitable for a different task, so long as the user has opened an account with each service he attempts to access.

Proprietary software

'Off the shelf' proprietary software has the attractions of (a) guaranteed delivery date and (b) costing much less than the development of an in-house system. On average, if it must be tailored for a user it is likely to cost about half as much as a purpose built in-house system. However there are always hidden costs such as the often considerable cost of changing corporate procedures to suit the package or the cost of training staff, unless this is included within the contract.

There are two types of proprietary software: computer-oriented software such as compilers, operating systems and general utility programs; and user-oriented software, whether scientific or commercial, of which the most widely used must be the standard packages for payroll. A general file interrogation package and a computer audit enquiry package are examples of proprietary software. Whether the package is to be used in-house or at a bureau it is essential to confirm that it is suitable. Care should be taken with packages which were originally developed to fit one user's requirements and were later marketed, with or without modification, as general packages. These in particular may have to be modified extensively before they are suitable for use. The modification process may be costly, and care should be taken to ensure that the contract with the supplier of the package covers subsequent maintenance; it may not, particularly if the package has been modified substantially.

Support for packaged software

It is difficult to overstress the importance of after-sales support. There are all sorts of reasons why software has to be modified or amended, of which the most important are the following:

1 To correct obscure errors found during the course of extensive use.
2 To reflect changes made necessary by external, particularly legal, factors (e.g. changes to provisions for collection of indirect taxation; changes to public reporting requirements).

3 To permit the software to be used in conjunction with upgraded hardware or enhanced operating system software.
4 To reflect increased expectations of technical performance of software in general.
5 To reflect increased expectations of the facilities of some particular category of software.
6 To incorporate specific users' requirements.

Under no circumstances should anyone acquire packaged software without knowing how it will be supported. Support may be provided by the software house or a third party: this is not a material point, though it must ultimately be the supplier's responsibility if no one else will undertake it. But the user must be satisfied that whoever provides the support is sound financially and technically and that the support, when required, will be provided efficiently and at a reasonable cost. (It should be free if the need for it is the supplier's fault or to improve the supplier's ability to sell the software elsewhere, but a charge is obviously reasonable if the need arises from external factors).

A prospective user of a package should always, if possible, consult some existing users about their own experiences of the package, particularly in relation to the supplier's support capability.

A prospective user should steer clear of packages which are not in use elsewhere, with *identical or near-identical facilities available on the same hardware configuration*. Attempts should be made to establish to what extent the package depends upon one or two programmers at the software house or bureau and might become impossible to maintain should they leave. The warranty of the software house relating to maintenance support must be adequate. Avoid packages developed by lone consultants unless they provide an invaluable service not available elsewhere. An application package marketed by another user who developed it for his own use and then decided to offset the cost by marketing it, is also risky—it may be too specialized and the company may lack experience of after-sales service.

If the user can persuade the supplier to part with complete documentation of the system there will be more security for the user as he could maintain the system himself or use outsiders to assist him. It is unlikely that a software house or bureau will part with a complete copy of the system documentation; were they to do so they would run the risk of illicit use of the package elsewhere. Further, the terms of the contract may preclude maintenance of the package by anyone other than the supplier. There is, however, no excuse for not providing a comprehensive user manual with the package.

The best compromise is to seek lodgment of a copy of the software with a third party (e.g. a bank, accountant or solicitor) who is empowered to release it to users in the event of the supplier going out of business or being otherwise unable or unwilling to support it. (This procedure is sometimes described as holding the software in 'escrow').

Implementation assistance and training

One aspect of the use of a software package which often causes particular problems is its initial installation. The supplier should be able and willing to assist the user to install the system, and to provide advice on associated functions such as initial file loading and use of the operating system software.

The supplier should be able, if required, to provide technical information about such matters as hardware functions and communications facilities.

The supplier should also be prepared to provide or recommend a source of initial training in the use of the system, and also ongoing training if required, at a reasonable cost.

Evaluating packaged software

Leaving aside matters relating to the supplier environment, there are certainly a number of identifiable characteristics of good commercial software. Broadly, they might be said to include reliability, security, efficiency and flexibility. However, these criteria are abstract, and people prefer something concrete. What they seek to evaluate are not in fact the criteria of good software but good practical factors like:

1 whether it is efficiently parameterized (so that it can be used flexibly);
2 whether it can interface with other software (like a spreadsheet or a word processing package, so that its efficiency is maximized);
3 whether it is integrated with other related packages (the purchases system and the sales system with the nominal ledger, for example, so that one item of input will generate all the associated file updates);
4 whether it is capable of producing easily understood reports, or includes a report generator;
5 whether it is well documented;
6 whether good training is available in connection with it;
7 whether it has a good audit trail (i.e. whether it can produce visible evidence of the way each transaction has been dealt with at all stages of processing);
8 above all, if it is a business information system, whether or not it incorporates good programmed control procedures, and/or features to facilitate good clerical control.

The trouble is that the relationships between the criteria of good software and the features which actually get evaluated are not simple. Certain desirable features are influenced by marketing techniques that are devised to sell as much as possible and therefore follow fashion. For example, perhaps, the use of graphics or split screens.

Also, the qualities of good software are independent of each other (a package can incorporate good control features but no one knows about it because they are badly documented). So assessment, as in so many other contexts, is partly a question of deciding the best mix of qualities (again, in the end, a subjective judgement).

Certain features are universally acknowledged as desirable, but can be implemented in so many ways that their desirability does little to assist the actual selection process. Such multiple options do not lend themselves to independent evaluation by those who are not going to make the choices. Examples of such features are good 'audit trail' and documentation.

Audit trail

Is it really necessary to have a system which will print everything out in the form (unchanged in principle for at least one century) of a full 'double-entry' set of books? If so, it is worth considering that, even under clerical systems, such full sets of books have never been maintained all that often (accountants are very familiar with 'incomplete records'). More importantly, a full print-out system—using the computer simply as a glorified typewriter—is not really taking proper advantage of even quite elementary data processing techniques. Why does it *need* to be printed out if it can be kept on magnetic media? (People have been known to lose accounting records on paper, as well). Surely, what is important is that it should be possible to determine from the records, in whatever form they are maintained, how transactions have been processed. And this capability is the essential feature of a good 'audit trail'.

Documentation

Is it necessary to have a system which comes with a detailed set of written instructions (unchanged in form since Caxton)? If so, again, this does not make use of the technical capability of a system to provide its own 'documentation' in the form of on-screen help facilities, programmed validation aids and on-line error diagnostics. It may be, of course, that separate textual documentation comes cheaper—if so, fair enough. But why else is printed documentation needed, if the essential features of documentation can be maintained on magnetic media? Surely, what is important is that it should be possible to discover, at moments of difficulty, how the system works—and that is the essential feature of documentation.

Reliance upon controls

There are various ways in which these two matters are particularly important. For example, the user may be ignorant, through poor documentation and/or training, of the detailed internal functionings of the package. If so, this is a control problem as well as an audit problem. It makes it much more difficult, if not impossible, to be able to rely upon controls built into the computer programs themselves. The audit approach may tend to be more of a 'black-box' approach of auditing round the computer. Likewise, effective management control may tend to be achieved by greater reliance upon manual accounting controls over the system. Whatever the case, it must be easy to control the system by reference to the audit trail produced by the system.

Packaged software—the user environment

The most difficult aspect of software evaluation, is that the quality of a piece of software is only partly intrinsic. There are several other factors to be taken into consideration. Firstly, it also partly depends on how well the software fits in with the environment in which the customer wants to use it, and what he wants it for. Secondly, different potential users have different expectations of software. 'I want all the figures at the touch of a button' is heard less often nowadays, but still not infrequently. Thirdly, everyone wants software to be 'user-friendly'. But some people make friends more readily than others, and good relationships are sometimes elusive. Fourthly, different people have different absolute requirements. They simply do not all *want* the same features, whether those features are available or not. Fifthly, different people have different-sized budgets. In the end, this may be the most significant factor in the evaluation.

The auditor should therefore pay particular attention to the following matters, in any context in which software packages are used:

1 whether the software does what it purports to do;
2 whether it does what the user *expects* it to do;
3 whether it does what the user *requires* it to do;
4 whether it does what the user *wants* it to do;
5 whether it can cope with the user's *data volumes*;
6 whether it can cope with the user's *data sizes* (e.g. it may cope with millions of pounds, but the user may want it also to deal with thousands of millions of lire: can it do so? Will it cater for the length of the user's reference numbers? Will it cope with the user's requirements for maintenance of names and addresses?);
7 whether it can cope with the user's requirements for *data analysis* (e.g. can nominal ledger sub-totals be produced if required?);
8 whether it can cope with the user's requirements for permanent data storage (e.g. how much on-line reference information does the user need?);
9 whether it can cope with the user's requirements for security and back-up (how easy is it to copy whole files onto off-line file media? How easy is it then to restore them for processing on-line if required?);

10 whether use of the software *can* be controlled (see chapter 7);
11 whether it is compatible with the user's methods of working and systems of internal control, and if not which should be changed, the software or the methods?
12 whether the user has suitable and competent personnel to operate the system and *enable* it to be controlled.

If the real answers can be obtained to these very simple questions (if possible, *before* a software package is acquired, not afterwards) a great deal of operational error, inconvenience, lack of control and risk of loss can frequently be avoided or minimized.

Use of a computer bureau

If a computer bureau is used, control over input and output may present a greater problem than with in-house systems as there is the physical problem of controlling the data in transit between the two locations. Interception of input for illicit alteration is a common means of perpetrating a fraud. Likewise interception of output may lead to disclosure of confidential information. The basic control principle remains unaltered: it is the user department's responsibility to control their system and they *must* be satisfied that they have the means to do so.

Time-sharing services are often used to process sensitive corporate data—perhaps data on market research, corporate planning, corporate modelling or sales forecasts. This sort of data is exactly the data which would be of value to competitors, most of whom are probably making use of the same time-sharing services. So it is important that corporate data on a time-sharing bureau is secure. A prospective user should satisfy himself about the security arrangements of the time-sharing service which should be guaranteed in its contract with the user. What stops others gaining access to the user's data? The basis of control will be a password system but how secure is it?

Data may be encrypted for transmission, and data left at the bureau could also be encrypted. It is often sensible to make it a rule that no data will be left on bureau tapes or disks: it should be wiped off before the user signs off. It is also wise to ensure that data is referred to by codes rather than by narrative descriptions which would be immediately intelligible to an unauthorized reader. The periodic invoice from a time-sharing service will show the access time charged: this can be reconciled to in-house records of terminal access in order to spot unauthorized access to confidential data, as well as to pick up overcharging.

The standing of the bureau or software house

As the user is committing his business affairs to the bureau or software house it is essential that he is satisfied with the standing of the bureau in particular so that he has assurance of continuity of processing. He should also be satisfied with the contract terms, which must be studied carefully, but the terms of the contract will be scant protection if the bureau turns out to be unreliable. The user should ensure that his insurance protection is extended to cover consequential loss caused by any failures at the bureau. It is generally better for the *user* to carry out this insurance than to depend upon the bureau's insurance.

The user should examine the bureau's own standby arrangements. It is important to know whether the bureau is making a guarantee of the provision of a stated service and what sort of obligations the bureau will honour if the user is late submitting input or if he requires additional processing time.

In investigating the standing of a bureau the following should be considered:

1 The age of the bureau.
2 Its reputation.
3 Whether it belongs to a satisfactory trade association, such as the UK Computer Services Association, which has its own code of ethics to regulate its membership of a large proportion of UK software houses and computer bureaux. There is an equivalent US body.
4 Its financial backing—in terms of share capital or membership of a larger group.

The user should give consideration to the issue of ownership of files and programs. Users have burnt their fingers in the past when their bureau has gone into liquidation and the user has then discovered that he has no further access to his own data or use of the package.

Bureau standards

Not only does the user have no control over, nor complete knowledge of, the controls which are built into the bureau's software—he also has no control over the general procedures or installation controls in force within the bureau. There is of course a pressing need for the user to be satisfied about these controls. It is impractical for bureaux to give free access to all users and their internal auditors in order that these may satisfy themselves about the bureau installation controls. Before a contract is signed with the bureau, the prospective user may have an opportunity to write into the draft contract a reasonable right of access for his internal and external auditors. He will probably have to pay a price for this; it would be an intolerable overhead for the bureau should all users insist on the same provision.

By some means the user must have the opportunity to reassure himself about the standard of bureau installation controls. Many bureaux are aware of this problem. Their own auditors will be reluctant to issue a certificate to users and to user auditors which states that in their opinion the controls are adequate: this may cause problems with the external auditor's own costly professional indemnity insurance. An auditor would certainly be reluctant to commit himself to the continued adequacy of controls as a result of one specific audit. Alternatively the auditors of bureau users may appoint one of them, or another auditor, to conduct a 'third party review' on behalf of all the auditors. Neither of these methods is completely satisfactory for two reasons:

1 It may not be practical to pass judgement on the adequacy of installation controls without detailed knowledge of the extent to which each user depends upon them.
2 The third party review is at a specified time which may not be appropriate for all the users' auditors. One review time may, in any case, be inadequate.

Computer bureaux may be willing to state their installation standards and commit themselves contractually to complying with them, but even this is an inadequate reassurance for a user who is dependent upon the bureau. To date the only satisfactory approach to this problem, from the user's viewpoint, is for the terms of the contract to allow the user's auditors the access they consider they may require.

Recently there has been talk about bureaux obtaining certificates from accountants to the effect that the proprietary software they are marketing is soundly designed and incorporates satisfactory controls. The writers know of only a few examples where such a certificate has been given. It is risky for an accountant to take on this job without qualifying his opinion; whether or not the built-in controls of an application are adequate will be influenced by the manual controls that the user applies. Nevertheless the auditor will want some means of satisfying himself that the programming standards of the software house are adequate.

Audit methods

The auditors will want the contracts with a bureau to allow them access to client files at the bureau. Some bureau systems have enquiry facilities available which auditors can use. The auditor may also want to use his own enquiry package on his client's data. This could be done at the bureau, provided the auditor could satisfy himself, usually by attendance, that the enquiry was made under his exclusive control. If it were done in this way there would be a need to establish in advance that the bureau would be amenable to this. Alternatively, copies of the user's files could be made and the test conducted elsewhere. In this case the auditor would need to satisfy himself that the copy files were exact replicas of the production versions, and once again bureau consent at the contract stage would be advisable.

If enquiries prove inadequate or impractical, the auditor may resort to the test data method. The methods are not interchangeable for all purposes but for some audit work either method may suffice.

Discussion topics

1 Is it reasonable to have weaker control over computer systems processed at bureaux? State your reasons.

2 Why is it often difficult to evaluate a proprietary software package?

3 What are the special problems relating to control and security with respect to bureau and time-sharing operations?

4 In general, what would be your approach to the audit of:
(a) proprietary software?
(b) bureau-based processing?

17 Auditing Databases

Summary

For all the advantages of databases, there are control and audit problems. Centralization of so much data under the control of a few key personnel exacerbates the risks to which the organization may be exposed. There is a high degree of dependence upon a piece of software—the database management system. Here we look at some of the problems and suggest some solutions.

'A database is a collection of interrelated data stored together without harmful or unnecessary redundancy to serve multiple applications; the data are stored so that they are independent of programs which use the data; a common and controlled approach is used in adding new data and in modifying and retrieving existing data within the database. The data is structured so as to provide a foundation for future application development. One system is said to contain a collection of databases if they are entirely separate in structure.'
(This definition is from Martin, *Computer Data Base Organisation* (Prentice-Hall, 1975, 1977.)

Where possible, data is held on a database once only and may be accessed by a number of different computer applications. In practice an organization may have more than one database. Even if this is the case, an effort will be made to ensure, wherever practical, that the same item of data is not duplicated between the databases. Whereas traditionally each application had its own set of master files holding the 'permanent' or 'standing' data, under a database system a number of applications share one database.

Control aspects

Responsibility for data

This gives rise to possibly the greatest control problem of databases: whose data is it? With batch processing systems it is a key control principle to assert that the system and its computer files are the *user department's* in the sense that:

1 The user department is responsible for the correctness of processing.
2 The user department is provided with the evidence which enables it to discharge this responsibility.
3 The user department actually *does* discharge its responsibility to ensure correctness of output; and, as part of this, to confirm the continued reliability (i.e. 'integrity') of the computer files.
4 Steps are taken to make the system 'transparent' (i.e. hidden) to data processing staff and to discourage any suggestion that responsibility for confirming the correctness of output and integrity of the computer files is vested in them. Of course the data processing department is responsible for ensuring that they have done their data processing task correctly, but they should not take over from the user department the ultimate responsibility for the integrity of permanent data and the reliability of output.

In other words, with traditional computer systems, the systems are *user department systems*, with data processing providing a systems development service (in collaboration with users) and a processing service. This is a sound principle as the user who is functionally responsible for the operation (whether production, sales accounting, payroll, etc.) should also have ultimate responsibility and authority over the processing of data which is associated with the operation. A production department has a vested interest in efficient production; it would be unsatisfactory to deprive them of control over the means of achieving their objectives. So would it be unsound to relieve them of responsibility for their systems. *This is exactly what database threatens to do.*

Since data is held only once on a database, an item of data is likely to be shared by several different responsibility areas within the concern. There is therefore no natural way of assigning responsibility for that item of data. For instance, stock numbers may be accessed by purchasing, production, sales and accounts departments. Looked at in total, how can it be said that responsibility for the integrity of the database is vested with the user when there are a large number of users all using the same data? Taken a stage further, how can the users be held responsible for the correctness of outputs when this depends upon the integrity of data which may be added to, amended or deleted by other users? So this principle of *control by user* may be threatened, and may certainly be much more difficult to achieve, if databases are not used in a way which eliminates this potential problem.

The database administrator

Partly in response to this problem, the role of the database administrator has been established. Where a large database is in use, or a number of associated databases, there will be a number of staff making up the database management team. Programming and systems analysis experience are usually regarded as essential for a database administrator, and he invariably belongs to the data processing department though ideally being segregated, for control purposes, from applications development programmers, analysts, computer operators, media librarians and other control section staff.

It is essential that someone should be assigned formal responsibility for the integrity of the database and, because of the problems outlined above, this is the database administrator rather than the user departments. There is a potentially grave weakness of control if no one person has overall responsibility for the entire database. The consequence will be that there is no one in authority to whom reference can be made when problems arise, and users as well as systems designers will give up trying to solve their problems if there is no one who can act as a focal point. If no one person can be *held accountable* for the continued integrity of the database it is almost certain that nobody will *feel responsible* and the quality of the database will not be maintained.

It is unfortunate from a control perspective that responsibility for databases, being vested in database administrators, has shifted from the user, who had responsibility with conventional computer systems, to the data processing department. This deprives the user a bit more of his opportunity to control what he is held accountable for—namely, the satisfactory functioning of his operation.

Minis and micros

This trend is behind the backlash towards mini- and microcomputers located, operated and controlled within user departments. There is, of course, no reason why minis and micros also should not use database file organization: if the mini or micro is dedicated to a particular user department's processing, its database can be administered by the user department which can thereby re-establish control where it ideally should be. The disadvantage of a distinct database for each user department is that the economies and efficiencies of integration are lost.

Reliance upon the database administrator

Tackling the control problem of an integrated database by appointing a database administrator has led to other control problems. One traditional control technique is to segregate knowledge on a *need to know* basis. Unfortunately the database administrator needs to know everything about the database so control is potentially weakened. He has both the *knowledge* and the *opportunity* to cause chaos within the database, either deliberately or accidentally. His opportunity for concealed fraud is probably unparalleled. His function has been described as optimizing the storage of data on the database. To do this he needs access to the software of the database management system in order to maintain it. He also requires access to the data on the database so as to assist in determining the existence of errors and their cause, and to make corrections. Finally he has access to system documentation, as he has to assist in designing cost-effective data structures. He knows how often data items are accessed; he knows the restrictions on access to data; he knows the methods of processing by application programs; and he knows which applications use which data. It cannot be claimed either that he is debarred from operating the computer: he invariably has the authority to instigate computer runs. Via his own terminal, coupled with his complete knowledge of the systems, he is probably in a position to conduct any operating steps (e.g. add, delete, modify) which any of the users is authorized to do. The rule which existed with traditional computer systems that data processing staff should not, and should not be in a position to, amend data on user department files has been breached where a database is in use.

It will be apparent that corporate dependency upon the database administrator (DBA) is acute. It is certainly not alarmist speculation to assert that many organizations could be driven into liquidation by their database administrators.

'After-the-event' authorization of DBA activity

The key to this control problem is an effective 'after the event' authorization process by users. Evidence of what the database administrator has done should be printed out and checked, preferably by user departments. While responsibility for the integrity of a database shared by many users has to reside with the database administrator, responsibility to check his work should be allocated between users wherever possible. The basis of allocation should be determined according to which user is most dependent upon the data in question. The database administrator should also be effectively supervised within the data processing department. Each organization should have fall-back staff who would be available to man the database administration task in emergencies; each concern should also have a contingency plan to be used in the event that the database was rendered inoperable.

Permissible activity

Users themselves should be restricted in what they are able to do to the database. The ideal is that any category of action should be restricted to one program only: for instance, deletion of particular data should be possible via only one program under the control of preferably one authorized user. While the database administrator would also be able to delete data, the changes he made would be printed out or otherwise displayed for the authorized user or users to review. The range of possible activities are:

Read only
Read and add new data
Read and amend
Read and delete
(No access)

If each of these activities except the last can be limited to one program ideally under the control of one user, then control is strengthened. In practice, reading data will tend to be done by several users and possibly by several programs. If it can be restricted to one program (even if used by several users) then control is improved as in practice it is difficult to keep control of permissible activity by programs.

Audit aspects

The external-audit interest

The external auditor's overriding concern is that the year-end results show a true and fair view. In so far as these results depend upon a database or a series of databases, his principal concern about the database is likely to be to satisfy himself that the database is complete and correct and completely accessible. All the control techniques which contribute to the integrity of the database are therefore likely to be of interest to the external auditor. Where there are control problems with respect to the integrity of the database these are likely to be audit problems as well, but it is not intended to go over all the control problems again.

The external auditor has an additional problem over and above those of internal auditors. The internal auditor may be working with only one database and is able to develop sophisticated auditing facilities appropriate to his installation. These may include resident monitors and patches, both protected by the operating system which we discuss later. On the other hand the external auditor has to be able to audit many different databases. As early as 1975 there were over eighty database management systems available. It is natural that the external auditor would favour the use of 'transportable' audit software as he has done in the past. Thus enquiry packages are currently favoured. But many consider they will become increasingly impractical. We shall discuss the snags of enquiry packages for databases later.

In the long term the external auditor has two alternative approaches to relying upon his own transportable interrogation software. He could instead rely upon the internal auditor, as he may already do in other areas, to develop audit aids tailor-made for the client's database. Unfortunately, although they have the better opportunity, on the whole internal auditors are in the stone age with respect to auditing databases. Alternatively, or as well, the computer industry could allow for a standard audit interface to their databases so long as auditors could agree amongst themselves and with the computer industry as to what is required. With this standard audit interface, audit interrogation packages as well as more advanced auditing methods such as audit monitors could all be accommodated. Litecky and Weber ('The Demise of Generalized Audit Software', *Journal of Accountancy* November 1974) first suggested that there were three possible approaches to these problems, viz: 1. Modification of existing audit software to access the database directly, 2. Modification of the DBMS to include audit functions, 3. Development of standard audit interfaces in DBMS.

The internal audit interest

The internal auditor exists, at least in part, to reassure management that the information submitted to management for control purposes (i.e. monitoring) is of high quality (correct, complete, accurate, timely, relevant and so on). So the internal auditor is equally concerned with the integrity of the database. The internal auditor is also an auditor more generally of 'the 3 E's'—efficiency, effectiveness and economy; his purview of the database has a wider perspective than that of the external auditor. He would, for instance, want to confirm that his concern had invested in an economic database whereas the external auditor would be unlikely to go further than satisfying himself that the database was reliable.

It is currently being suggested that one consequence of the control problems associated with databases, in particular the problem of user control, is that information quality assurance needed by users may increasingly have to be provided by internal auditors. Ward [1] has suggested that this is compatible with the internal auditor's responsibility to secure the installation of soundly-based systems of control. He goes on to suggest that the prime control requirement is that the computer systems are inherently auditable. From the point of view of the auditor, he considers that auditability implies the facility for a competent and qualified professional independently, within reasonable time limits and without undue difficulty, to convince himself of the proper design and functioning of the system and its internal controls, and form an opinion on the propriety of generated information for the decision purposes of a user or group of users. From the viewpoint of a systems designer, he considers that auditability requires that the designer be able to convince an auditor that the system under review is sound and under control.

Audit independence

One of the audit problems is the extent to which the auditor can achieve independence in his audit of the database. The internal auditor needs independence; it is inappropriate for him to rely exclusively upon information provided by management using their own systems. Management may deliberately be withholding information from the internal auditor—and this applies even more to the external auditor. Alternatively management may be depending upon systems which, unknown to them, are unreliable and are not producing accurate information. Internal audit exists to reassure management that the information which management receives is reliable for control purposes. It is therefore incumbent upon the internal auditor to have his own independent means of obtaining data.

The external auditor's reasons for not wishing to be at the mercy of management's systems need no elaboration, and amount to the main drawbacks to depending upon the internal auditor's audit aids.

Using the database control program for auditing

One useful tool for the auditor is the database control program, or the query/report generator. This program exists for the database administrator to check the integrity of the database. The auditor may use it in several respects similarly to a conventional computer audit enquiry package—with the exception that it does not have specific audit-oriented routines built in. He is likely to find it easier to learn to use than an audit enquiry package and it will do most of what an enquiry package can do.

The basis question is 'to what extent can the auditor rely upon the control program?' The extent to which he may rely upon it will be enhanced if he checks it out in detail initially and thereafter keeps his own copy in secure conditions for his own use. As this aid in fact generates a program from parameters specified by the user it is unlikely that it would be unreliable, in particular through deliberate corruption. This is fortunate as 'program auditing' (the analysis of program coding by the auditor in order to find incorrect, inefficient or unauthorized logic) has suffered a body blow with the advent of databases: it is virtually impossible for the auditor to analyse DBMS program code. There may, however, still be a place for computerized program auditing using code comparison programs.

Using the computer as an audit tool

It used to be said of computer auditing that an auditor who could not use an audit enquiry package was the equivalent of a blind auditor asking management to read out to him the manual accounting records. Auditors must certainly use the computer as an audit tool to assist their audit of databased systems. Audit enquiry packages are not, however, such a promising audit tool for the audit of databases. The following is a list of some of the disadvantages of audit enquiry packages for databases:

1 With so many different DBMS, and a lack of standardization of data description languages, transportability of an audit enquiry package is not practically achievable where databases are in use.
2 Standard database query/report generators can do most of what a generalized audit enquiry package might be able to do, without serious loss of audit independence.
3 The practice of converting database entities into conventional sequential files of discrete records has a number of disadvantages:
   (a) The auditor may rely upon installation software to do this for him such as the standard back-up or dumping utility, with a consequent degradation of audit independence compared with the use of interrogation software on conventional systems.
   (b) If the auditor writes his own program to do this conversion he may have to learn a new programming language, e.g., a data manipulation language, which causes data to be transferred between the database and an application program.
   (c) Converting from entities to records is an unnatural and cumbersome audit step which may result in unreliable output, defective in terms of both accuracy and completeness. At best it is a temporary interim audit dodge to extend the life of their existing audit tools. It is rather as if the auditor was constructing a set of manual accounts from a computerized system so as to avoid the need to 'audit the computer'.
   (d) It would often be impractical. For instance one typical database has been said to take up twenty 2400 ft long magnetic tapes when converted to conventional sequential file layout which would lead to a processing time for audit purposes of several weeks (quoted by Ward, op. cit.).
4 Interrogations of single databases might take hours of computer time, be difficult to implement and prove expensive! It is not really practical to audit the database management system itself to satisfy the auditor that it is extracting all the data the auditor is interested in, and accurately.

Integrated audit monitors (or resident audit monitors, etc.)

To meet the need for developing new audit tools for databases, and to compensate for deficient audit trail, the auditor may think of using an integrated audit monitor, protected by the operating system or by being built into the database management system. This provides a measure of protection against unauthorized scrutiny or amendment. As such it is different from audit code resident in application programs. It acts as a monitor of processing. It takes copies of data which fit a profile specified in advance by the auditor. In essence this is a 'real time' auditor as it detects conditions of interest to the auditor *at the time that they arise during processing.* It has the particular attraction of spotting the condition at the time, and before it may be concealed by subsequent processing; it makes the existence and reliability of audit trail superfluous as the auditor is creating his own trail.

These audit monitoring systems work faithfully on behalf of the auditor even in his absence. It is a type of exception reporting. This general method of auditing is an appropriately advanced family of techniques for the audit of what are, after all, advanced data processing systems. In practice a problem is that there seems to be a built-in inertia against the development of technically sophisticated methods for auditing advanced computer systems. There is the added problem that these methods require co-operation from the client who must be fully involved: it can be argued that this reduces the value of the test as the auditor's independence is compromised to an extent. If the auditor's module is to be protected by the operating system or by the database management system it also requires the active interest and support of the manufacturer or software house who provides the database: in this respect it presumes audit involvement when the database is being designed—which, as we shall see later, is highly desirable for several reasons but can cause practical problems.

Once the auditor's module is operational there is the on-going overhead of additional run time and perhaps additional data storage space (where tagging is done) but this should become less of a problem as hardware becomes cheaper. With an integrated audit monitor working on the 'tagging' basis, the following may occur: 1. A null tag is linked physically or logically to each database entity to be monitored either when the entity is created or later, 2. Tags may be activated on direct audit command or in response to internal system events, 3. While a system is live, software *in the operating system* tests each entity for an active tag, 4. Other software reports active tags, their associated data entities and what caused them to be active. Even today what claims to be the first resident audit monitor for a database has been found to impose no appreciable overhead on run times. While the database is nominally larger because of the presence of tags, as these are only half a character in length the total storage overhead is only 1/2000th of the database.

The main problem of resident audit monitors is the software cost of developing this audit facility in the first place, which is likely to be prohibitive for the external auditor with many clients. There is scope for standard integrated audit monitors to be developed which, as with audit enquiry programs, could be adapted simply for each application and even for each database. This would require that the developers of database audit software provide a standard audit interface to convert generalized audit commands into database audit software. Integrated audit monitors are in many ways the equivalent of conventional audit enquiry programs but for on-line, real-time systems. Based on Ward (op. cit.) we can list the advantages of the integrated audit monitor working on a database as:

1 It is protected by the operating system which is understood in detail by relatively few people, hence it is in a protected area.
2 There is a degree of independence by virtue of the monitor being provided by a manufacturer or software house which is independent of the organization being audited.
3 The monitor exists once and does not have to be built into each application. It is independent of applications.
4 The monitor is 'hidden' in the operating system.
5 As such, the monitor is not subject to any other software.
6 The monitor is relatively inaccessible to users, as the operating system is a protected area.

It is also possible to use the monitor to inhibit the processing of transactions found by the monitor to be exhibiting a particular profile which is clearly invalid and dangerous. Many might feel that such an action would be outside the scope of internal audit but that depends upon the circumstances and the laid down scope of internal audit. It would, however, be beyond the scope of external audit.

Operating system patches

It is feasible to build into operating systems coding which would subsequently allow the auditor to instruct the operating system to report on particular activity which is taking place in the computer. A *negative* patch would trap an unauthorized instruction and report on the location at which it occurred, the operator password used, and so on. A positive patch would trap a specific command which, though possibly correct, should be reported—such as the use of superzap. This method is closely related to tagging except that activities, not data conditions, are here being monitored.

Test databases

The test data method of auditing may be feasible through the constructions of an audit test database. Set up by the auditor using the DBMS this will be adjusted from time to time to incorporate the conditions the auditor wishes to test. The application programs are used against this test database and the output reviewed by the auditor. The test database can be maintained by the auditor, so it is a much more effective audit method than the one-off test data shot.

Pre-event auditing of databases

The auditor must decide whether to be involved at the development stage of a database. Apart from the incorporation of resident audit aids, each of the following seven areas of audit interest are matters on which he could constructively contribute if he were involved at the design stage. Each also poses problems to the auditor in satisfying himself at the design stage that the arrangements made are adequate, and after the event that they are functioning satisfactorily and have not been changed:

1 *Validation procedures:* to ensure that adequate tests are provided for, and are conducted, prior to potentially erroneous data being used in processing or in output reports.
2 *Permissible activity:* to ensure that (a) operator access to terminals, (b) terminal access to programs and (c) program access to data, are restricted and controlled and that evidence is available to demonstrate this.
3 *Data definitions:* to ensure that a procedure exists and is followed which will ensure that consistent data definitions are used for each data element, and that unnecessary duplication of data is avoided.
4 *Responsibility:* to ensure that evidence of proper performance of all key functions is provided to those responsible for the correct results of those functions; and to ensure that all responsibilities are appropriately assigned, in particular that overall responsibility for the database is vested appropriately and that different sections of the database are the clear responsibility of different user departments.
5 *Audit trail:* to ensure that by logging and copying recovery is possible, and that adequate records of the system are provided.
6 *Contingency planning:* to ensure that appropriate measures have been developed and tested to handle all possible contingencies with respect to malfunctioning or complete failure of the database.
7 *Control totalling:* to ensure that proper provision of data has been made for the regular totalling of segments of data and values in order to confirm the continued integrity of the database.

Control of the auditor

In conclusion there are two remaining problems which confront the auditor of databases. First there is the problem of restrictions being placed upon his own actions by control-oriented management who are, after all, only insisting upon the best practices that audit recommend to them. In practice, for instance, the auditor may find management reluctant to allow him to be one of the authorized users of a database. Certainly the auditor should be prepared to be restricted to 'read-only' status unless he is operating within an integrated test environment—with all its associated problems and limitations from an audit viewpoint. An integrated test facility, despite its limitations, may be an effective way for the auditor to test the controls built into database systems. However, the need for higher levels of built-in integrity when databases are in use may make the test data method and the integrated test facility even more unpopular than they are with conventional systems.

Audit competence

Secondly, there is the problem of audit competence. While it is true to say that today all auditors must be computer auditors as most systems are now computerized, it is also true that audit firms and departments also need *specialist* audit competence—particularly if they are to cope with the audit problems of advanced computer systems, including databases. It is unlikely that this competence will be developed except in someone who has worked in a computer department for perhaps two years at least. There are problems in attracting such people to audit, but this is the way forward. There are then problems in keeping the computer audit specialist up-to-date with data processing developments. The workable solution is to return him to data processing after from two to four years in audit to enable him to 'recharge his batteries'. There is also the problem that he may not make a good auditor and, in the case of internal audit, it may be difficult for him to stand at arms length from the data processing department. The solution to this lies partially in recognizing that audit competence is found in an *audit team* and not within one individual auditor.

Reference

1 G. Ward: *The Audit of Database Systems* (Sixty-fifth Infotech State of the Art Conference, Paris, 14–16 November, 1979).

18 Networks and Teleprocessing

Summary

Digital processing techniques may be applied to a wide variety of functions. These often involve the use of networks and distributed processing. Control over distribution of files and programs is considered, together with other auditing considerations and problems in respect of networks.

Digital processing techniques

It is not just words and figures which can be represented in binary digital format but also sound, pictures, mechanized processes and indeed professional and technical thought processes or any other form of coherent information.

This convergence of hitherto different technologies makes possible the introduction of largely electronic offices and factories and the co-ordination of different but related functions by programmed means.

Many of these functions have been performed for a long time by older technologies, such as telegraph, telex, telephone, radio and television, machine tools and physical analogues, or clerically. What is fairly recent is the opportunity to perform all of them by different applications of the single technique of digitized information processing.

The functions which may be performed by such applications are themselves closely connected. For example, point of sale systems are in operation which permit the functions of selling, inventory control, cash control, dispatch scheduling and sales analysis to be integrated, by reference to the scanning of an electronic bar-code on the side of the product.

Such applications include the following:

Voice communications.
Facsimile transmission.
Electronic mail and document filing.

Filing, indexing and cataloguing of reference material, on-line information retrieval systems.
Message switching.
Teletex, viewdata and electronic telephone exchanges.
Point of sale data capture, electronic funds transfers and automated banking.
Automated manufacturing and warehousing.
Expert systems.
Artificial intelligence.

Many of these possibilities are interrelated. For example, public viewdata systems are also closely associated with telephone exchanges because the information available on viewdata systems is accessed via telephone lines. Viewdata can be used for the transmission of text, as can facsimile transmission. Facsimile transmission may be used to transmit printed copies of documents filed either clerically or electronically. The contents of documents may also be made available within an organization by means of an electronic mail service.

Networks

The use of such functions presupposes the availability of a network to distribute digitized information from its source to its destination. If it distributed to a number of different destinations, the system may be described as a distributed processing system. Such distributed processing systems may use a network linking remote users to a central computer but not directly to one another (which may be depicted as a sort of star system—see Fig. 7), or a network where each user is linked to all or several others—see Fig. 8. Such a network may incorporate the use of a central computer system exercising a significant degree of control over the network as a whole (the Systems Network Architecture approach). However, this need not be the case: it is possible for the system to be much closer to a network of equals. The auditors should always be clear about the configuration of the network, otherwise its potential, as a source of either reassurance or concern, may not be fully appreciated.

Distributed processing

The factors relating to control of distribution are the same whatever the number of destinations, even if there is only a single recipient of the information. Distribution, however, does not necessarily require a network: it may be achieved by sending information physically from place to place, for example on a floppy disk.

It is also important to differentiate between distribution of data, and of access to the programs which may be used to process it, and distribution

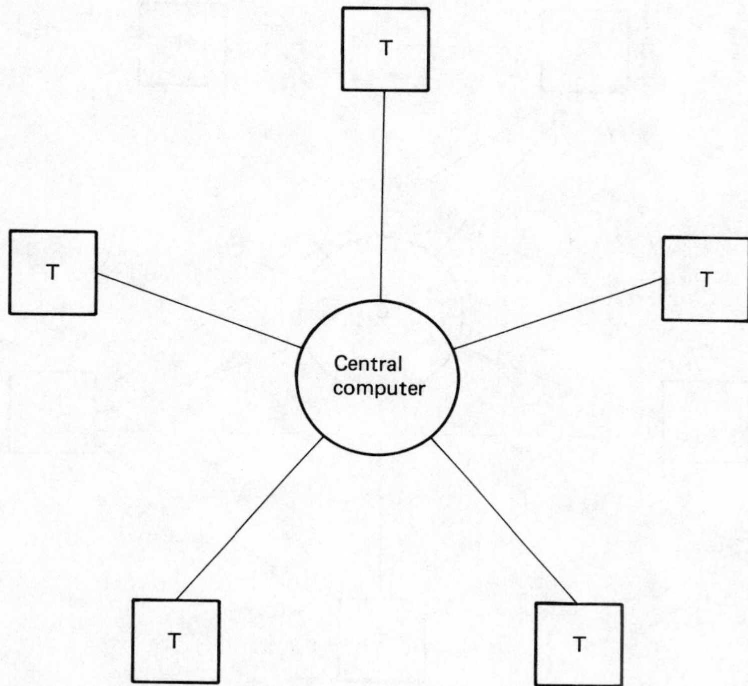

Fig. 7. Network linking remote users to a central computer.

of the programs themselves in such a way that they can be changed at their destination. Again, such distribution may be achieved physically rather than via a network. If a program, however transferred, can be changed at its destination, it cannot be assumed that the functions of that program will always remain identical at both its source and its destination. If the auditor needs to examine the functions of the program in one place, its functions in the other will almost certainly need to be examined separately.

Likewise if the data, however transferred, is distributed in such a way that it is retained on a separate file at its destination (i.e. it is downloaded from its source and retained separately) and can be altered in both locations, there is no guarantee that the two versions of the data will remain identical. Indeed the prima facie assumption is that they will not. The auditor should always bear this in mind.

Whatever the method of distribution, controls are desirable over the separate and distinct functions of: (a) access to and (b) amendment of: (i) programs and (ii) data.

If a network is used, a large measure of such control may normally be achieved by passwords (i.e. identity codes), as discussed in chapter 7.

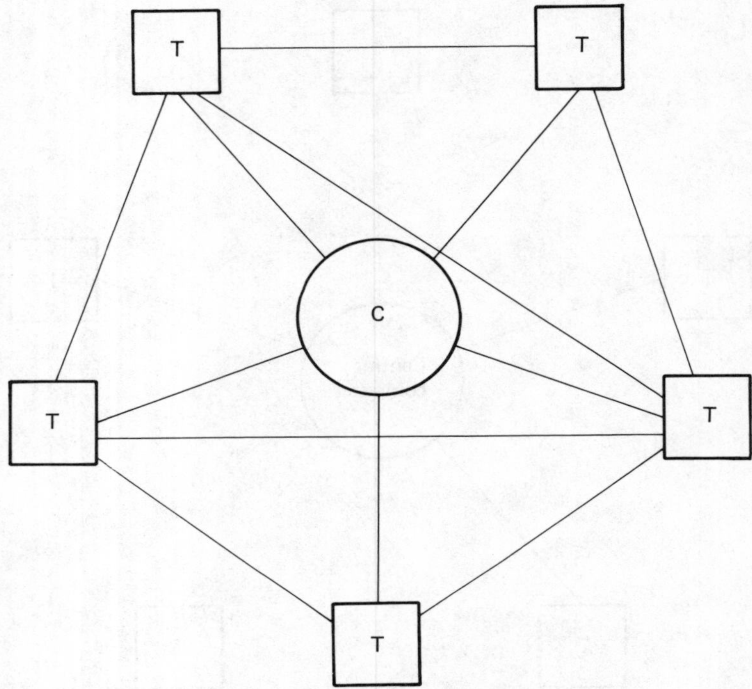

Fig. 8. Network where each user is linked to several others.

Local Area Networks

Local area networks operate within a limited physical area such as an office or a factory. Such networks use coaxial cables to which terminals, minicomputers or mainframes may be connected and, provided the relevant network control software is available, intercommunicate.

Such networks may be either 'closed' (i.e. allowing the use of a range of equipment from a single manufacturer) or 'open' (i.e. allowing the use of equipment from a variety of sources).

Apart from being more informal (and therefore more difficult to control), local area networks do not differ in principle from more widely distributed networks.

Auditing considerations

The main auditing principles for networks (whether distributed or local) are clear and consistent with those applicable to other methods of data processing. The auditor should find out the purpose and use of the network, the characteristics of the messages passing through it, and seek the appropriate degree of control over the various categories of message. Particularly sensitive messages are likely to include accounting and other commercial data. In such instances the individual terminals and other equipment attached to the network must be adequately controlled.

The most important aspect of networked data processing, from the auditor's point of view, is control of the information passing through the network. For example, all networks, in one way or another, use programs and data files. The following matters are therefore important:

1 Back-up for programs and files.
2 Archiving procedures.
3 Systems support procedures.
4 Controls over access to files.
5 A contingency plan in case files or programs become unavailable.
6 Segregation of duties.
7 Controls over the use of programs.

Control must also be exercised over access to the modems and communications controllers (if it is a distributed network), the public or private lines and local cables used for data communications.

All communications must be logged by the system. The auditor should examine such logs and enquire into any apparent discrepancies. It may also be appropriate to use some of the computer-assisted audit techniques described in chapters 9–14.

If the information is sufficiently sensitive, then the only answer is to encrypt it (i.e. scramble it) before it leaves its source, so that only authorized recipients have access to the codes by which it can be decrypted (i.e. unscrambled). The decryption is normally performed by computer programs, which themselves must of course be kept secure.

Encryption is a means of maximizing the security of the information itself. Whether the information is encrypted or not, it may also be *authenticated* by the application of a programmed formula (an algorithm) mutually agreed beforehand between the originator and recipient of any communication. If the recipient's application of the algorithm does not yield the expected results, the recipient will have reason to suspect that the communication did not originate with its purported source.

The auditor should ensure that full consideration is given to the desirability of encrypting data or authentication of communications. If either is desirable, then the auditor should be fully involved in the discussions about the means of implementing it. Once it is implemented, the auditor should then undertake tests of its effective operation, in the same way as for any other control procedure.

In general, the auditor should be concerned with the objectives, technological characteristics and method of use of a network, and its cost-effectiveness, but most particularly with the risks and control procedures associated with its use. However, the auditor, particularly if personnel resources are limited, should not be over-ambitious. Certainly, as we have already discussed, auditing is not something which always has to be done only by qualified professional accountants, except in external audit contexts to the extent that the law requires. However, an auditor should also remember that there must always be reasonable limits to the function of auditing. These limits do change as time goes on. In 1896 Lord Justice Lopes decided that an auditor was not an inventory checker and that it was not an auditor's duty to verify the accuracy of the inventory check at the accounting year-end: clearly, no judge would be likely to reach the same conclusion today. But, by analogy, an auditor today would scarcely be regarded as a communications engineer, and would not necessarily be expected to be able to detect, much less prevent, certain advanced forms of electronic intrusion or wire-tapping. In this connection the auditor, like everyone else involved in the use of a public network, has to accept that such a network is indeed public. This means that, like any radiated or cabled information, it can ultimately be intercepted by anyone with the mechanisms to do so, whether legally or otherwise, at any time after it has left its source.

Nevertheless, it should be noted that the UK Audit Commission, in its recent report, draws attention to its view that 'the shift towards an increased dependence upon telecommunication facilities is certain to increase the risk of fraudulent activity. Those organizations whose day-to-day business stability is based upon the ability to initiate large scale financial transactions via fast computerized communication links must be concerned that their protective measures are absolutely safe and secure'. The auditor must be involved in this process.

19 Systems Software

Summary

This chapter considers various types of systems software and what they achieve. Operating systems and job control language are particularly important. They present a number of problems for auditors and offer a number of opportunities, particularly in connection with efficiency auditing and fraud detection. The auditor should be in a position to use systems software for audit purposes and to analyse and evaluate its use in other circumstances where appropriate.

Power, capacity, speed—how much does it really matter?

Computers are often marketed with reference to their technical characteristics. It is worth noting the extent to which these may or may not contribute to the effectiveness of one computer over another in terms of what it will achieve for you. The main factors are:

1 The power of the computer's processing unit. A 32-bit computer has the capacity to process data more quickly than a 16-bit computer (though how much more quickly depends on what sort of processing is involved).

2 The size of the main memory. A 128K RAM machine has the capacity to process twice as much data as one of 64K (though whether this is worthwhile depends on whether the larger amount of data is more useful than the smaller).

3 Storage capacity. The more on-line storage is available (like a 10 megabyte disc), the more processing is possible, because program instructions can be transferred back and forth between the main memory and the on-line storage, thus enabling the main memory to be used more efficiently than would otherwise be possible.

4 The efficiency of the operating system. The OS is the set of programs that handles general functions such as reading data off files, printing and

enabling two or more programs to be executed simultaneously.

5 The speed of the peripherals. If you have a slow printer, the most powerful computer in the world will not make it any faster. Although the efficiency of the operating system may help you to mitigate the problem, it is likely to be better just to get a faster printer if what you mostly want to do is printing.

But in the end the characteristics of the computer are less important than the quality of the programs that do the work you want done. If the accounting programs or the payroll programs or the production control programs function incorrectly, a more powerful computer will simply give you the incorrect results more quickly. This is why software quality is so important, and is the first, rather than the last, of the characteristics of a system with which you should be concerned.

Functions of systems software

'Systems software' is an umbrella term covering the software used to perform a number of different functions which are not specifically related to any particular user's computing requirements but are of general applicability. This is in contrast to software, often described as 'application software' which supports the application of the computer to the particular requirements of a specific user or users (such as storekeepers, production managers or credit controllers).

Systems software always includes an *operating system*. It may also include, in any given installation, such items as database management software (DMBS), communications and teleprocessing monitors and software to support time sharing and transaction processing. It also embraces such software as compilers, assemblers and interpreters (to convert programs from the form in which they are written into a form in which they can be run on the computer), file library management software (to record and maintain information about the contents of the magnetic files) as well as software to diagnose processing errors and to record and analyse hardware utilization and performance.

Another category of software under the same general heading is 'utilities' dealing with such matters as sorting, merging, copying and reorganizing files. A very important sub-class of utilities permits direct access to records without invoking the regular access-handling software. The auditor should take particular care to ensure that, if possible, such file amendment software (typified by 'superzap' and 'DFU') is either completely unavailable or is available only under the most stringently controlled circumstances. This approach should be adopted in relation to all forms of *system* software which permits unrestricted and uncontrolled file amendment. It should be noted that the approach is not possible, and indeed is not even desirable, in relation to files created and maintained by spreadsheet packages and other forms of proprietary *application* software of which *the whole purpose is to facilitate file amendment*. In such cases the auditor should adopt procedures which are based on examination of the data, and which do not imply an assumption that the data is likely to be correct.

Operating systems

In any installation, the software usually known as the operating system performs the functions which permit coherent computer processing. For example, a computer system may often be used by more than one person. These users may either:

1 all be using the same program, e.g. order clerks receiving and entering orders received from customers (a 'multi-user' environment); or
2 all be using different programs to carry out separate and distinct functions (a 'multi-processing' environment); or
3 some combination of both.

In a multi-user environment, the operating system therefore should prevent direct conflicts between different users (e.g. more than one user seeking to update the same record simultaneously). In a multi-processing environment, the operating system incorporates routines to pass control from one program to another and to determine priority of processing between different programs.

Other operating system functions include:

1 Scheduling jobs to be run in a multi-processing environment when it is not possible for them all to be run (in effect) simultaneously.
2 Loading programs.
3 Handling files (e.g. in such a way that they are not corrupted or improperly overwritten).
4 Input/output handling.
5 Controlling the transfer of data to and from the central processing unit and the peripheral equipment.
6 Handling the 'paging' of program instructions and operational data into and out of the central processor when multi-processing is being carried out.
7 Handling 'interrupts' (i.e. if a program ends, or a piece of hardware functions, abnormally).
8 Job control, using a 'job control language' (JCL).

Job control language

The JCL is necessary in order to provide the operating system with instructions about the task to be performed. Mainframe and minicomputer JCLs have long been noted for their general obscurity and lack of machine compatibility, although microcomputer JCLs are more standardized. Nevertheless, job control is an integral part of all aspects of computing. Job control is therefore a potential source of danger through restriction of significant levels of knowledge to a limited cadre of specialists whose work is nevertheless of wide general relevance. Also, lack of JCL knowledge may compromise an auditor's independence in the performance of a computer-assisted audit procedure or in the review of a computer system.

Privileged access to data

The auditor should closely consider the responsibilities, scope, management and method of operation of technical support specialists with some privileged access, either through terminals or directly, to the files or databases of the system. The following passage from the American ICPA Statement on Auditing Standards 3* is particularly relevant to this matter:

> 'Supervisory programs are used in some EDP systems to perform generalized functions for more than one application program. Supervisory programs include (a) "operating systems", which control EDP equipment that may process one or more application programs at a given time and (b) "data management systems", which perform standardized data handling functions for one or more application programs. An individual who can make unapproved changes in supervisory programs has opportunities to initiate unauthorized transactions that are like those of a person who can make unapproved changes in application programs or data files; he therefore performs incompatible functions.'

The key word in this paragraph appears to be 'unapproved'. In order to monitor adherence to this principle, the auditor must therefore enquire into the procedures to enable the work of system support specialists to be approved and controlled, and the evidence of adherence to those procedures.

In practice, this aspect of the auditor's work is extremely difficult. Sometimes such procedures do not exist. Even if they exist, they may be generally ignored or applied haphazardly. Such support specialists are often extremely reluctant to be controlled. Since they work at the leading edge of the technology, their skills are bound to be scarce and highly valued. Management may be unwilling to impose irksome disciplines on them, for fear that they may respond perversely, perhaps by changing their jobs.

Even if evidence of the work of support specialists is available, the auditor may not have the necessary experience to monitor it confidently. Because the necessary technical skills are scarce in any case, and because the auditing profession may not necessarily seem very attractive to those who have them, an audit team may have significantly less skill in this connection than those

* Now superseded (see SAS 48), but still of relevance.

whose work it is trying to audit. In fact, although long-term career prospects may sometimes present a problem, a career or a period of experience in auditing may well be rewarding for them, both generally and technically.

However, this may not be possible to arrange as often or as satisfactorily as would be desirable.

Even if the audit team is technically capable of keeping up with the support specialists, and even if the necessary evidence is retained, it may be difficult to monitor the sheer range and volume of work which they perform.

Efficiency

Systems software auditing, however, may be required more often than not as an aspect of an efficiency audit. The efficiency or otherwise of functions in the systems software may have a disproportionate effect on the overall efficiency of processing. For example, poor input–output handling routines will slow up processing which involves a lot of input and output, no matter how fast the central processor or how efficient the application program. This effect may be mitigated, however, if extensive multi-processing is taking place and the paging routines are good. In practice, therefore, it is often extremely difficult to determine, even by bench-marking, the effect on the overall efficiency of processing of any significant change in the mix of use of different operating system functions. Also, systems software functions are only partly responsible for processing efficiency. It is also directly influenced by the efficiency of the hardware and by that of the user program being run: again, while these can to some extent be individually evaluated (in the case of the hardware, by technical bench-mark testing), the effect of combining (or changing the combination of) these factors cannot always be predicted with any confidence. A change in one of these factors may generate an unforeseen change in the effect of their mix.

Attention to audit objectives

In any case, the auditor should ensure that the objectives of auditing the systems software are well defined. For example, whether it is to be audited independently of the user-related systems, perhaps as part of an efficiency audit, or whether it is to be audited only in relation to its possible effects on the accuracy of the accounting or other commercial records. In the latter case, it may not be necessary to audit it at all (for example, because the accounting procedures exercised in the user departments are sufficient to impose the necessary degree of control without reference to the systems software). Because of the difficulties associated with the audit of systems software, the auditor should always consider whether and how the relevant auditing objectives could be achieved by alternative methods involving either systems-based reviews and procedures or by computer-assisted audit techniques directed towards the users' files or the application programs.

The audit procedures will depend on the particular controls that are used to safeguard the integrity of the systems software, and these will differ from installation to installation. Before devising audit procedures the auditor should seek full information about the functions of the systems software, the efficiency and effectiveness of each, and the methods used to control its operation.

It may be possible to narrow down the scope of a systems software audit, even where it is considered essential. For example, apart from efficiency, the other most likely reason for an extensive systems software audit is fraud detection. This will usually be directed to some particular area of suspicion or special concern, and this will in itself determine the functions to which most attention ought to be directed.

Audit procedures

Whatever the precise objectives, the audit procedures associated with operating systems will be based on the use of the following:

1 Program-generated logs of system activity such as CPU, peripheral and terminal usage, program execution, file accesses, abnormal interrupts and operator intervention. These may come in the form of job control logs or output from more specialized monitoring programs incorporated into the operating system. (N.B. Such programs might be prepared by the auditor if this is really considered to be an optimal use of audit resources.)
2 Manually produced records of system support activities, including all direct intervention by support specialists to the files, application programs or systems software itself. Records of the take-on of new operational programs, and the removal of superseded programs, should also be carefully examined. The system-generated catalogues of current operational programs and files at different dates should also be compared, including the details of their labels, sizes and update history if available.
3 The use of test data and test access procedures by the auditor, to test and evaluate the various operating system functions. The principles are as described in the chapter on the use of test data, although the required degree of technical skill may be much greater.
4 The use of audit software (possibly embedded in the operating system itself but more likely used independently) to extract information directly from the files used to produce the program-generated system activity logs, or to create files of comparable data by directly monitoring the use of the system in a particular way (e.g. the messages being transmitted to and from a particular location or the records being accessed and for what

purpose) over a specific period of time (say a day). The information collected by the auditor in this way could be examined directly, compared with corresponding information collected on a previous occasion, or compared with the relevant logs generated by the system itself.

The difficulty of controlling system support specialists has already been mentioned. However, the position is often made even worse than it need be. Even the most straightforward forms of control over systems support functions are often overlooked. For example, the relevant control procedures (e.g. passwords giving privileged access) should be changed whenever any person with previous knowledge of those procedures is reassigned from technical support functions, or leaves the organization, and the auditor should enquire into the relevant arrangements. This is simplicity itself, and yet it is a control discipline which is widely ignored by both management and auditors alike. (To a lesser extent, it is also relevant when any user of a password-controlled access system leaves the organization or is reassigned, but this is more a matter for individual management discretion, depending on the scope of the person's previous responsibilities).

Audit use of systems software

Auditors can often use systems software to their own advantage in other ways. They can use utilities, for example, to sort and copy files and to alter their format so that they can be more conveniently interrogated. They can also sometimes use utilities to add their own records to files, so that they can be more readily processed in conjunction with other files at a later date. (However, this is undesirable if it makes use of software which ought to be generally unavailable, even to auditors, or available only under direct and specific management control).

Auditors obviously use the facilities of the system in the course of such activities as compiling their own audit software, using a telecommunications network or accessing records in a database. Special aspects of the use of DBMS software, for database access, are discussed in the chapter on the audit of databases. Audit software itself also makes use of the other normal features of the operating system as discussed above. Auditors therefore need to have a good understanding of the relevant job control language and of the reports generated by the system in respect of any particular program execution, so that they can:

1 set up their own software without any help from systems support specialists, other programmers or operators, or at least be able to evaluate the likelihood that the help they receive is satisfactory;
2 determine whether their audit software has apparently functioned as intended from a technical point of view (e.g. that it has accessed the right files and has not terminated abnormally or been interrupted).

Discussion topics

1 Under what circumstances is it worthwhile for auditors to concern themselves with operating system functions?

2 Which system software functions are likely to be most important? Which are likely to be most sensitive?

3 Which system software functions are likely to be most useful to auditors? In what particular contexts?

4 Why does system software present difficulties for auditors? What are the implications of these difficulties?

20 Protection of Personal Data

Summary

In keeping with other countries which have ratified the Council of Europe's 1981 convention on the protection of individuals with respect to automatic processing of *personal data*, the UK now has its Data Protection Act [1984] which is designed to comply with what have become known as the *Data Protection Principles*, the 8th Principle being that personal data must be secure against unauthorized access, alteration, disclosure or destruction, and against accidental loss or destruction.

This is the first time there has been a specific legal requirement to implement computer security arrangements and this is of the utmost significance for auditors. Since, within most integrated computer systems, personal data tends to be held on the same files and databases alongside other types of data, those responsible for compliance with this Act are advised to ensure that the general principles relating to data security which are requirements of the Act are observed for *all* the computer systems for which they are responsible. In practice, this is likely to be the only way of ensuring that the Act is complied with. It is also recommended that data users apply for registration in all cases where there is any doubt as to whether registration is strictly required, as it is better to comply with the Act unnecessarily than to commit an offence by not complying.

The discussion which follows sets out the main requirements of this Act. It makes no difference whether the computer is a mainframe or a micro—the provisions of the Act apply to both extremes. Terms set in bold type are defined in the glossary of terms at the end of the chapter.

Registration

Data users, unless exempted, must apply for registration of each system separately to the **Data Protection Registrar**. The Registrar's Guideline No.

1 on the operation of the Act was published in April 1985.

Applications for registration should give the name and address of (a) the data user and (b) the person to whom **data subjects** should apply for access to the data, a description of the data held and the purposes for which it is held or used, a description of the source or sources from which the data may be obtained and the types of people and countries to whom it may be disclosed or transferred. This information will all be included within the entry which will be made in the Register. Dissemination of data to a country or territory outside the UK would only be permitted if the country or territory is named in the registered entry.

The Registrar is not empowered until 11 November 1987 to refuse an application for registration except on grounds of incomplete information, nor to issue deregistration notices, transfer prohibition notices or enforcement notices.

The Act provides for a Tribunal to consider appeals of data users in dispute with the Registrar.

Compensation rights

From 12 September 1984 data subjects have legal rights including a right to compensation for damages as a result of loss or unauthorized disclosure of **personal data**. So data users must take special care to ensure that the **Data Protection Principles**, incorporated into the Act, are being complied with—in particular that the uses to which the data are put are limited, that the data is up to date and accurate, that it is secure against unauthorized access and protected against accidental loss.

After registration, a data subject will more readily be able to sue for damages for losses incurred if the information has been disclosed in ways not covered by the registration entry. From 11 May 1986 data subjects will be able to sue for damages caused by inaccurate data (as well as having the right to apply for its rectification or erasure). Data subjects will also be able to sue for damages incurred with respect to uses of computerized personal data on unregistered databases.

Access rights

Data subject access provisions come into force two years after the date (11 November 1985) appointed by the Registrar for the commencement of main provisions of the Act, at which date (11 November 1987) the Registrar's enforcement powers also come into effect.

A data subject will then be entitled to know within 40 days of a request whether the data user holds personal data on the data subject and, also within

40 days of a request, to receive a copy of such data in an intelligible form.

Computer bureaux

Computer bureaux are caught by the Act and must apply for registration where personal data is processed either by the bureau or by other persons using the bureau's equipment. A bureau's application for registration need only give its name and address.

While the first seven **data protection principles** apply to data users but not to bureaux, the eighth principle applies to both: a bureau is thereby restrained by the Act to disseminating personal data only with the prior authority of the person for whom the bureau's service is being provided. The bureau does in addition have a legal obligation under the Act to make sure that those using the bureau's services are themselves properly registered as users. Of course, if the bureau is itself a user of personal data processed automatically, it must seek registration in the same way as any other data user.

Exemption from registration

1 There is no need to register if the data includes no personal data or is not processed automatically on a computer.
2 Payroll and pensions personal data are exempt from the registration requirement if they are held and used only for these purposes, and are not disclosed to anyone except to the payee, to another party (such as a bank, bureau or pension fund) to enable the remuneration to be made, to auditors or actuaries, to someone to whom the payee has agreed that disclosure may be made, or for the purpose of giving information about the financial affairs of the *data user's* enterprise (as opposed to the financial affairs of the data subject).
3 Accounting and stock recording data provided disclosure is only made to the auditors or for the purpose of giving information about the financial affairs of the *data user's* enterprise (as opposed to the financial affairs of the data subject).
4 Personal, family, household, recreational data.
5 Unincorporated members' club data (provided the data relates only to members who have been asked and have agreed to the data being held).
6 Names and addresses and other necessary information relating to distributing things to people, provided the data subjects have been asked and have not objected.
7 If the data consists of information which you are obliged to disclose under other laws.
8 If your systems are certified by a senior Minister of the Crown as being for the purpose of national security.

Exemption from right of access

Subjects have no right of access to data held for:

1. Certain statutory purposes.
2. In the interests of national security or for the prevention or detection of crime.
3. The assessment or collection of tax.
4. Certain health and social security purposes.
5. Statistical preparation and research if the results are in a form which makes it impossible to identify the data subject.
6. Making judicial appointments.
7. Purposes the Home Secretary may specifically exempt (particularly to help prevent fraud).
8. Calculating pay or pensions only.
9. Accounting purposes only.
10. Most home computer purposes.
11. Use by an unincorporated members' club.
12. Distributing or recording the distribution of articles.
13. Purposes which can claim legal professional privilege.
14. Back-up purposes.

Usually the data subject still has a right to have erroneous data rectified or erased, and to apply to the Court for this to be done, and also to sue for damages for any losses incurred. This would only be practical if the data subject learns from some other source about the faulty contents of the data.

Exemption from non-disclosure provisions

Data users will not be in breach of the Act if they disclose personal data for various legal purposes or to protect national security; to aid the prevention or detection of crime or the assessment or collection of tax; to enable pay or pensions to be calculated or paid; for audit purposes; for distribution purposes only if the individuals do not object; and a few other purposes.

The position as regards other countries

Personal data on computer files may not be transferred from the United Kingdom to other countries except in accordance with the details registered. However, the UK Data Protection Act does not apply to a *data user* in respect of data held or to a person carrying on a *computer bureau*, outside the United Kingdom. The Act also does not apply to *data processed* wholly outside the United Kingdom unless the data are used or intended to be used in the United Kingdom.

Where a person who is not resident in the United Kingdom controls the use of data or runs a computer bureau through a servant or agent in the United Kingdom, the Act applies as if the control were exercised or the bureau run by the servant or agent acting on his own account. The servant or agent has to register (but may be described for the purposes of registration by the position or office which he holds).

The European Convention

The Council of Europe has prepared a Convention on Data Protection which was opened for signature in January 1981 and was signed by the United Kingdom in May of that year. In addition the Organization for Economic Co-operation and Development prepared guidelines on privacy protection and transborder data flows which the United Kingdom endorsed in September 1981.

Article 5 of the Convention states that personal data undergoing automatic processing must be:

1 obtained and processed fairly and lawfully;
2 stored for specified and legitimate purposes;
3 not used in a way incompatible with those purposes;
4 adequate, relevant and not excessive in relation to the purposes for which they are stored;
5 accurate and, where necessary, kept up to date;
6 preserved in a form which permits identification of the data subjects for no longer than is required for the purpose for which those data are stored.

Article 6 states that personal data concerning certain special categories of data may not be processed unless appropriate safeguards are provided. These categories of data are in respect of:

1 racial origin;
2 political opinions;
3 religious or other beliefs;
4 health;
5 sexual life;
6 criminal convictions.

Article 7 states that appropriate security measures must be taken for the protection of personal data stored in automated data files against:

1 accidental or unauthorized destruction;
2 accidental loss;
3 unauthorized access;
4 unauthorized alteration;
5 unauthorized disclosure.

Article 8 states that any person must be enabled to establish the existence of an automated personal data file, its main purposes, and who controls it. A person will be able to find out at reasonable intervals and without excessive delay or expense, whether personal data about him or her are stored in an automated data file, and the content of those data in an intelligible form. If they are not held in accordance with the law giving effect to Articles 5 and 6, the subject of the data must have the right to require the data to be corrected or erased.

Article 9 states that any country may provide for derogation from the provisions of Articles 5, 6 and 8 when such derogation is held to be in the interests of:

1 State security;
2 public safety;
3 the monetary interest of the State;
4 the suppression of criminal offences;
5 protecting the data subject or the rights and freedoms of others.

Automated personal data files used for statistics or for specific research purposes may also be exempted in appropriate instances.

Austria, France, Denmark, Iceland, Finland, Luxembourg, the Netherlands, Norway, Portugal, Spain, Sweden, Switzerland, Turkey and West Germany, as well as the United Kingdom, all have forms of data protection legislation either in force or in prospect. Not all these countries have yet signed and ratified the Convention.

Computer users and auditors in these countries should ascertain from their own Interior Ministries the precise state of progress towards adherence by their own country to the terms of the Convention, and the enactment of its provisions in their own domestic laws.

Glossary of terms

DATA PROTECTION PRINCIPLES

1 Personal data must have been obtained fairly and lawfully.
2 Personal data must be held for lawful purpose(s) disclosed in the Register.
3 Personal information must only be disseminated for the purpose(s) disclosed in the Register.
4 Personal data must be adequate, relevant but not excessive for the purpose(s) held.
5 Personal data must be accurate and, if applicable, up to date.
6 Personal data must be kept no longer than is necessary for the purposes for which it is held.
7 Personal data subjects have an entitlement to know what data is held on them and to apply to have it corrected or erased if appropriate.

8 Personal data must be secure against unauthorized access, alteration, disclosure or destruction, and against accidental loss or destruction.

DATA PROTECTION REGISTRAR
The Data Protection Registrar has the responsibility to maintain a Register of personal data users and computer bureaux which hold personal data and has powers to ensure that personal data is used in accordance with the data protection principles. The Registrar's functions include considering any complaint that any of the principles or any of the provisions of the Act has been or is being contravened.

DATA SUBJECT
An individual upon whom personal data is or may be held automatically.

DATA USER
Someone who is designated as the person who holds personal data for automatic data processing and has the responsibility to control the contents and use of the data.

PERSONAL DATA
Data relating to a living individual who can be identified from the data.

Part 5 **Computer Crime and Abuse**

21 Computer Crime and Abuse

Computer crime and abuse may be fraudulent or non-fraudulent. Non-fraudulent abuses include damage to hardware, programs or files, occupation of the computer centre to prevent its use, or the straightforward misappropriation of materials or information without any attempt at concealment. 'Fraud' is not a very helpful term: its essential meaning is 'dishonesty', but generally we think of fraud as also implying a measure of at least attempted concealment and certainly an intention to gain on the part of the defrauder.

We must also allow for the fact that many abuses against the computer may not be criminal or, if criminal, may not obviously be so, and the appropriate redress may be to sue for civil damages. For instance, information may be copied without any theft of materials. Information is perhaps the organization's most valuable resource: a very wide variety of information could be of value to third parties and must therefore be kept securely.

A 1981 UK survey refers to the common difficulty of presenting the courts with firm, admissible evidence, and this alone would sometimes deter a company or other enterprise from seeking to prosecute. We shall be referring to this survey by BIS Applied Systems Limited [1] and also to the 1985 survey by the Audit Commission for UK local authorities [2].

There are other factors which discourage companies from seeking to resolve the issue through the courts, and we shall refer to these later.

Not all computer fraud is computer-dependent, this term being reserved for those frauds which would not have been feasible were it not for the fact that a computer is in use. There is little distinction between the terms computer-related and computer-assisted fraud, unless it is that the first merely involves the computer whereas the second is helped by the presence of a computer system though it is not dependent upon the computer.

Whether dependent, assisted or related it makes little difference from an audit and control viewpoint as the systems controls to prevent such frauds, as well as the techniques to detect them, are likely to be the same whenever a computer is in use.

Likewise these controls and detection techniques are likely to be just as effective to prevent and detect other forms of error and loss. It has been shown that accidental losses due to human error and omission account for fifty per cent of avoidable loss, malicious damage fifteen per cent, hazards such as fire and flood twenty per cent and fraud and theft only fifteen per cent.

The perpetrator's style

It is as well to know who is most likely to perpetrate computer crime and what are that person's preferred methods. In general we can say that computer crime is intelligent, white collar crime: it is surprising that so far there is little evidence that it is also so-called organized crime.

It has been pointed out that there are typical personality types amongst computer defrauders—the loner, the good guy, the 'perfectionist',* and the confused. Studies have also been done on motivations, which have been shown to include greed, gratification, revenge, self-protection or helpfulness. With respect to the last mentioned, forty per cent of the proceeds of employee frauds are said to be spent on favours for others.

Perhaps the most useful way to classify the problem is in terms of the relationship of the defrauder to the system. A study by the author of cases of computer fraud [3] allows some conclusions to be drawn.

The principal category of defrauder was found to be the computer specialist who favoured the technical means with which he was familiar and with respect to which he had the opportunity, such as the manipulation of computer programs.

In-house systems users were the next most frequent category: in general they neither had an opportunity, nor had the knowledge, to effect technical frauds—which tend to be computer-dependent—so their preferred methods were non-technical, such as manipulating the input to the computer application. This indicates that organizations tend to trust their employees and so leave them with abundant opportunity to perpetrate non-technical frauds.

The third category was the outsider, and here the interesting point is that most outsider frauds required a high degree of technical knowledge as well as know-how of the systems of the enterprise which was to be defrauded. Many outsider frauds were done by people who had acquired the necessary know-how as insiders at an earlier date—consultants or temporary staff in particular.

It must be admitted that an analysis by this writer of the cases given in the BIS survey shows that most (twenty-seven of the forty-five) cases were perpetrated by in-house systems users with only eleven being perpetrated by computer professionals. This reverses the ordering obtained in the author's own survey [3]. The disparity between these two surveys is probably due to different sample selection criteria: the more cases which are computer-related though not computer-dependent, the more likely it is that in-house systems users rather than computer staff will be the predominant perpetrators.

* A person who is intrigued by the *challenge* of computer fraud.

Computer fraud by computer staff tends to be computer-dependent as it often involves manipulation of the programs or unauthorized use of computer resources. In all the surveys the outsider was found to be the third category of defrauder, being responsible for only eight cases reported in the BIS survey. One of the outsiders in the BIS survey had been an insider, and this is a common feature to which we have already referred.

It would appear that corporations protect their systems against non-technical outsider abuse, even though they do not provide similar protection against insider abuse. The inferences seem to be: first, that no one trusts the outsider to be honest yet, secondly, that there is no general recognition that the technical competence of some outsiders is of an extremely high order. Just as our systems are wide open to non-technical insider abuse, so they seem wide open to technical outsider abuse.

In the writer's survey [3] the control point which was initially violated in order to give the defrauder an entrée to his fraud was usually computer input in some form (particularly for in-house user abuse); the installation itself was the next most important weak point (particularly with respect to occupation by outsiders). Manipulation of the software was a close runner-up. Output also featured as the entrée, though less commonly. This ordering is confirmed by a study of the BIS and Audit Commission surveys [1,2] with the exception that the BIS survey includes fewer cases of installation abuse than of software abuse. Once again this is probably due to different sample selection criteria, in this case the omission of physical abuses such as occupying the computer centre, as such abuses are generally not strictly 'fraudulent'.

All these surveys found that between two-thirds and three-quarters of all computer frauds involved fraudulent input. While this usually amounts to the corruption of input data after it has been made out, or the insertion of fictitious input data into the job stream, the fraud may be instigated at an earlier stage. For instance there is one case on record of new, unused bank deposit slips having been personalized with the account number of the defrauder and then left on the tables at a branch of a bank, in order that other customers would use them unwittingly to deposit money into the defrauder's account.

Personal account manipulations have been shown to be involved in eighty-five per cent of all computer frauds. In particular, sales ledger frauds are very common. The examples in the BIS survey show that while in some twenty per cent of cases goods or services were the immediate object of the fraud, in most cases it was cash that was embezzled.

Collusion is also a common feature. It appeared to be a necessary component of sixteen of the forty-five BIS cases, and an inessential feature of others. This is unfortunate as most of our systems controls are only effective if collusion does not occur.

Two special types of computer fraud deserve particular mention: first, the valid balance embezzlement where, although funds have been misappropriated, the accounts still show the picture as it was before the fraud, at least at account-end times; secondly, indirect frauds such as inducing an error on a government return so that the value of an equity stock drops, so allowing the defrauder to buy at a cheap price before the error is spotted and corrected on the next issue of the return.

Risk, damage and cost

White collar crime is increasing, and so is the use of computers. One director of internal auditing of a building society has said that his organization has about three hundred cases of computer fraud every year. In these cases, since all systems are computerized, most, if not all, frauds are at least computer-related. Computer fraud is also bound to become much more prevalent with the growing use of microcomputers.

It would be a mistake to consider, since most corporate fraud is now likely to be computer fraud, that we can cease to be concerned *specifically* about computer fraud. Computers provide their own special opportunities for fraud and will do so even more in the future. Concealment is easier. The period of exposure during perpetration is minimal. There may be a total absence of human monitoring and supervision. Centralization of records enhances the opportunity to perpetrate and conceal the fraud. Automation makes the infinitely small fraud worthwhile when repeated on countless occasions. The fraud can be 'set up' to function indefinitely, with the defrauder having left the scene of the crime.

It is unlikely that it is the largest computer frauds which attract media attention. The data for eighteen of the forty-five BIS cases was obtained from private sources, although this writer is aware that some of these received media attention. There appears to be no tendency for the largest cases in the BIS survey to be those which had been reported in the media. Losses in the cases surveyed by BIS ranged from £100 to £2 000 000, the latter case being the value of cannabis smuggled through customs by manipulating a computer. In 1979, the eleven cases surveyed ranged from £118 to £53 000 with an average loss of £22 000. The average loss in the Audit Commission survey was £14 700.

These losses may not appear very large, but we must remember that they represent only the losses which are known about in the frauds which have been detected. In any case, the twelve largest frauds identified in the Audit Commission report [2] total just under £1 000 000. But what about unknown losses in both detected and undetected fraud? The writer's survey [3] found that most computer frauds were discovered by accident, which seems to imply that most are not known about. The analysis also showed that most computer frauds are continuous, having been 'set up' at an earlier date and thereafter carrying on working on behalf of the defrauder. It is possible that, due to the continuous nature of most computer frauds and the fact that most are discovered by accident, the largest ones are perhaps not even known about. However, we should point out that the Audit Commission [2] noted that within their sample the longest frauds were surprisingly not of highest value.

In this writer's own analysis of the forty-five cases written up in the BIS survey [1], only three were 'smash and grab' taking place once at an instant of time; all the others were continuous, typically over a one- to three-year period. Rather similarly, the Audit Commission survey shows that most were continuous with fifty-seven of the sample of seventy-seven lasting for one to two years.

The information given in the BIS survey makes it quite clear that at least twelve per cent of their cases were discovered by 'pure chance'. In most of their other cases suspicions were aroused, but it is not often possible to discern from the data whether suspicions were aroused due to carelessness of the defrauder, to a chance happening, or to the proper functioning of systems controls. Of course one would expect the 'smash and grab' cases to be detected by systems controls, as it is of their nature that detection is expected shortly after they are perpetrated. Certainly, in the cases surveyed by District Audit, twenty-three of the seventy-seven were detected by 'other means' rather than by audit or control. 'Other means' means 'accident'.

If most are continuous and if most are not known about, it indicates that most are getting bigger and bigger, which suggests that the largest computer frauds have not yet been discovered. Other specialists on computer crime concur with this view*. Most authorities consider that only a small fraction of known computer fraud is reported to the authorities.

Whether most or just many computer frauds are discovered by accident, it is indisputable that most are continuous rather than 'smash and grab'. These considerations suggest that the iceberg effect applies to computer fraud: it is unlikely not to be a problem to your organization, it is more likely that you have not yet noted the problem. Neither can we console ourselves that this is a peculiarly American problem. The BIS survey reports forty-six UK cases, though one is reported twice and another appears to qualify only because it was discovered by computer auditors. The survey is dated 1981 and we can expect it to be biased towards the inclusion of the more recent cases. Even so it is impressive that all but five occurred in the 1970s or 80s, with six in 1978, eleven in 1979, a further two in the 'late 70s' and two in 1980—all within the UK. The dates of three were unspecified.

Prevention and detection

While there is no panacea against computer crime, there is much that can

* This is not, however, borne out by a comparison of the Audit Commission survey [2] and their previous survey in 1981, which tends to suggest a more static situation.

be done to contain the problem. In particular it is recommended that specific responsibility should be designated to a senior manager to detect computer crime: it may be surprising how much comes to light! Detection is perhaps the best form of prevention as it acts as a deterrent to others and also highlights necessary improvements in the system of control.

It is also wise to have a widely known corporate policy of full disclosure and instant dismissal as this has been found to be a deterrent to many. The alternative policy of sweeping it under the carpet in order to save face and to save executive time is a recipe for future problems. With opportunities for criminal restitution it can no longer be said that disclosure prevents restitution. Restitution through the courts is generally much to be preferred to restitution in the form of a deal with the defrauder. The BIS survey reported several cases where partial and complete restitution was made, and it is clear from the survey that the usual practice is instant dismissal of the culprit from his employment, though there was the occasional case reported where the individual was given the opportunity to resign, as well as the occasional case where the culprit obtained similar employment elsewhere—apparently even with the help of glowing references from the victim employer!

In some cases there may be an understandable reluctance to attract public attention to the fraud, either because there is no wish to attract other would-be defrauders or because of a fear of losing customers and public confidence. There have even been occasions when the courts have criticized the company, not for bringing the action but for having lamentably poor controls which put temptation in the way of staff. Light sentences meted out by the courts have been the order of the day, and this is another disincentive to take the matter through the courts. However, sentences will tend to be light as most computer defrauders appear to be first offenders.

Of the forty-five different cases outlined in the BIS survey [1], it appears that prosecutions took place in at least twenty-six: incomplete information does not allow us to conclude how many of the remainder led to prosecutions. At least nineteen of these twenty-six cases led to jail sentences, though these were sometimes only suspended sentences; four defendants were fined only—from £15 to £1000—and one offender was put on probation.

As several of the BIS survey computer frauds involved collusion, in some of the hearings there were multiple defendants. Of all the defendants, seven received suspended sentences. Of the custodial sentences, the longest was for four years (two cases) and the shortest for six months (one case) with most between one to three years.

Loose control and poor records create a potential fraud situation—a situation in which the fraud is likely to be written off as just one of many unexplained losses. Prerequisites to effective control are a strong, involved top management team which takes the problem seriously, and alert, capable, independent auditors. It has often been suggested that auditors are ineffectual with respect to discovering fraud, but this does not appear to be the case;

in one of the surveys we are using [1], auditors, both internal and external, led to the discovery of seven of the forty-five cases; in another of the surveys [2], nine of the seventy-seven cases were discovered by audit.

However, the Audit Commission survey [2] also emphasizes the often overlooked point that 'auditors are often criticized for failing to discover computer frauds but this fails to recognize that one of the primary duties of auditors is to encourage management to install and maintain effective internal control mechanisms. The main responsibility to prevent and detect fraud lies with management and there is no measure available of the numbers of frauds prevented thanks to the imposition of effective controls'.

Auditors should certainly not be complacent, but neither should they be disheartened if they are not constantly detecting fraud: *their work may well be preventing it*. As noted by the Audit Commission, 'the Code of Local Government Practice for England and Wales refers specifically to the responsibilities of the auditor in relation to fraud'. The code affirms that 'the integrity of public funds is at all times a matter of general concern and the auditor should be aware that his function is seen to be an important safeguard'.

Following a systems analysis approach to computer abuse, it is wise to shield the 'entry points' to the abuse, that is, prevent the defrauder from getting started. One of the principal entry points is the manipulation of input data, another is doctoring the programs, another is unauthorized access to the computer area. Different categories of defrauder have their preferred entry points, so control can be directed accordingly.

Because of the widespread use of personal accounts to perpetrate fraud, it is wise to monitor closely the personal accounts of employees in key positions of trust, particularly those of (a) computer specialists, and (b) in-house system users who have personal accounts which relate to the system(s) they administer. One very basic requirement is to segregate the setting up of an account from the processing of transactions against that account. Safe custody of passwords and of authentication codes has also been indicated as important.

It is also wise to guard the exit points. For instance, if the end-product of a fraud is likely to be an invalid cheque, perhaps there should be a pre-audit of payments before they are made.

Between the entry and exit points there should be a comprehensive system of manual and programmed controls designed to make it exceedingly difficult for the fraud or other abuse to be perpetrated.

In order to achieve such a system it is necessary to set up and apply a formal project of fraud control. This involves identifying the corporate assets at risk, analysing the threats, establishing appropriate personnel policies, introducing effective internal control and monitoring, developing and using detection techniques and having a plan for handling discovered fraud.

Note also that while the conversion of a system from a manual basis to a computer system has sometimes revealed an existing fraud, systems conversion sometimes ends any chance of detecting an established fraud.

We have already touched on the need for appropriate personnel policies. The objective should be to recruit personnel to key positions who are trustworthy but not trusted. The backgrounds of applicants should be thoroughly checked. Systems should be designed to confirm the employees' honesty.

There are many tell-tale signs which may be indicative of a defrauder at work. Altered attitudes, extravagant life style, questionable friendships, self-contained behaviour, excessive private phone calls, irregular private life, poor job performance, appearance of being under pressure on the job and unclear explanations for exceptions are some of the signals that all may not be well. The risk is that they will be overlooked by trusting colleagues.

Controlling the environment

For the most part, therefore, hackers and other computer fraudsters succeed because other people let them. Computer users just do not impose the simple disciplines which would either prevent abuse altogether or at least confine it to the most determined.

Of course, if you are using a public network to transmit messages, that information is vulnerable to unauthorized interception. The only way to protect it is by scrambling it, and even then (as military cryptologists as well as philosophers are aware) there is no such thing in the end as a totally private language. It is also possible to detect and interpret radiation from a video terminal (as those who have not paid their TV licences may discover). But this does not prevent you from using a password system which is actually effective, as opposed to being futile. Choose a password which no one else is likely to guess, so it must be sufficiently lengthy (more than just three or four characters) and sufficiently meaningless (not the name of your spouse or dog, or your birthday). If you bother to use a password at all, make it a real control, not just a formal ceremony.

Also, in relation to output, don't forget that the easiest way of getting one's hands on information is to pick up a piece of paper and read it. If you leave printouts lying around, or throw them away without shredding them, someone other than you and your staff will probably read them. You may not care if they do. But if you don't care about printouts then you probably don't need to care about hackers or passwords either.

Conversely, if you object to your printouts being seen by unauthorized eyes, you need to pay as much attention to their security as to that of your computer files and accounting input. But if you *are* concerned about these things, remember that a person does not have to be very clever to be a hacker. You do not normally have to do very much to foil one. All you have to do is exercise good controls, and there are probably four particular areas over which control should be exercised. These are in respect of:

1 Transactions input.

2 Processing and output.
3 Continuing correctness of reference files.
4 The computer(s), terminals (if any) and files in use.

Transactions input

In many cases controls will be carried out interactively as input takes place, but nevertheless may involve batching (for example, of cash input). Common validation checks are:

1 Password authentication.
2 Matching input from different sources (e.g. records of deliveries and original orders) before data is used for up-dating files.
3 Checking sequential reference numbers of input data.
4 Verification of the presence on master files of data relevant to particular updates (e.g. whether there is a record of a customer from whom an order has been received).
5 Format, completeness and reasonableness validation.

Try to ensure that your computer system provides as many of these 'self-checking' controls as you believe you need. Concentrate also on the design of the clerical procedures that are to be carried out in conjunction with the computer system. These are often not considered until a very late stage in its implementation. Sometimes consideration is deferred until after live running of the system has begun. This very often leads to a situation where they are never properly defined at all, or where the actual procedures applied are ineffective. This causes many problems as the processing of data proceeds. The worst case of all is if the system is actually uncontrolled but is *believed* to be controlled. Such a situation often arises because, for example, everyone knows that input control reports, daybook listings and audit trails are produced by the system, but no one ever actually looks at them to ensure that there are no inconsistencies or error conditions, until it is too late. It sounds so silly, but it happens over and over again.

In such an environment, it is possible for assets to be lost or misappropriated, for very misleading management information to be produced, and for extensive recriminations to take place between the user and the computer supplier, software house or programming department.

Reference files

You will need to specify controls to ensure that reference files (of names and addresses, for example) get updated accurately. If everyone, even within a small organization, has a free hand to update, amend and delete such data without reference to anyone else, it will swiftly become inaccurate. For example, it may be possible to get access to stock records from terminals located in several different parts of geographically separated stores or warehouses. No one may be imposing overall control over the regular input of stock movements. It may also be impossible to insist on the effective implementation of a set of control standards at every terminal.

It is therefore necessary to provide for the clerical and programmed validation controls required to ensure that records are not introduced, deleted or altered in an unauthorized or incorrect manner. Much the same considerations apply as in respect of transactions input, only even more so. An error in the input of a transaction affects only that transaction. An error in updating a reference item will affect every transaction which uses that reference. A couple of simple examples. If the price of a stock line is wrongly recorded, all invoices for sales of that stock line will be wrong and you may lose (or even unintentionally gain) a lot of money. If a delivery address is wrongly recorded, goods may be delivered to the wrong place and you may not get paid for them (this could be the basis of a very simple fraud indeed).

Processing and output

There should also normally be controls over processing. For example, verification by program that useful control information (e.g. total customers'

Table 16. Computer auditing techniques

Potential for the detection of fraud, including the ability to detect programmed manipulation or falsification of data. (Scale: 1 (poor) to 5 (good))	
1 Generalized software	2
2 Generalized computer audit enquiry packages	5
3 'One-off' tailored audit enquiry packages	5
4 Integrated audit monitors	3
5 Parallel simulation and normative auditing	5
6 The test data method	2
7 Integrated test facility	2
8 Program auditing	2
9 Code comparison programs	4
10 Logic path analysis programs	1
11 Tracing and mapping	1

Table 16 incorporates the perceptions of the authors.

balances) is derived from the records whenever they are all accessed together for whatever purpose (e.g. analysing the debts by age or producing monthly statements to customers). It should be possible for this to be related to the clerical system of accounting controls. There should also normally be output controls to ensure the proper distribution and adequate examination and scrutiny of all significant tabulations produced as output from the system. Very often, control can be exercised in relation to detailed tabulations of information which have been processed at an earlier time, by means of managerial or clerical scrutiny. However, in many cases, and ideally in fact, it may be possible to exercise control by reference to exception reports. There is no reason why, if such control procedures are implemented with the appropriate degree of forethought, they should not be both effective and useful. However, if clerical control procedures are ill-defined, or are not properly interrelated with programmed controls, they will inevitably be ineffective.

There are a great many more things which can be said about these aspects of control but these are among the most important.

Discussion topics

1 Do you consider computer fraud and other abuse to be a real problem, or is it exaggerated in your view?

2 Discuss the ways in which computer abuses may impact upon computerized systems. What would you regard as potentially the most damaging impacts?

3 Who defrauds the organizations via the computer and what are their favoured methods?

4 Provide a classification of computer abuse which assists in getting to grips with the problem.

5 Explain the distinction between computer-assisted abuse and computer-dependent abuse. Give examples.

6 What is the internal auditor's responsibility in the area of fraud?

7 What preventive measures may be taken to safeguard computer systems against fraud?

References

1 Wong, K. (1981) *Computer-Related Fraud Casebook*, BIS Applied Systems Limited.

2 Audit Commission UK. (1985) *Computer Fraud Survey*, H.M.S.O., London.

3 Chambers, A. D. (1981) *Computer Auditing*, Pitman, London, and Commerce Clearing House, USA, Canada, Australia and New Zealand, pp. 165–187. See also Computer control and fraud, *The Computer Journal*, Vol. 21; No. 3, August 1978.

Part 6 Computer Flowcharting for Auditors

22 Computer Flowcharting for Auditors

Summary

Auditors should be familiar with computer flowcharting. They should concern themselves with three types of flowchart. Here we consider the system summary flowchart which the auditor may design for himself in order to obtain a 'birds-eye view' of a system. We also examine the system flowchart of the systems analyst as well as the programmer's flowchart—both of which the auditor must be able to interpret. Examples and exercises are provided.

Introduction

There are three methods of flowcharting computer systems which should be familiar to the computer auditor. They all use the rectangle as the basic symbol to denote an operation and the principal logic flow is from 'north' to 'south', that is from the top to the bottom of the page. They are:

1 System summary flowcharting
2 System flowcharting
3 Program flowcharting

Most computer auditors will find it sufficient to be able merely to interpret system flowcharts and program flowcharts, as these will usually have been designed by EDP staff. They should, however, be able to design system summary flowcharts for themselves.

System summary flowcharting

Rather than show each program of a system as a separate process, it is often convenient to lump *all* programs into a single process symbol and simply to show all input and output of the system as input and output of a single process symbol. This technique is useful to auditors in documenting the essential features of the system in overall terms. This method of charting was devised by auditors to assist them in getting to grips with many of the essential features of a system while avoiding the technicalities. During the fact-finding stage of the audit the auditor may draw up a system summary flowchart of the system and, by examining it carefully, work out whether he has found out the whole story of the system in so far as it concerns him.

Four examples of system summary flowcharts are shown as Figs. 9, 10, 11 and 12. The systems charted in Figs. 9 and 10 feature later in our discussion

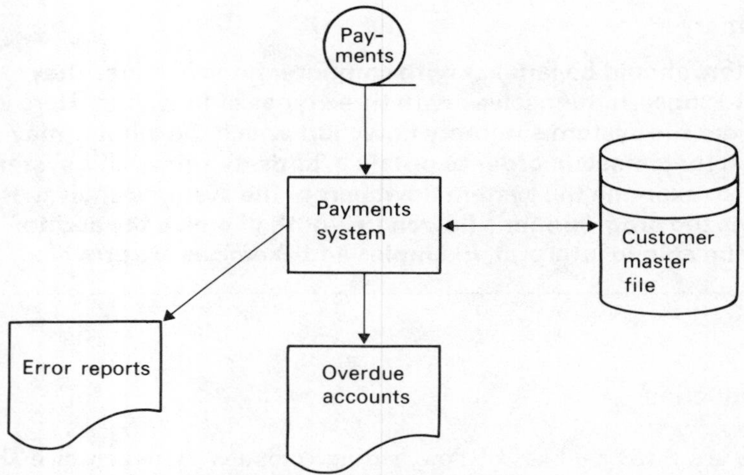

Fig. 9. System summary flowchart: payments processing.

of system flowcharting as Exercises 1 and 2: Figure 9 is a system summary flowchart of a very simple application which reads payment records, reports any error in these records and then updates the customer accounts with these payments. Figure 12 shows system summary flowcharting in use to describe the hardware of a computer centre rather than an application processed using that hardware.

System flowcharting

System flowcharting uses some of the symbols of program flowcharting (see Appendix 2). It is simply a means of charting the computer programs processed by the system, having regard to the sequence in which the programs are processed and showing the input files and output files of each program.

By way of example, Fig. 9 provides a suggested system summary flowchart to the following exercise:

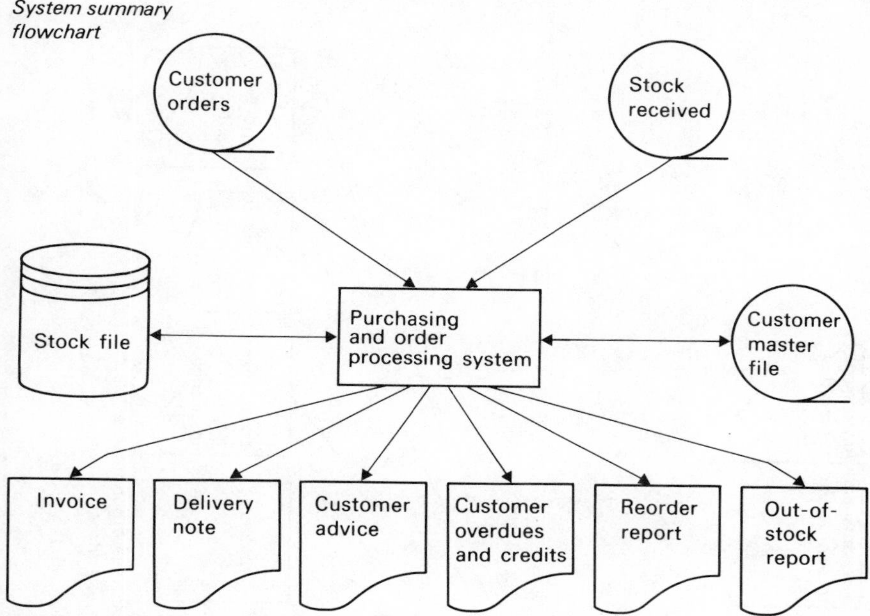

Fig. 10. Purchasing and order processing system.

First exercise on system flowcharting: payments processing

Flowchart a simple computer system of programs for which the system summary flowchart is shown as Fig. 9. The system has the following programs:

Program 1: Read payments records and report errors. Correct and re-submit reported errors. Transfer correct records to another magnetic tape file.

Program 2: Sort the magnetic tape into customer account number sequence.

Program 3: Update the customer master file (held on disk) from the magnetic tape of payments, and report any outstanding accounts.

This first exercise may be worked through with the suggested answer (Fig. 13) in order to give a general understanding of the method. Then the second, more complex exercise may be attempted without reference to the suggested answer which is given in Appendix 3.

Second exercise on system flowcharting: purchasing and order processing system

The problem

A manufacturing company intends to put its sales accounting system on its

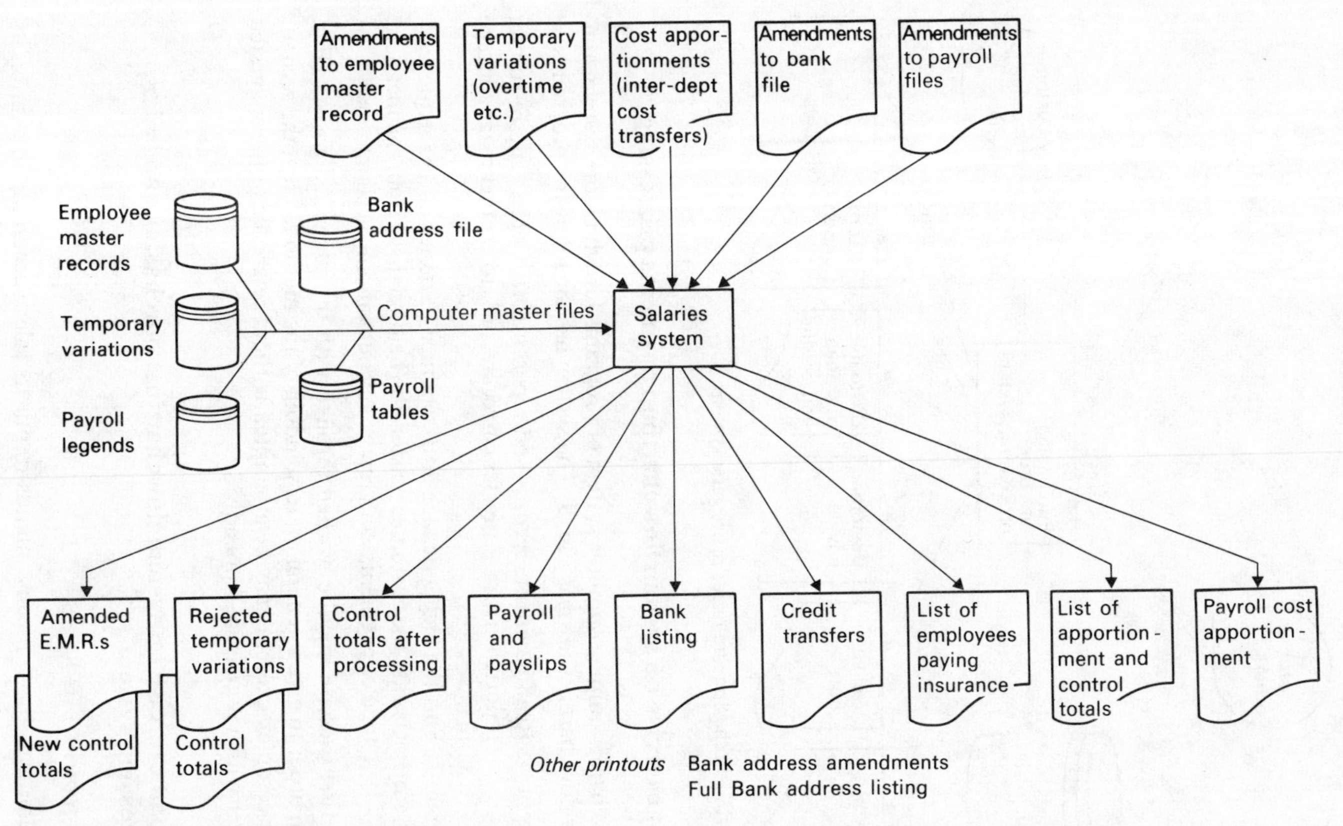
Amendments to employee master record
Temporary variations (overtime etc.)
Cost apportionments (inter-dept cost transfers)
Amendments to bank file
Amendments to payroll files
Employee master records
Temporary variations
Payroll legends
Bank address file
Payroll tables
Computer master files
Salaries system
Amended E.M.R.s
New control totals
Rejected temporary variations
Control totals
Control totals after processing
Payroll and payslips
Bank listing
Credit transfers
List of employees paying insurance
List of apportionment and control totals
Payroll cost apportionment
Other printouts
Bank address amendments
Full Bank address listing

Fig. 11. System summary flowchart: salaries.

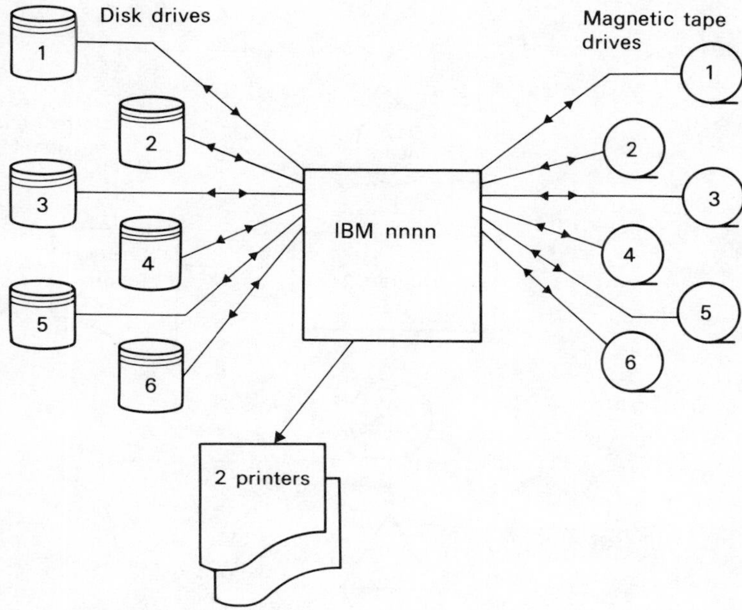

Fig. 12. System summary flowchart: hardware configuration.

computer and the system analyst in charge of the project has suggested that only two 'permanent' (or 'master') files need be maintained: one for stock items and the other for customer accounts. There will also be work files for customers' transaction data (i.e. orders), and for management reports. The daily processing will be:

1 Update the stock file for receipts of goods into stock from the factory.
2 Produce invoice sets for customer orders with notification if items are out of stock.
3 Update the stock file to reflect the assignment of stock to customer orders (as in 2 above).
4 Update the customers' accounts file (known as the 'customer master file').
5 Report any customers whose credit limits have been exceeded or who are overdue with their payments.
6 Print out items in need of re-order and out-of-stock as a result of the day's run, in item number order. Report out-of-stock items in customer number order (i.e. in sequence of customers who have ordered these items).

To keep the exercise relatively simple, out-of-stock items are lost once they have been reported (see 6 above). Part deliveries will be made where possible.

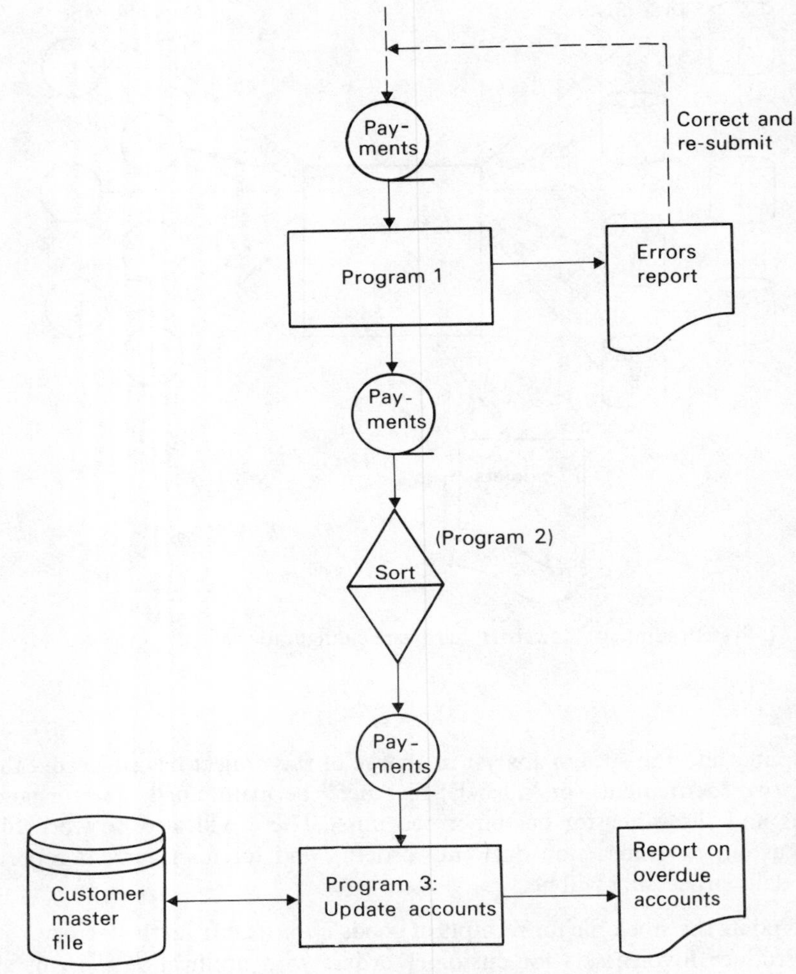

Fig. 13. First exercise on system flowcharting: suggested answer.

The company has a small computer with four cassette tape drives, one disk drive, and one line printer. The company also possesses off-line peripherals such as magnetic tape encoders. For the purposes of this exercise, assume the company 'pre-invoices', that is produces delivery notes, customers' advices and invoices at the same time when processing the order. Assume random processing of the stock file in 1 and 3 above. The stock file will be restored off magnetic tape at the beginning of the day and dumped at the end. Assume maintenance of the customer accounts file is carried out separately and is not part of this exercise, and that adjustments due to discrepancies between computer stock figures and actual stock are done manually and posted to the customer account file during the maintenance run. This means, for instance, that the addition, deletion and amendment of customer details should not be incorporated into the system you are being asked to design. The only exception to this is that you are asked to show the updating of customers' accounts to reflect accepted orders.

To do

Draw the system flowchart (that is, the schematic of the computer runs). *Suggested Answer:* see Appendix 3.

Program flowcharting

Sometimes an auditor will need to 'read' the flowcharts which exist as part of the computer program documentation and were designed either by the computer system analyst or the computer programmer. These program flowcharts describe the detailed logic of the program, and are sometimes known as logic diagrams.

The symbols used are shown in Appendix 2 and examples are given in the two following exercises. Suitable templates are sold by computer firms (ICL, IBM, etc.).

Readers will note that whereas the *system summary flowchart* uses one process symbol (rectangle) to denote the entire system, the *system flowchart* uses one process symbol for *each program* of the system and the *program flowchart* uses one process symbol for *each process* within one program.

An apparently rather complex example of program flowcharting is given as Fig. 14. In fact this merely shows the programming logic for handling input from two sequential files, and omits any of the logic associated with processing once a 'match' between the two files has been achieved. Readers are recommended to endeavour to obtain an understanding of Fig. 14 before attempting the exercise on program flowcharting.

Handling input from two sequential files (Fig. 14)

Notes:

1 It may be considered that File A is a Master File (such as a Product MF). File B is a Transaction File with one record for each product ordered. Both files have previously been sorted into the same sequence (i.e. Product Code Sequence).
2 Despite prior sorting into the required sequence, the program must check that records are in the correct sequence (flowchart boxes 6 and 12) as

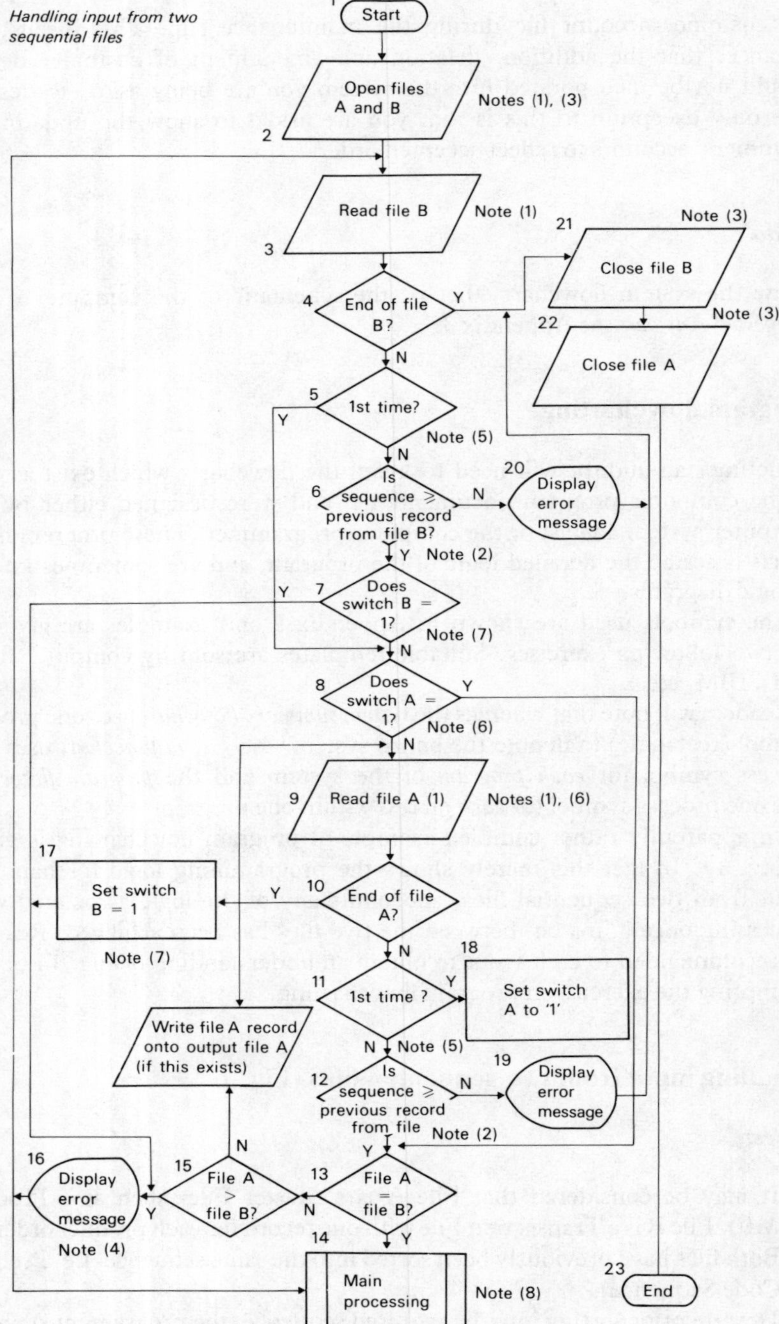

Fig. 14. Handling input from two sequential files.

there is no hundred per cent certainty that correct sequence has been achieved: unpredictable, nonsense results would occur if out-of-sequence files were processed. Error messages will be displayed (boxes 19 and 20) and the job abandoned if an out-of-sequence condition is detected.

3 Open and close files (boxes 2, 21 and 22) are necessary before and after reading records from the files. 'Open' results in the computer attempting to locate the file on the expected volume and notifying the operator if it cannot be found. The 'read' instruction fetches the next record on the file.

4 It is assumed that not all Master File records will have a match on the Transaction File. All Transaction records should have a match on the Master File (if not there is an error—boxes 15 and 16). There may be more than one matching Transaction record per Master Record but it is assumed there will only be one Master Record of each sequence number.

5 First time switches (boxes 5 and 11) by-pass logic inapplicable to the first pass.

6 Switch A (boxes 8 and 9). Initially zero. On each pass of the logic a test is made of this switch after reading the Transaction File but before reading the Master File. First time through, on finding 'zero' in Switch A the program will go straight to read the Master File (for the first time). On subsequent passes Switch A will equal '1' and the program will by-pass reading the Master File and branch to test whether a new record from the Master File is required.

7 Switch B (boxes 7 and 17). Initially zero. Is set to '1' when all records on the Master File have been read. Any further sequence numbers on the Transaction File will be in error and will be reported (box 16).

8 Main processing (box 14) includes all the operations performed on the data from the two files as well as the instructions necessary to control output (whether to files or to the printer).

Exercise on program flowcharting

Edit and print: the problem

1 Draw the programmer's flowchart of a COBOL program to read a file on disk and print the contents of each record on continuous stationery in a formatted fashion. The system flowchart is shown in Fig. 15.

(a) You should program the following validity checks:

(i) that each record read is of a higher sequence (as shown in the sequence field) than the previous record;

(ii) that the amount field of each record is numeric.

(b) Invalid fields, see (a) above, should be asterisked immediately beneath where they appear on the printout.

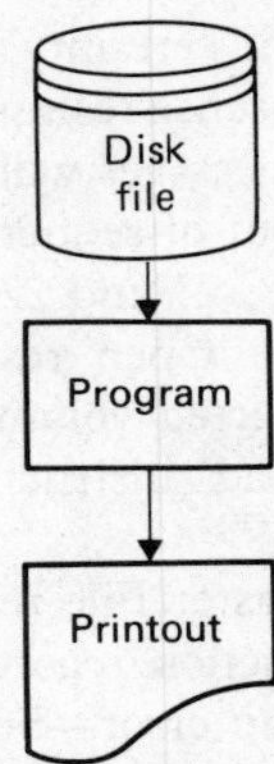

Fig. 15. System flowchart for a COBOL program.

(c) Valid amounts are to be accumulated and the total printed out at the end of the report.
(d) If a record fails the sequence test, the amount on that record should still be accumulated unless it is invalid, and the sequence number should be stored for comparison against the next record to be read.
(e) For your guidance the record layout is shown in Fig. 16.

Sequence no.	Amount
Characters 1 to 3	Characters 4 to 7
(numeric)	(numeric)

Fig. 16. Record layout.

SUGGESTED ANSWER: see Appendix 4.

Appendix 1 **Suggested Solution to the Enquiry Program Case Study** (Chapter 13)

Field name (Mnemonic)	Audit samples	Reperformance of calculations	Items not conforming to system rules	Items conforming but of audit interest	Totals and analyses	Comments
SI	A (1 in n) E (1 in n) S (1 in n)		Not A, E, S.		Cost (or valuation) and accumulated depreciation (CD + DC)	Analysis for Companies Acts Notes to Accounts. Samples for tests to additions (perhaps related to cost). Samples for physical verification. Samples of scrappings (perhaps related to cost, or odd disposal value).
AN		Check digit calculation	Not numeric, duplicate			
AD			Blank			
AL			Blank		Analysis of depreciation charge by cost centre	If detailed table of cost centres available then a more sophisticated test could be performed.
AC			Not FH, LL, SL, PM, FF, MV		Cost (or valuation) and accumulated depreciation (CD + DC)	Analysis for Companies Acts Notes to Accounts.
DR			Not in accordance with AC per table.			
DB			Not in accordance with AC per table.			

Field name (Mnemonic)	Audit samples	Reperformance of calculations	Items not conforming to system rules	Items conforming but of audit interest	Totals and analyses	Comments
DU			Invalid or future date. Not current year if SI = 'A'.			
OC			Negative, zero.	Large items		
RC			Negative, zero if RD ≠ blank.	Large items		
RD	Current year		Blank if RC ≠ 0	Revaluations varying by x% from OC	Total of this year's revalued items	
DD			Invalid or future date. Blank if SI = 'S'	Date in use and date of disposal in the same year.		
DP				Selection of large profits/losses on disposal (with cost or revaluations as appropriate).	Aggregate profit/loss on disposal	For checking to Profit and Loss Account
CD			Not 0 if SI = 'A'. Negative or zero.	CD + DC greater than cost or revaluation	Total	For checking to previous years accounts.
DC		Recalculate DC with reference to appropriate dates and fields (on cost or valuation).	Not numeric ≠ 0 unless disposed in period 01		Total for the year	For checking to Profit and Loss Account.

N.B. The above tests are not exhaustive but indicate the types of tests that can be performed.

Appendix 2 **Program Flowcharting Symbols**

Program flowcharting symbols — examples

Basic symbols (These symbols conform to the British Standard (BS), International and American National Standards)

1 PROCESS
(See also 4 to 11)

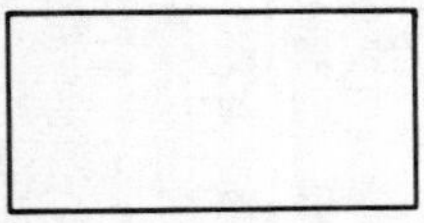

2 DECISION

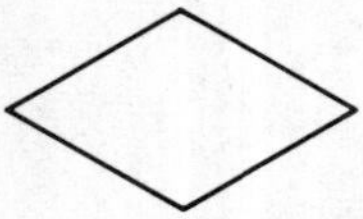

3 INPUT/OUTPUT
(See also 12 to 23)

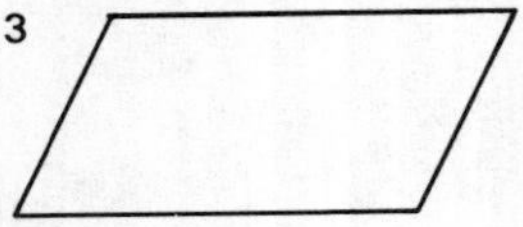

Special process symbols

4 PREPARATION
i.e. modification:
e.g. set a switch, initialize a routine etc.

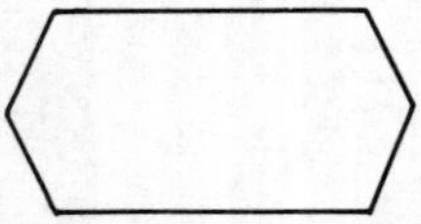

5 PREDEFINED PROCESS

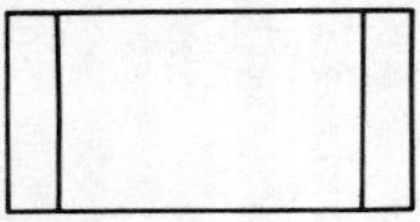

6 MANUAL OPERATION
(any off-line process)

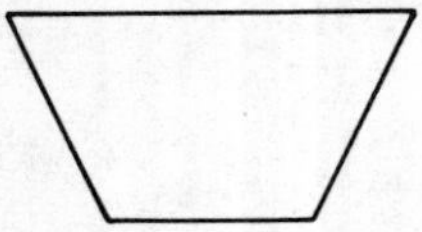

7 AUXILIARY OPERATION
(not an on-line operation, nor a manual operation but 'an off-line operation performed on equipment not under direct control of the central processing unit')

8 MERGE

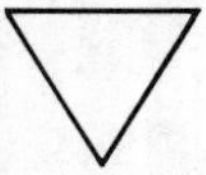

9 EXTRACT

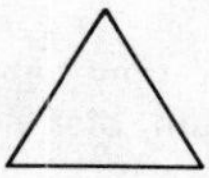

10 COLLATE
(MERGING with EXTRACTING: forming of two or more sets of items from two or more other sets)

11 SORT

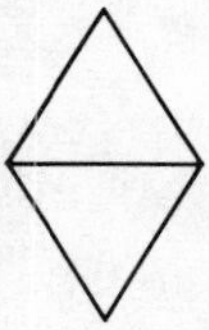

Special data symbols

12 DOCUMENT

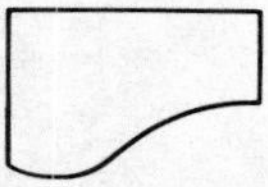

13 MAGNETIC TAPE

14 MAGNETIC DISK

15 CENTRAL PROCESSOR

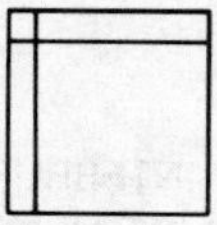

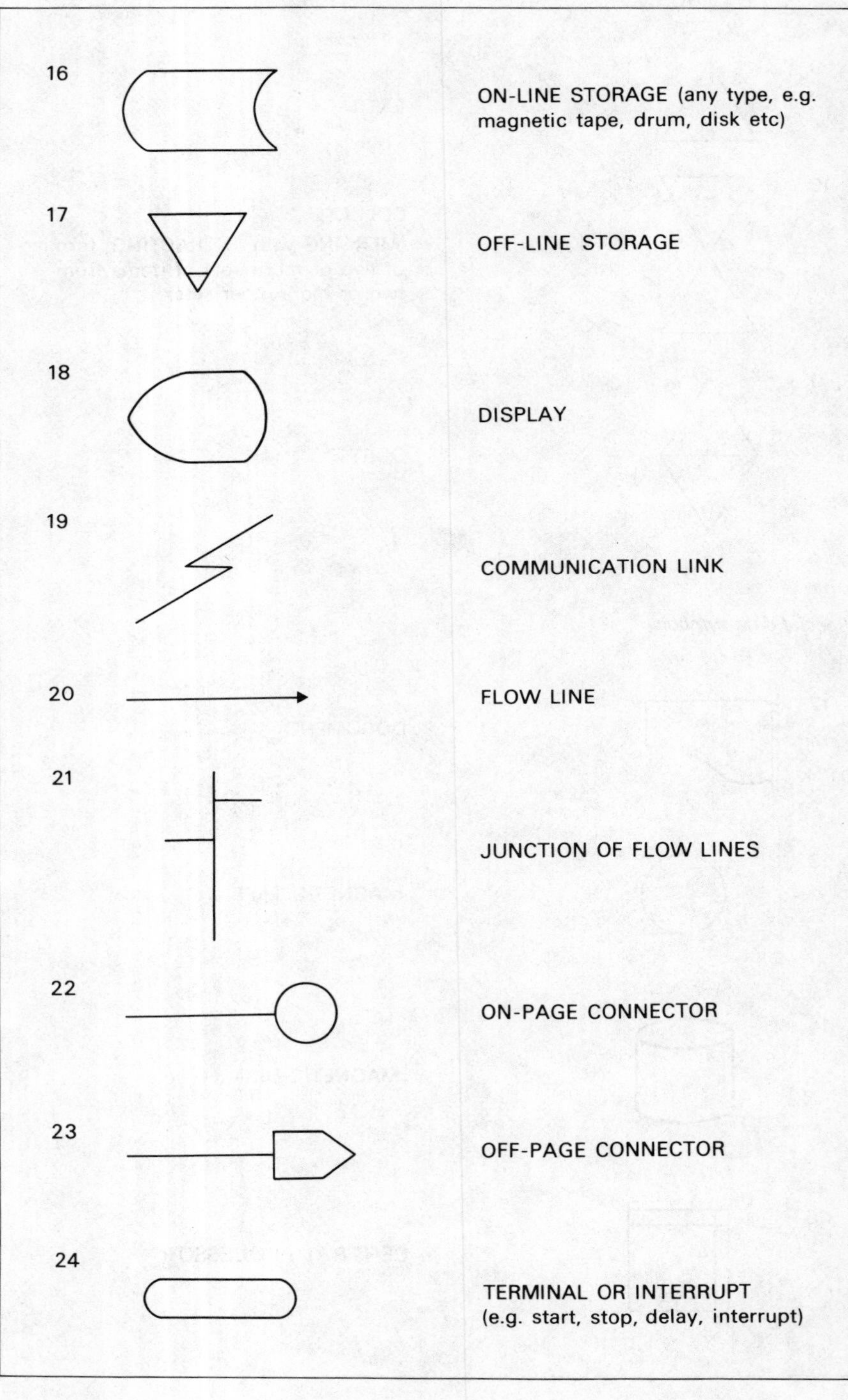
16
ON-LINE STORAGE (any type, e.g. magnetic tape, drum, disk etc)
17
OFF-LINE STORAGE
18
DISPLAY
19
COMMUNICATION LINK
20
FLOW LINE
21
JUNCTION OF FLOW LINES
22
ON-PAGE CONNECTOR
23
OFF-PAGE CONNECTOR
24
TERMINAL OR INTERRUPT
(e.g. start, stop, delay, interrupt)

Appendix 3 **Suggested Solution to the Second Exercise on Systems Flowcharting in Chapter 22**

Purchasing and order processing system—System flowchart

Purchasing and order processing system — System flowchart

(This is a suggested answer to the second exercise in section two on System Flowcharting in Chapter 22)

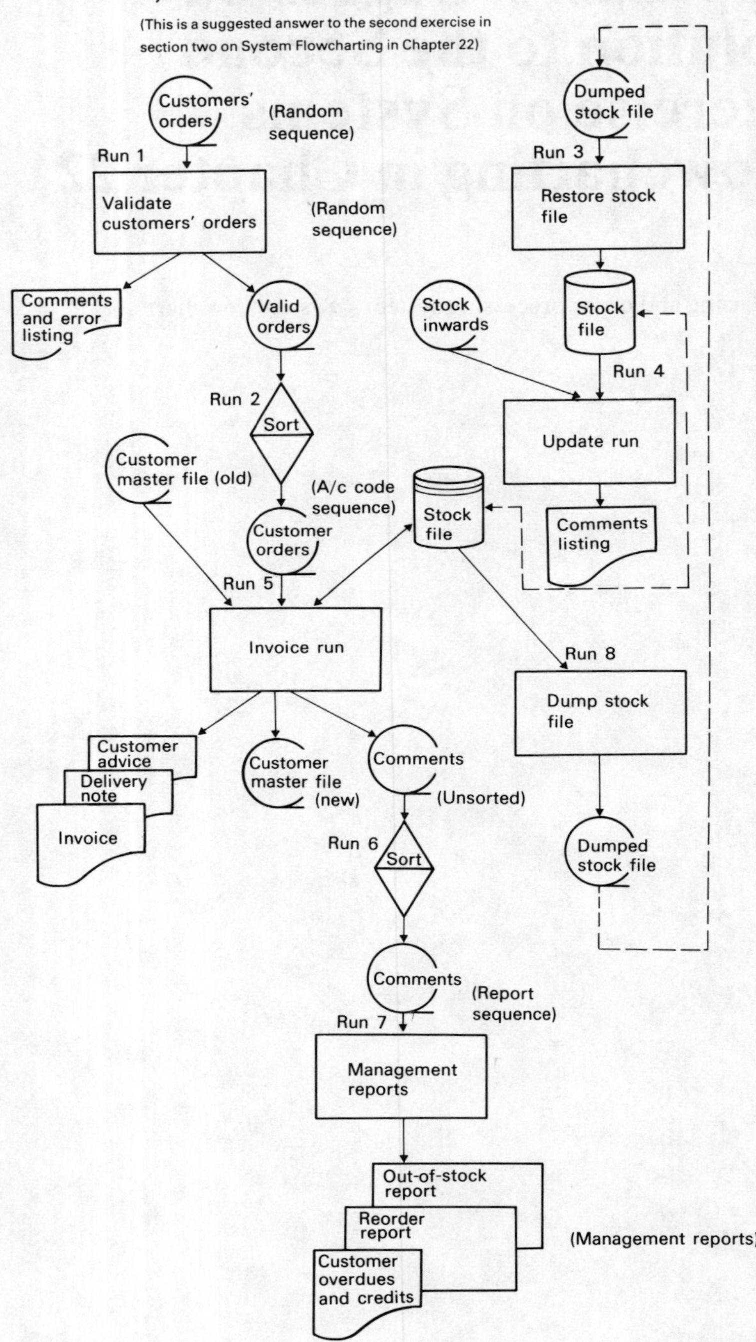

Appendix 4 Suggested Solution to the Exercise on Program Flowcharting in Chapter 22

Records edit and print — Program flowchart

(This is a suggested answer to the exercise in Program Flowcharting given in Chapter 22)

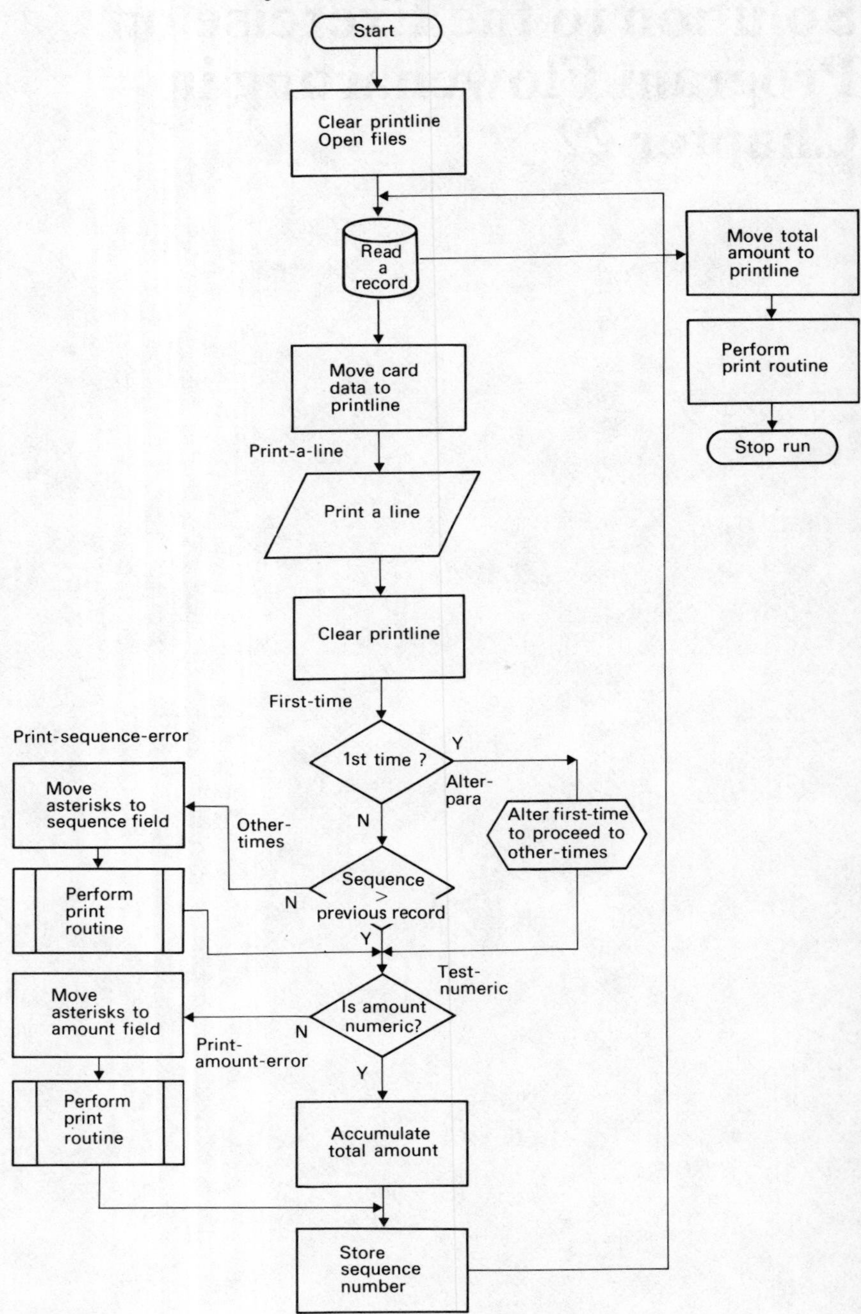

Select Bibliography

Books

American Institute of Certified Public Accountants: *Audit Considerations in Electronic Funds Transfer Systems*, in the Computer Services Guidelines series (24 pp) (1978)

American Institute of Certified Public Accountants: *Auditor's Study and Evaluation of Internal Control in EDP Systems*, 67 pp (New York, 1977)

American Institute of Certified Public Accountants: *Computer-Assisted Audit Techniques*, 102 pp (1979)

American Institute of Certified Public Accountants: *Control Over Using and Changing Computer Programs* (New York, 1979)

American Institute of Certified Public Accountants: *Statement on Auditing Standards No. 3, 'The Effects of EDP on the Auditor's Study and Evaluation of Internal Controls* (New York, 1974)

J. M. Court (ed.): *Audit and Control in a Complex Computer Environment* (Institute of Chartered Accountants in England and Wales, 1985)

G. B. Davis, D. L. Adams and C. A. Schaller: *Auditing and EDP*, American Institute of Certified Public Accountants (New York, 1983)

K. W. Davies and W. E. Perry: *Establishing the Audit Base* (John Wiley, New York, 1980)

I. J. Douglas: *Audit and Control of Mini and Microcomputers* (NCC Publications, 1982)

J. Fitzgerald: *Internal Controls for Computerized Systems*, 93 + ix large pp (Fitzgerald, 1978)

Halper, Davis, O'Neill-Dunne, Pfau: *Handbook of EDP Auditing* (Warren, Gorham & Lamont, Massachussetts, 1985)

Home Office: *Report of the Committee on Data Protection*, (Chairman Sir Norman Lindop), 460 + xxiv pp (H.M.S.O. December 1978)

H.M.S.O.: *The Data Protection Act 1984* (1984, chapter 35)

Infotech: State of the Art Report (Series 8, number 8) on Computer Audit and Control (2 volumes), 1980

B. G. Jenkins, R. C. L. Perry and P. J. Cooke: *An Audit Approach to Computers*, The Institute of Chartered Accountants in England and Wales, revised edition (London, 1986)

L. I. Krauss and A. MacGahan, *Computer Fraud and Countermeasures*, 509 + xv pp (Prentice-Hall, New Jersey, 1979)

W. C. Mair, D. R. Wood and K. W. Davis: *Computer Control and Audit*, 489 + xvii pp (The Institute of Internal Auditors, Inc., 1978)

A. Meadows and C. L. Malcolm: *Audit of Small Computers*, (Institute of Chartered Accounts in England and Wales, Acc. Digest 131; 1983)

NCC Publications: *Audit and Control of Systems Software*, 1983

W. E. Perry and J. F. Kuong: *Generalized Audit Software—Selection and Application* (Management Advisory Publications, 1979)

J. M. Ross and G. J. Collier: *The Data Protection Act 1984* (Institute of Chartered Accountants in England and Wales, Acc. Digest 165; 1985)

G. Simon: *Choosing Accounting Software for your Microcomputer*, (Collins, 1985)

The British Computer Society: *Audit of Control of Database Systems*, 163 pp (July 1977)

The Canadian Institute of Chartered Accountants: *Computer Audit Guidelines* (1975, reprinted several times)

The Canadian Institute of Chartered Accountants: *Computer Control Guidelines* (1970, reprinted several times)

The Institute of Internal Auditors, Inc.: *Systems Auditability and Control Study* (1977), 3 volumes, viz.: *The Executive Report*, 20 pp, *Control Practices*, 149 pp. *Audit Practices*, 219 pp

G. Ward and D. Marshall: *Recommended Codes and Practices for the Audit of Data Processing Activities*, Handbook No. 1, The Institute of Internal Auditors—UK. 156 + ix pp (January 1980)

Update services

Auerbach Publishers Inc.: *EDP Auditing*, an update service launched in 1978 (ed. W. E. Perry)

Management Advisory Publications: *Effective Computer Audit Practices (ECAP)*, devel. by W. E. Perry and J. F. Kuong, (1979, and added to)

Periodicals

Computer Fraud & Security Bulletin, published by Elsevier.

Computer Security, Auditing and Controls, published by Management Advisory Publications (known as 'COM-SAC').

Computer Security Newsletter and *Computer Security Manual* (373 pp) published by the Computer Security Institute.

EDPACS (The EDP Audit, Control, and Security Newsletter), published by the Automation Training Center, Inc.

EDP Analyzer, published by Canning Publications, Inc.

Information Privacy, published by the IPC Press.

The EDP Auditor, journal of the EDP Auditors' Foundation for Education and Research.

Addresses

American Institute of Certified Public Accountants,
1211, Avenue of the Americas,
New York, New York 10036. USA.

Auerbach Publishers, Inc.,
6560 North Park Drive,
Pennsauken,
New Jersey, 08109, USA.

Automation Training Center, Inc.,
11250 Roger Bacon Drive,
Suite 17,
Reston, Virginia 22090, USA.

British Computer Society,
13 Mansfield Street,
London, W1M 0BP, England.

Computer Security Institute,
5 Kane Industrial Drive,
Hudson, Massachusetts 01749, USA.

EDP Analyzer
Canning Publications Inc.,
925 Anza Avenue,
Vista, California 92083, USA.

Van Nostrand Reinhold (UK) Co. Ltd.,
Molly Millar's Lane,
Wokingham,
Berkshire, RG11 2PY, England.

(H.M.S.O.)
Her Majesty's Stationery Office,
49 High Holborn,
London, WC1V 6HB, England.
and in principal cities throughout the UK.

IPC Press,
Guildford, Surrey, England.

Jerry Fitzgerald & Associates,
Management Consulting,
506 Barkentine Lane,
Redwood City, California 94065, USA.

Management Advisory Publications,
P.O. Box. 151–44,
Washington Street,
Wellesley Hills, Massachusetts 02181, USA.

Prentice-Hall, Inc.,
Englewood Cliffs, New Jersey, 07632, USA.

The Canadian Institute of Chartered Accountants,
250 Bloor Street East,
Toronto, Canada, M4W 1G5

The EDP Auditors Foundation for Education and Research,
The EDP Auditors Association, Inc.,
7016 Edgebrook Lane,
Hanover Park, Illinois 60103, USA.

The Institute of Chartered Accountants in England & Wales,
Chartered Accountant's Hall,
Moorgate Place,
London, EC2P 2BJ, England.

The Institute of Internal Auditors, Inc.,
249 Maitland Avenue,
Altamonte Springs, Box 11119, Florida, 32701, USA.

The Institute of Internal Auditors—UK,
82 Portland Place,
London, W1, England.

The National Computing Centre Limited,
Oxford Road,
Manchester, M1 7ED, England.

Index

Index